Praise for *Catch the Fire*

We need to do a better job of engaging future generations. *Catch the Fire* gives us hope for a future where young people and all of us are better able to access our humanity and creatively respond to the challenges we face. I encourage anyone who seeks to work across generations to build a more compassionate and empowered world to read this book.

— Bishop Desmond Tutu, South African social rights activist and retired Anglican bishop

The arts are the languages of the soul that express and define the best and worst of what we are and could be. They are also powerful tools for change. *Catch the Fire* is full of living examples of how the arts enable us to connect deeply with our own humanity across generations and cultures, while providing us practical tools that can transform us, our communities, and the world around us. (PYE power!)

— Peter Gabriel, musician

Catch the Fire is contagious, hot, transformative. If you want to ignite creativity, cooperation and collaboration, if you are engineering world change, this is your guidebook.

— Marika Partridge, Radio Producer, former Director of NPR's "All Things Considered"

PYE has impacted the lives of hundreds of vulnerable young people in the Eastern Cape of South Africa. *Catch the Fire* brings the underlying principles of the Creative Community Model to life and makes them accessible and engaging. It's a must read for anyone involved in youth development.

— Priscilla Higham, Founder and Program Director, African Solutions to African Problems

I've seen the positive, health enhancing effects of the Creative Community Model first-hand through my daughter's participation in Power of Hope Camps: increased confidence, personal growth, and enthusiasm for life. *Catch the Fire* is now making this approach widely available for anyone who wants to have a positive impact on the lives of young people. I highly recommend it.

— Andrew Weil, MD, leader and pioneer in the field of integrative medicine, author of numerous books including *Spontaneous Healing*

Some people think education is about filling buckets. Peggy Taylor and Charlie Murphy know it's more about lighting fires. *Catch the Fire* is an unmatched tinderbox for kindling fires of creativity. Proceed without caution. Don't keep away from children.

— Eric Utne, founder, *Utne Reader*

Catch the Fire shows you how to tap into the deeper streams of meaning in your work with youth and adults in a way that is joyful and transforming for you as well as those you work with. The Creative Community approach that Charlie, Peggy and their team have honed over the years is both practical and soulful. I believe in these people and this work, and I wholeheartedly endorse this powerful guide to awakening hidden wholeness across the generations.

— Parker J. Palmer, educator, activist and author of *Let Your Life Speak*, *The Courage to Teach*, and *Healing the Heart of Democracy*

In *Catch the Fire*, Taylor and Murphy make the powerful argument that not only are the arts an important part of human development, they are essential to being alive. This practical handbook helps us find our way back to ourselves…and each other. And through sharing their experiences of creating spaces that change the world, teach us how to do the same in our own work and lives. A gem of a book.

— Priya Parker, MBA, Innovation Consultant, Founder, Thrive Labs

Every young person deserves to discover the vision and creativity that is uniquely theirs. I know no better magicians that can show us how to do that than Peggy Taylor and Charlie Murphy. *Catch the Fire* is the essential guidebook for anyone who cares about young people.

— Joanna Macy, PhD, environmental activist, Buddhist Scholar, author, *Active Hope: How to Face the Mess We're in Without Going Crazy*

Peggy Taylor and Charlie Murphy's unique approach to empowerment and leadership unlocks the creative potential within young people helping translate their gifts into real-world outcomes. I have directly witnessed the impact of their model on young people and have been thoroughly impressed. I also have personally experienced their approach when applied with adults. As an experienced intercultural leadership and diversity trainer, facilitator and consultant, I am thankful for the new and innovative approaches that Peggy and Charlie are introducing to the world through this important book.

—Amer F. Ahmed, educator, intercultural diversity consultant, urban arts and social justice activist, poet

In *Catch The Fire*, Peggy Taylor and Charlie Murphy offer an inspirational and eminently practical arts-based guide for helping young people heal from trauma, tap into their creativity and aliveness, and move forward with new passion and purpose. By integrating the honoring spirit and practical tools in this true gem of a resource, organizations that serve adolescents will be given the means to turn up the heat—providing a dynamic program that results in more compassionate, hopeful, and engaged young people and staff.

— Robin Casarjian, Executive Director, Lionheart Foundation sponsor of The National Emotional Literacy Project for Youth at Risk, co-author of *Power Source: Taking Charge of Your Life*

Catch the Fire is filled with thrilling, enlivening and deeply transformative stories that speak to the power of practices and ideas that fuel capacities for powerful social change through inter-generational connection. It illumines the essence what we human beings can create when we experience ourselves as part of communities that are nurturing, curious, strong, ingenious and filled with the power of love in action. Thank you Peggy and Charlie for providing a map into new territories - both the inner and outer landscapes of a bolder and more beautiful tomorrow.

— Shakti Butler, PhD, social justice scholar, filmmaker, and speaker; Founder, World Trust Educational Services, Inc.

In my thirty years as a teacher and school administrator in Canada and Asia, this is the most exciting and successful model for working with young people I have encountered. I have seen it work it's magic in such diverse settings as a camp for youth on a farm in rural Canada, a gathering of young people affected by HIV/AIDS in Uganda, a weekend program for teenage urban women, and a class of seventh graders in an International School in Vietnam. While built around the arts, the creative community model is about connecting young people to one another, awakening them to the power within themselves and helping them see the potential they have to positively impact the world around them. *Catch the Fire* is a must have book for anyone who works with youth.

— Donna Bracewell, former principal of Linnaea School in British Columbia, Canada; teacher at the United Nations International School of Hanoi, Vietnam

Charlie and Peggy's approach is empowering not just for middle class youth and adults in North America but is transformational for youth who live in poverty in different parts of the world in a wide range of religious and cultural contexts. It is magical to see divides dissolve as youth experience their shared humanity and acceptance in mixed income groups. In *Catch the Fire* they now generously make available the tools they use to create unbounded joy and possibility where ever they work.

— Deepa Narayan, PhD, international poverty, gender, and development advisor, author of forthcoming book, *Stirring India's Soul.*

Charlie Murphy and Peggy Taylor honor young peoples' yearnings to build a more just and peaceful world by proclaiming: "We don't have to just consume the culture we have. We can co-create the culture we need." By bringing the expressive freedoms of rock & roll to the passionate desires of soul & role, they show how social arts and inner work empower cultural creativity in young leaders—and in everyone willing to *Catch the Fire*.

— Rick and Marcy Jackson, Co-Founders, the Center for Courage & Renewal

Catch the Fire is an extraordinarily important book. Peggy Taylor and Charlie Murphy have crafted an arts-based method for creating transformative community for young people. The method works equally well for people of every age. I have witnessed their work and it is amazing. *Catch the Fire* shows you how you can adopt the method to your group work.

— Michael Lerner, PhD, President, Commonweal, a health and environmental research center in Bolinas, California

Peggy and Charlie's programs work brilliantly. I have experienced them myself and seen amazing positive transformations in my sons and other young people. These two remarkable leaders have gone further by making their skills transferable, very effectively training others to lead empowering programs. *Catch the Fire* takes the process yet further, making their insights and experience widely accessible. It is engaging, clear, practical and inspiring. A treasure trove.

— Rupert Sheldrake, PhD, biologist and author of *A New Science of Life* and *Science Set Free*

Peggy Taylor and Charlie Murphy have created a methodology for unleashing the human spirit that is sheer magic. They are igniting cultural evolution in a way that is teachable and scalable. This book shares their secrets in accessible, generous and effective language and style. The creativity and unleashing of the human spirit they empower, will be one of the emotional revolutions of these times. Every teacher, ceo, counselor, politician, medical professional, and wealth manager needs to read this book.

— Joel Solomon, leader in socially responsible business, President, Renewal Partners

Everywhere we turn, we find that people are ready to create the future they are dreaming of by rebuilding communities. *Catch the Fire* offers practical and inspirational tools for teachers, community leaders and ordinary folks to empower communities to come together and engage in fun, creative activities that will build the foundation for greater personal self esteem and dynamic, vital human connections and community engagement.

— Edgard Gouveia Júnior, architect and urbanist, co-creator of the Oasis Game, and Fellow of the Ashoka Foundation

The Creative Community Model has been a game-changer at Dream A Dream. It has helped us transform our philosophy and approach to "Building a Community of Change-Makers" starting with ourselves. It has brought more authenticity in our work and helped us create powerful transformatory experiences in thousands of young people across India.

— Vishal Talreja, Executive Director, Dream a Dream, life skills program in Bangalore, India

Filled with moving examples of how the arts can change the world, *Catch the Fire* tells the inspiring story of one of today's most innovative and successful examples of social artistry: Partners for Youth Empowerment. Taylor and Murphy's excellent book is also a practical guide in how to use the arts for empowerment and community building, complete with innovative and easy-to-use tools and exercises so that you too can help your groups *Catch the Fire.*

— Robert Gass, EdD, Co-Founder Rockwood Leadership Institute

Peggy Taylor and Charlie Murphy teamed up 18 years ago, blending their talents and experience to help youth find confidence, leadership, and motivation through arts-based learning. Their approach is magical in its ability to access youth, who universally claim they receive hope, strength, new skills, and love at programs based on these methods. *Catch the Fire* is a generous book full of wisdom, fun activities and practical tools to assist anyone wanting to use arts-based teaching with both youth and adults. It makes a real contribution in how to help youth grow into happy and successful people. And it's all generously laid out for you to work with and make your own.

— Torkin Wakefield, Co-Founder, Bead for Life poverty eradication program

catch the fire

An Art-Full Guide to
Unleashing the Creative Power
of Youth, Adults and Communities

PEGGY TAYLOR and **CHARLIE MURPHY**
Cofounders of PYE: Partners for Youth Empowerment

new society
PUBLISHERS

Cover design by Diane McIntosh.
© iStock: Hand illustration: kyestudio; Background pattern: penfold.

Printed in Canada. First printing November 2013.

New Society Publishers acknowledges the financial support of the Government of Canada through the Canada Book Fund (CBF) for our publishing activities.

Paperback ISBN: 978-0-86571-757-2   eISBN: 978-1-55092-550-0

Inquiries regarding requests to reprint all or part of *Catch the Fire* should be addressed to New Society Publishers at the address below.

To order directly from the publishers, please call toll-free (North America) 1-800-567-6772, or order online at www.newsociety.com

Any other inquiries can be directed by mail to:

New Society Publishers
P.O. Box 189, Gabriola Island, BC V0R 1X0, Canada
(250) 247-9737

LIBRARY AND ARCHIVES CANADA CATALOGUING IN PUBLICATION

Taylor, Peggy, 1946–, author
Catch the fire : an art-full guide to unleashing the creative
power of youth, adults and communities / Peggy Taylor and Charlie
Murphy, cofounders of PYE: Partners for Youth Empowerment.

Includes bibliographical references and index.
Issued in print and electronic formats.
ISBN 978-0-86571-757-2 (pbk.). — ISBN 978-1-55092-550-0 (ebook)

1. Community arts projects.   2. Arts—Social aspects.
3. Creative ability—Social aspects.   4. Creation (Literary, artistic,
etc.)—Social aspects.   I. Murphy, Charlie, 1953–, author   II. Title.

NX180.A77T39 2013   700.1'03   C2013-906158-4
                                               C2013-906159-2

New Society Publishers' mission is to publish books that contribute in fundamental ways to building an ecologically sustainable and just society, and to do so with the least possible impact on the environment, in a manner that models this vision. We are committed to doing this not just through education, but through action. The interior pages of our bound books are printed on Forest Stewardship Council®-registered acid-free paper that is **100% post-consumer recycled** (100% old growth forest-free), processed chlorine-free, and printed with vegetable-based, low-VOC inks, with covers produced using FSC®-registered stock. New Society also works to reduce its carbon footprint, and purchases carbon offsets based on an annual audit to ensure a carbon neutral footprint. For further information, or to browse our full list of books and purchase securely, visit our website at: www.newsociety.com

We dedicate this book to our friend and colleague, Susan Bamutenda,
lead facilitator and program coordinator for In Movement,
our partner organization in Uganda. Susan passed away unexpectedly on
February 27, 2010 in Kampala. Her joyful spirit, passion for change,
and deep caring for everyone—youth and adults alike—defined what it
means to be a social artist. Susan, your life set a loving vibrant tone
that continues to resonate in the lives of so many.

We also dedicate this book to Mateo Utne and Olivia Vance
(Peggy's grandchildren) and all of the children who
are being born into this time in history.
May you see the dawning of a more just and peaceful world.

Contents

PART 4: FACILITATION TOOLS

Acknowledgments

The seeds of this work were planted with a call from Joanna Macy to Peggy Taylor in 1995. "You must come over to the Deep Ecology Summer School tonight," Joanna said. "I want you to meet my friend Charlie Murphy." Thank you, Joanna, for putting all of this in motion. The book and the growing body of work it represents has been influenced and formed by so many people we cannot mention you all here. We hold you in our hearts. Special thanks go to our colleagues at the Whidbey Institute, where Power of Hope began, and our friends at Hollyhock and Linnaea Farm on Cortes Island, who insisted that the camps needed to be in Canada as well. And mega thanks to Ian and Victoria Watson, who are the force behind the founding and ongoing work of PYE Global. Your wisdom and generosity know no bounds.

Big gratitude to every person who has served—or currently serves—on the staffs or boards of Power of Hope in the US and Canada, PYE Global, Young Women Empowered and all of our partner organizations around the world. You are the unsung heroes of this work. And special thanks to the ever-growing community of artists, educators, facilitators, camp staff and volunteers who carry on arts-empowerment work with youth. You inspire us with your integrity, passion, inventiveness and generosity of spirit. We are continually enlivened by the ways you have deepened and spread this work far and wide. And the biggest thanks of all to the young people who have attended creative community programs and taken what you've learned out into the world. When we see so many of you return years later to mentor the next generation, we know we have done our job well. None of this would be possible without our large and growing community of donors who have faithfully walked with us for over 17 years. You form the protective outer circle through your abiding commitment to providing young people with transformational learning programs. Thank you for your consistency and your faith in us.

And now to the book itself. Big thanks go to Lynn Willeford, editor extraordinaire, friend and gentle task master. Thank you for seeing this book through from start to finish and for telling us, "It sounds great!" whenever our inner critics got the best of us. Hanif Fazal, your thoughts and ideas show up throughout this book. Thank you for mastering the art of training facilitators and taking the work with young people to ever-deeper levels. Magdalena Gomez, thank you for giving us a vision for how to use theater improvisation to build community. For our colleagues who helped out with specific chapters—Nadia Chaney, creative writing; Jackie Amatucci, visual arts and crafts; Eric Mulholland, theater; Erica Helm Meade, storytelling; Cilla Utne, working with diverse groups; and Evan McGown, theme-based session—thank you for your generous feedback and your camaraderie in this work. Thank you to Richard Russell for your wise counsel in helping us articulate the Creative Community Model and drawing the process maps that appear in this book. And to Leslie Cotter, thank you for saying yes every single time we asked, "Can you just drop everything for a minute and read this one chapter?" Our PYE staff members Gwyn Wansbrough, Katie Jackson, Silvia Giovannoni and Marjorie Triplett helped us immeasurably throughout the writing process. Thank you for all you do to make PYE thrive. Special thanks as well to all of you photographers who so graciously donated your images to the cause. Thanks to Larry Ravitz and Marika Partridge for commissioning Sam Bartlett's theater improvisation cartoons. And a big thanks to our colleagues at New Society Publishers. We have been so happy with our experience working with each and every one of you.

And finally, of course, love and deep gratitude to our families: Rick, Leif, Cilla, Mateo, Eric, Amy, Steve and Olivia. You make our hearts sing.

Introduction

Who would ever imagine that a pile of paper and some crayons could transform lives?

After Hurricane Katrina devastated New Orleans, thousands of families ended up living in horrific conditions in the Houston, Texas, Astrodome. Sanitation was poor; people didn't feel safe; and there was little hope in sight. Nearly everyone, including many children, suffered from trauma. People in Houston helped in all kinds of ways, but the work of a group of four stay-at-home Texan moms particularly caught our attention.

These four women gathered piles of crayons, markers and paper and headed to the stadium. They invited children to draw pictures of their experiences and talk. While their first pictures were filled with terror, over time their images turned brighter and more hopeful, as the sun and rainbows adorned the pages.

"Just by listening and sitting with them while they drew, we saw how amazing the transformation occurred with the children," Sue Jensen, one of the four moms, told NBC News.[1] They called their ad hoc initiative the Katrina Kid's Project. The drawings made their way to the national news, and some were even sold to raise money for schools for Katrina survivors. These women were not social workers, and they weren't psychologists.

They simply cared and believed that the act of making art might help kids find a way to process their experience and get their feet back on the ground.

This simple story illustrates what motivated both of us to leave our jobs mid-career and devote ourselves to working with young people through the arts. Our life experiences had shown us that young people around the world, from all cultures and socioeconomic classes, are a wellspring of hope and resilience. Furthermore, we had witnessed over and over again that making opportunities for creative expression within a context of care and connection is a seemingly magical key for unlocking that hope and resilience. And it doesn't require the work of experts. We can all do this.

We entered our work with youth, arts and empowerment from different directions but with a common concern for the environment that today's young people are growing up in. Youth are surrounded by a seamless web of media images and messages that tell them who they are, what they should look like and how they should act. They live in a world that is experiencing dramatic demographic shifts that too often lead to misunderstanding, conflict and injustice. Severe stress upon our natural environment is causing upheavals that will increasingly affect the upcoming generations. And these are just a few of the big issues young people face.

Millions of us are busily working on ways to address these issues, but too few of us spend time sharing our wisdom and passion with the upcoming generations. Vipassana meditation teacher Sharon Saltzberg said, "It's as if the transmission of knowledge from one generation to the next has broken down in our modern world."

We have found that the arts and creative expression serve as an incredibly effective bridge between generations as well as between cultures and socioeconomic classes. Creative expression ignites joy and hope; develops empathy, teamwork and collaboration; and fosters the desire to live meaningful lives. We see it as a power tool for the kind of social healing and positive change called for in our world.

A lot of attention is being paid to creativity these days; bookstore shelves are increasingly populated with new titles promoting the concepts of creativity, imagination and "right-brain" potential. Theoretical treatises on creativity and related subjects, however, leave many feeling on the outside of this new wave of understanding. Those who lack artistic experience, or who don't think of themselves as talented, are left searching for a way to experience their own creativity. What's needed are easy and safe opportunities to jump in and get started.

In the past 18 years we have learned again and again that the arts and creative expression are the birthright of every human being. We all get to play in this realm, and it's through doing so that we learn how creative we really are. That's why we take a very practical and participatory approach to creativity. At our trainings and youth programs—all based on a learn-by-doing model—we have the pleasure of seeing person after person awaken to innate creativity. And once recognized, that creativity can never hide again in quite the same way. Our work is about re-enchanting the world through arts for everyone.

 ## Who We Are

Charlie spent his early years working as a professional musician, leading a popular Seattle band called Rumors of the Big Wave. At 40, he left the music business to become cultural coordinator of the Earth Service Corps, a national YMCA teen environmental organization. Curious whether the skills he had learned as a poet, songwriter and performer might be useful for young people, he started leading creativity-based programs with youth throughout North America and internationally. He was heartened by young people's willingness to take creative risks and their desire to make a positive difference in the world, whether they came from the inner cities, the suburbs or rural communities, from detention centers, impoverished high schools or fancy private academies. It turns out that young people really do want to express themselves fully and make their lives count.

Peggy worked off and on for 20 years as the editor of *New Age Journal*, a US magazine that covered emerging progressive movements barely noticed by the mainstream press. She left the magazine for a few years to earn a Master's of Education in Creative Arts in Learning at Lesley University Cambridge, Massachusetts, where she focused on the role the arts can play in building strong people and connected communities. Back at the magazine, she became fascinated by the stories that came across her editor's desk about grassroots organizations successfully using arts-based approaches to help their communities deal with catastrophes such as shootings and natural disasters, to decrease rates of incarceration and keep young people out of gangs, and to build alliances across cultures and generations. She left the magazine in the mid-1990s determined to find a way to work with creativity to help youth and adults live more fulfilling lives and to build stronger more resilient communities.

In 1996, we tried an experiment on Whidbey Island in the northwest corner of the US. We convened a leadership gathering with 28 teens from diverse backgrounds and fourteen adult artists, youth workers and community leaders. We spent five days exploring our values and our hopes and dreams. We played, danced, made art and music, wrote poetry and told our life stories. We climbed into the trees on a high-ropes course, immersed ourselves in the natural world and learned from people very different from ourselves. Youth and adults alike left the camp brimming with self-confidence and a network of new allies, ready to take on the world.

The gathering gave us a glimpse into a whole new world of possibility for working with youth and spurred us to begin the body of work represented in this book in the spring of 1997. We started a non-profit program, called The Power of Hope: Youth Empowerment through the Arts, in the US and Canada to put on arts-based leadership camps. A decade later, in 2006, we began to work in Uganda and then in the UK where Charlie worked with Lucy Sicks to start a youth program called LIFEbeat. With our friend and collaborator Ian Watson we formed PYE: Partners for Youth Empowerment to respond to the growing demand for similar programming around the world. Through PYE we partner with communities around the world to train leaders who can provide transformative programs for teens. We currently work in the UK, Uganda, India, South Africa, Brazil, Canada and the US and continue to develop new partnerships with organizations that are motivated to release the creative potential of young people. In 2009, Peggy, Jamie-Rose Edwards, Leslie Cotter and a group of women from Power of Hope founded Young Women Empowered, a creative leadership program for teen women from diverse backgrounds in the greater Seattle area. And this is not to mention all of the initiatives, programs and organizations started by our colleagues.

What has put the wind into the sails of this work is the amazing network of dedicated artists, youth workers, teachers and activists we have met along the way. We call these people—and ourselves—social artists, because we apply our creative zeal to the healing of the world, using society as our canvas. We dedicate ourselves to developing arts-based group-facilitation skills and finding ways to apply our skills to increase the effectiveness of programs for youth and adults all over the world. As far as we can tell, social artists exist in every community, in every nation on this planet, ready to be recognized and deployed.

Nadia Chaney is a perfect example. Nadia was working as a spoken word and performance installation artist in Vancouver, British Columbia, paying the bills by washing dishes in a café. "The first time I came to a Power of Hope camp, I realized that living my dreams didn't necessarily mean living the life of a starving artist," she said. "I went to more camps and trainings and expanded my definition of myself to include social artistry. Not only did I continue working as a performance artist, I started using my creativity to work with youth in schools, juvenile detention centers and community centers. It wasn't long before I left the restaurant job, and I've been doing this work ever since." A few years later, she and three colleagues started Metaphor, a performance troupe that has positively affected the lives of over 60,000 teens in British Columbia through hip-hop-based empowerment programs. Nadia is now a lead trainer for PYE and has led initiatives in India and South Africa.

David Kafambe, a social worker in Kampala, Uganda, came to social artistry from the other direction. When he attended our Creative Facilitation training in 2007, he was working with youth for the Ugandan Ministry of Gender, Labour and Social Development and with DSW, a German NGO that focuses on the sexual and reproductive health of youth. Prior to the training, David had not considered creativity as a focus for empowerment work; nor had he imagined using the arts as a tool in his work with youth. Once he saw the impact of creative expression, though, David applied himself to becoming an excellent facilitator. Several thousand Ugandan young people have now attended creative empowerment camps that David has organized and facilitated, and he has trained hundreds of youth workers and peer leaders in East Africa and beyond. David proudly calls himself a social artist and has been invited to join several international youth empowerment initiatives in other parts of Africa, Europe and India. Meeting David, one is struck by a sense of irrepressible joy and clarity of purpose. These are common characteristics of the people we are fortunate enough to meet through our work, and they make our lives a constant pleasure.

You don't have to be a full-time facilitator to be an effective social artist, however. You might be a teacher who finds ways to slip creative practices into the classroom or a businessperson who uses arts-based practices to lead exciting and motivating staff meetings. Maybe you are a community organizer who strengthens the bonds among people in your neighborhood by staging participatory community arts events. Or a youth worker, social worker, educator or government official who brings new life into your workplace by injecting the arts and opportunities for creative expression. Or a parent or grandparent who plays with your children in ways that nurture their creative spark.

 ## Why This Book

Our work with creativity and communities reflects what we feel needs to happen in the world. We offer this book as our best effort in support of a massive shift that is trying to happen in our time. We see ourselves as fellow travelers with many millions of people around the world engaged in the high-stakes adventure of securing a just and healthy world for future generations.

The challenge that humanity faces has been described in countless ways. Kenny Ausubel, a cofounder of the Bioneers—a leading organization supporting the emergence of a thriving, Earth-friendly society—captures our predicament as a species with a powerful metaphor. He equates the challenge facing humanity to being travelers on a massive, smog-belching, ironclad cargo ship, heavy in the water, charging headlong in the wrong direction. What's more, only a fraction of the wisdom, compassion and energy of the passengers is being called upon. And we (the collective we) have been given a challenge: somehow we've got to find a way to change direction while transforming this hulking mess into an elegant sailing vessel, equipped with the most innovative and nature-friendly technology imaginable. And all the travelers on the ship get to contribute the best of what they have to offer. This is our real-life adventure, serious, fraught, sometimes exhilarating and potentially full of joy—and there is room for everyone who wants to play. We need thousands, even millions, of social artists—engaged, confident, grounded, empathetic citizens—if we are to create that elegant sailing ship that can take us in a new direction. And that means you and me. You don't have to have experience with the arts to jump on board; you simply need a bit of courage and a taste for adventure.

In this book you will learn the basic tools for becoming a social artist—whether you work with youth or adults. We frame the book around our youth work, since that's where we formulated the model. But the principles and practices are applicable to adult groups as well, whether

Social artists in Cape Town, South Africa, relax after a training session.

Credit: PYE Global

it's a class, a work team, a community meeting or even a party. That's right, a party. This book prepares you to bring vitality into group encounters regardless of the context. Whenever people come together, there is an opportunity for creative engagement.

In Part 1, you'll learn about how the arts and creative expression are an overlooked force for positive social change. Through real-world examples, you'll learn about the Creative Community Model and how to use it in a wide range of situations with youth or adults.

In Part 2, you'll learn how to structure programs for success and how to integrate the arts into every aspect of your program.

In Part 3, you'll learn how to bring the worlds of visual arts and crafts, creative writing, improvisational theater, storytelling and song into your work through easy-to-lead activities. You need no prior experience in the arts to use them.

And finally in Part 4, you'll receive additional tips on facilitation and counsel on working in diverse cultures and intergenerational groups.

For over 18 years we've been blessed to work in an endlessly creative environment with a vast community of youth and adults who care about this world. We invite you to join the growing cadre of social artists working to transform the world through joy, imagination and compassion.

— Peggy Taylor and Charlie Murphy, 2013

A note on our sources: The activities in this book are, for the most part, widely known games with our spin added to them. We made every attempt to credit individuals when possible. If you find an activity in this book that you have personally designed, we apologize for the lack of credit. Please let us know and we will remedy this in future editions.

All proceeds from this book will support the work of PYE Global.

part 1

the call for
creative community

The Creative Imperative

A few years ago, we attended a spoken word show featuring young performers from Hip Hop Hope, a program led by Power of Hope, the teen arts organization we founded in 1996. One 17-year-old in particular mesmerized us with his powerful presence and eloquent words. As we watched him stride back and forth across the makeshift stage, we assumed he was a pro who had been performing for years. Exactly how long he had been performing? "Three months," he told us, "just since going to Hip Hop Hope." He confessed he'd been too shy to stand up in front of an audience before. "Now I'm performing all over Seattle," he beamed.

Popular belief tells us that this kind of transformation would be a slow incremental process, but in over 18 years of working with youth and adults in our creativity-based programs, we have almost come to expect such rapid change. In just one week of living in an arts-rich supportive community, we see people's empathy and self-confidence bloom, not to mention their desire to make a contribution to the world. It's as if a light comes on.

Again and again, young people defy the media stereotypes of the disaffected, uncaring, hard-to-reach generation. If you have fallen prey to the commonly held view, think again. Through poetry, creative writing, theater, dance and visual art they express the depth of their caring and concern. They step out of their cliques to befriend people from cultures and backgrounds different from their own. A recent Muslim immigrant in our Young Women Empowered program in Seattle told us, "Before this program, I only ever talked to people who look just like me. Now I can relate to anyone." They gain the confidence to bring their ideas and thoughts into the world. "I used to be silent in school," said another young woman. "Now my teachers can't keep me quiet!" Furthermore, they recognize that taking creative risks and becoming engaged citizens makes them happy. "I now have more fun taking big scary creative risks than I used to have doing things that were bad for me," enthused a young man from an urban neighborhood.

Adults in these intergenerational programs are similarly affected. As they push their creative edges, they discover parts of themselves long dormant, and many connect with this vibrant younger generation for the first time. "This camp reminds me of what it feels like to be fully alive," said a health care worker at a program in Uganda. And similar results have been borne out in the slums of Bangalore, the back country of Brazil and the war-torn north of Uganda as well as in inner cities of England, the US, Canada, South Africa and Italy.

 ## The Turning of the Tide—To the Right Brain

In the US, over three million students drop out of high school each year, with attrition rates in minority communities double and triple those of white students.[2] Of the youth who *do* stay in school, two-thirds say they are bored every day and 17 percent say they are bored in every class. Of those, nearly 40 percent say they are bored because the material isn't relevant to their lives.[3] It's as if there is no room in too many of our schools for the emerging souls of our young people.

David Whyte, a poet known for his work bringing poetry into the corporate world, speaks of a similar conundrum for adults. He suggests that people leave big parts of their souls in the parking lot when they go into their workplace. How many of us leave ourselves behind when we go to work, whether in a large or small company, a for-profit business, NGO, school or service organization?

Change is afoot, however. A growing number of neuroscientists and leading-edge thinkers in multiple disciplines concur that right-brain thinking—artistic, holistic, pattern-oriented—is the mode of thinking most needed in the 21st century. In his best-selling book, *A Whole New Mind*, social commentator Daniel Pink tells us that education that pays attention to the right brain is exactly what young people need in order to thrive in this new century. He writes,

> The keys to the kingdom are changing. The future belongs to a very different kind of person with a different kind of mind: creators and empathizers, pattern recognizers and meaning makers. These people—artists, inventors, designers, storytellers, caregivers, consolers, big picture thinkers—will now reap society's richest rewards and share its greatest joys.[4]

Pink identifies six attributes of right-brain thinking as essential to success in the 21st century: design, story, synthesis, empathy, play and a sense of meaning.

We believe that young people intuitively know this. They are voting with their feet as they contribute to the massive dropout rates in secondary schools that are run on the outmoded factory model of education. Today's learning needs to include a right-brained approach that engages young people and prepares them to be creative contributors to a world in flux. In our high-technology world, young people need first-hand— unplugged—experiences of themselves, others and the natural world. Expressing their own thoughts and feelings helps them make meaning of their lives; putting their voice out into the world promotes a sense of agency and personal power. And the research is now clear: social and emotional intelligence—right-brain intelligence—is a more reliable indicator of academic and life success than IQ ever was. Science is confirming what we've known for a long time. As far back as AD 100, Greek historian Plutarch claimed, "A young person is not a vessel to be filled but a fire to be lit." Education that activates the right brain is needed in order for young people to thrive.

Developmental scientist Peter Benson, in his book *Sparks: How Parents Can Help Ignite the Hidden Strengths of Teenagers* has this to say: "Thriving begins with the human spark—that which gives us aliveness, hope, direction and purpose."[5] Research conducted by the Search Institute, where Benson was director, confirms the effectiveness of creative expression and a multi-arts approach in helping young people find their spark. In a recent national study in the US, a substantial majority of youth reported that they feel most alive when they are expressing themselves creatively.[6] Using the arts is the best way we know of to activate the powers of the right brain.

Through our work with adults in training programs and organizations, we find that they are looking for the same thing as youth—a deeper connection with themselves and each other and greater access to their creative power. When we sing together, make art, write and read to one another, dance and drum, or play theater games, the two sides of our brain come into balance and the walls that separate us tumble. It's as if everyone in the room releases a collective sigh of relief and remembers what it means to be human.

"Creative expression is most often accompanied by a feeling of shimmering joy." –Rollo May

Credit: Sara Dent, Power of Hope Canada

One participant in an arts and leadership workshop we led at a major organizational development conference wrote, "If you would have described what we were going to do I might not have attended, thinking it might be too light weight for me. Well, I was wrong. You showed us beyond a doubt that the arts can be used to bring people together, to bond almost instantly and to overcome barriers of race, age and walk of life. I would not have believed it!"

Creative Expression Is the Secret Sauce

The arts provide powerful tools for transforming lives and communities. In the not-too-distant past—and in some cultures still today—creative expression was seamlessly woven into everyday life. Cross-cultural anthropologist Angeles Arrien tells us that in land-based cultures, when sick people went to the local healer, they were essentially asked four questions. She calls these the healing salves:

- When did you stop singing?
- When did you stop dancing?
- When did you stop telling your story?
- When did you stop sitting in silence?[7]

We Are All Creative

Creativity is one of our greatest sources of energy, and creative expression is what makes it operational in our lives. Unfortunately, too many people are cut off from this powerful force. "When I ask people in my classes who thinks they are creative, it's shocking to see how few hands go up," said Rebekka Goldsmith, a singer and vocal coach who leads vocal empowerment trainings in Seattle. We have this same experience again and again, particularly when working with adult groups.

We attribute this to the overidentification of creativity with art-making—and particularly professional art-making. If you can make great art, you're creative. If you can't, you're one of the great mass of uncreative people. Actually, we are all creative. Our creativity is simply our ability to think things up and make them happen. Cooking breakfast, planting a garden and coming up with a budget for an organization are all acts of creativity. Most of us express our creativity in small ways throughout the day.

Creativity, of course, also has to do with artistic expression, and studies show that we thrive when we express ourselves through the arts—especially when we are not under the pressure to be good. In a recent UCLA study of 25,000 youth over 12 years of age, James Caterall found that when young people are engaged in creating art at an early age, they outperform their peers in every category, including academics as well as life skills.[8]

Studies of US schools that integrate the arts into learning also paint a powerful picture. Schools, teachers and communities that use arts-based learning methods have consistently positive outcomes. The social and emotional climate in schools and classrooms improves, and students become better learners. Students typically:

- participate more in class
- become more interested in learning
- are more creative and self-directed
- develop communication and complex thinking skills
- have better relationships with teachers and other students
- are more likely to develop connections with community members

Teachers who use arts-based approaches are more creative and enthusiastic and develop higher-level thinking skills. They are more innovative, flexible, and more willing to improve their skills through professional development training.

Community organizations that work together to bring arts to youth become more collaborative and are more effective in generating resources and solving problems.[9] It's a win all the way around. "We should devote ourselves to developing the power of creativity and imagination as a priority," said noted British educator Sir Ken Robinson. "Creativity is as important in education as literacy and math."

You Don't Have to Be a Professional Artist to Use the Arts in Your Work

Opportunities to integrate creative expression into our personal and professional lives exist for all of us once we realize that we can lead arts-based activities with no training in the arts. You don't have to be an experienced painter to use visual arts activities. You don't have to be an actor to lead theater games. Nor do you have to be an author to engage people in creative writing. *All you need are some easy-to-lead activities and the courage to present them.* As you become proficient in leading arts-based activities, the response you get from your participants will reinforce your desire to find more and more activities to add to your toolbox.

Everyone Has a Valid Desire to Be Seen and Heard

The power of creative expression to transform is rooted in our human need to be seen and heard. We see this in the earliest days of a child's life. When we play with babies, what do we do? The baby smiles; we smile. The baby goes, *goo goo*; we go, *goo goo*. The baby frowns; we frown. As we mirror the baby's actions, our hearts open and the baby is bathed in love, connection and validation. As we grow older, we need to be seen and validated as well. The unheard child or adult suffers, often shutting down or acting out.

Playing a theater game in Uganda: we all have a valid desire to be seen and heard.

Credit: Autumn Preble

In arts-rich cultures, participatory arts provide people with a venue to be seen and heard—whether through drumming, dancing, singing or storytelling. Everyone gets to be part of the performance troupe. It's not about being a professional and it's not about being a master. It's just about being a human being exercising your birthright. Psychologist Rollo May put the power of art this way: "Self-expression is most often accompanied by a feeling of shimmering joy."

When you encourage a person to take a creative risk by making something up and then showing it to others without judgment, a cycle of affirmation develops. The action could be as simple as coming up with a movement in a theater game. The person makes up a movement and everyone repeats it. The appreciative response builds the courage to take

Why the Arts?

A growing body of evidence mixed with personal experience suggests that the arts are good medicine. Here's a short rundown of their benefits.

Elicits joy: Creative expression in a judgment-free environment is simply a lot of fun. Worries about the past or future disappear, and we find ourselves in the flow of the present moment. When we express ourselves without trying to be perfect, we experience happiness regardless of our circumstances.

Promotes health: Numerous studies point to the benefits of creative expression for health. Notable is the work of Dr. James Pennebaker, who found that writing with emotion about one's life experiences increases immune function and decreases reliance on health care.[12]

Builds confidence: Arts-rich learning communities provide opportunities for everyone to shine and be seen and appreciated by one another. When people take creative risks, and are appreciated by peers and mentors, their confidence jumps. Through repeated opportunities to take creative risks, self-confidence develops quite naturally.

Develops empathy: Neuroscientists have discovered that our brains have mirror neurons that fire off when we witness emotions in another. We drop into empathetic resonance when we hear others expressing authentic feelings through poetry, music and other arts.

more risks. Or someone with no previous musical experience might play in a drumming ensemble on open-mic night at a camp or an adult conference. The exhilaration of playing with others and then receiving the appreciation from an audience raises self-esteem visibly. Or someone stands up and reads a short personal piece about his or her life. A sense of intimacy and appreciation develops in the group and serves as fertilizer for forming souls.

The Arts Open the Door to the Inner Life

When we express ourselves creatively something even deeper is happening than being seen and heard. Creative expression opens the door to our inside world—our imagination, the soul, the spirit. "The aim of art is to

Brings learning alive: Creative expression creates relevance by putting us in touch with our thoughts and feelings. It creates excitement by putting us on our creative edge. It creates a sense of vitality by bringing our imaginations into play. Human beings are designed to make meaning of our lives, and much of this happens in the inner world of our imaginations, where heart and head work together.

Strengthens human connection: Creative expression brings down the walls and builds trust, connecting us across cultural, religious, socioeconomic and generational divides.

Provides opportunities to take creative risks: Young people love to take risks. The arts provide an adventure with no right or wrong answers and an outlet for positive risk-taking without physical danger.

Teaches 21st-century leadership skills: Through the arts we learn how to see the big picture, synthesize information, live with paradox, collaborate with others, tell our stories and so much more. These are all right-brain skills that leading thinkers claim are crucial for success in the modern world.

represent not the outward appearance of things, but their inward significance," wrote Aristotle. Whenever we enter into creative expression we walk into the inner world of imagination. It is here that we make meaning of our lives. It is here that motivation takes root, that we make core decisions about our lives. Theologians tell us that the teen years are a particularly rich time for spiritual exploration, for finding meaning. And yet, our schools generally don't nurture the rich terrain of the inner life.

Young people are capable of profound thought and deep compassion. Creative expression—in a judgment-free context—brings this out. At our camps we often find that the most broken youth flock to the art barn, where they are challenged to express themselves in a private way. As they play with paper and pastels, glue and magazine pictures, paints and sparkles, making meaningful objects, it's as if you can see their tenuous inner selves move back into coherence. As Karl Paulnak, pianist and director of music at Boston Conservatory, has said, "Music [and we would add all of the arts] has a way of finding the big, invisible moving pieces inside our hearts and souls and helping us figure out the position of things inside us."[10]

 ## Empowerment from the Inside Out

"The most important question you'll ever ask is whether the universe is a friendly place, " Albert Einstein once said. When it comes down to it, empowerment is all about moving toward an experience of life as a gift and of the universe as a friendly place. Given the seemingly intractable systems of oppression that operate in our world, and the crushing impact that injustice has on the lives of countless millions, this may seem like a weak-kneed response to the lack of empowerment experienced by so many. We believe, however, that for the individual, hidden or stifled potential is activated when we are able to enlarge our sense of possibility and claim our power to make choices in response to even the most dire of circumstances.

In the young people we work with we see this shift, regardless of their outward conditions. A young person who has lived through the greatest horror is as capable of moving toward love as a youth who has had great privilege. Empowerment at its essence is about envisioning our dreams and moving toward them, even in tiny steps. It's about acknowledging and building on our strengths and gifts, living with purpose and meaning. It's about taking a stand for justice and equity in the world.

Empowerment takes different forms for different individuals. For Anna, a young woman in Uganda, empowerment means going back to her HIV/AIDS teen club and speaking up for the first time. For Marquis, an inner-city youth from Detroit, it's mending a relationship with his family and deciding to stay in high school. For Taylor, a Canadian Power of Hope

Facilitating Empowerment

The chart below shows various manifestations of this move toward empowerment. When we facilitate from the right-hand column we are inviting people to move in that direction. This, of course, requires ongoing personal work for you as a facilitator.

From	To
Fear	Love
Protective Mode	Curiosity Mode
Persona	Essence
Victim	Personal Agency
Can't Do	Can Do
Ego-centric	Eco-centric
Ethno-centric	Ethno-relational
Focus on deficits	Focus on strengths
What's wrong?	What's right?
Extrinsic motivation	Intrinsic motivation
It's all about me	It's all about us
I live in a hostile universe	I live in a friendly universe

teen, it's starting an organization to help children internationally and continuing that work for years. For Bussie, an unemployed youth worker in the Eastern Cape of South Africa, it's releasing her shyness and getting a job with an AIDS outreach organization. For Robert, a high school teacher in Seattle, it's establishing a racial equity program in his school. For Fatuma, a low-income high school senior living in the US, it's raising $2,500 to help alleviate famine in her birthplace in the Horn of Africa.

What's missing in too many empowerment programs is the focus on the inner work needed to develop strong and purposeful leaders. Too often programs emphasize outward work in the community at the expense of the inner development required for transformational and lasting change. It is through knowing who we are on the inside that we get to deepen our understanding of how we have choice even in the most challenging situations. The core of inner work is the power that comes from a growing realization that most of the time we have a choice. Nelson Mandela's response to his long years of imprisonment stands as a powerful example for South Africans and the rest of humanity of the power that humans have to make choices in support of our higher selves and our dreams for the world. PYE advisory board member Deepa Narayan designed global studies for the UN and the World Bank on how people climb out of poverty. She found that the majority of those who overcome poverty report a decision or choice they made between the ages of 15 and 17 that was the key to their success. Our relationship to self and our view of what is possible are essential stepping stones on the path toward empowerment.

Through our work over the past two decades we have developed a model—the Creative Community Model—that provides a road map for integrating personal inner work with community involvement, for developing the social and emotional skills to be a healing influence in our communities and the world, for developing the right-brain, creative skills to address the issues of our times and for finding the compassion and motivation to live a life of purpose and meaning. The Creative Community Model provides a social learning laboratory in which youth and adults alike can practice building and living within social structures that enhance creativity, compassion and civic engagement.

The Creative Imperative

In *The Master and His Emissary: The Divided Brain and the Making of the Western World*, psychiatrist and author Iain McGilchrist shows how, in an ideal physiology, right brain is master and left brain is servant. The right brain has the qualities of the "leader," and the left brain works to support that leadership.[11] In our world today, the left brain seems to have the upper hand. With the support of science, the social application of the arts, and the growing number of social artists who are making creative expression operational in our families, schools, communities and public institutions, the tide could indeed be turning. This book is a call to action and a practical guide for transforming the very fabric of our lives personally and collectively.

An Arts-Based Model for Change

We are in Bahia, Brazil, and camp is about to begin. Brightly colored welcome signs hang from trees towering over a rambling Spanish-style ranch house. Blue marquees protect paper, cameras and oil pastels from the blazing sun. Twenty-five adults scurry around, hanging signs and laying out supplies. This unlikely group includes youth workers from local NGOs, teaching artists from Sao Paulo and Salvador, and seven employees from the corporate offices of Agrifirma, Brazil, the company sponsoring the camp.

The staff and volunteers share an easy camaraderie in spite of their widely diverse backgrounds. They have just completed four days of training in which they experienced a Creative Community camp themselves, and already hearts and minds have changed. Marianna Duarte, chief legal officer of Agrifirma, Brazil, said, "When I first heard about the program, I was skeptical. I thought it would be altogether too sophisticated for the young people in this rural area. By the end of the training, I knew we adults and the youth were in for a very special experience."

Before the youth have even arrived, the staff members of the Agrifirma, Brazil camp have accomplished a first and important task of what we call the Creative Community Model: setting the stage for a positive learning experience. Because they have stretched their own creative

Opening day at the Agrifirma Creative Community camp in Bahia, Brazil.

Credit: PYE Global

edges, connected across lines of difference and developed a sincere appreciation for one another, they are able to quickly set up the physical space of the camp to communicate "We are glad you are here."

An ad hoc welcome committee greets the young people as they tumble off the bus. They escort reticent teens to the registration table, pass out water bottles and help carry belongings to the sleeping areas. We have found that a warm welcome helps campers acclimate to what promises to be a very powerful experience. After stowing their belongings, everyone gathers under the marquees to make personal posters—called I-AM posters—that will introduce them to their fellow campers and the staff. The quality of gentle interaction that happens around the art tables provides a non-threatening way for both youth and adults to begin expressing their creativity and making themselves known to each other. At the end of this process participants tape their posters to a big wall, providing a mosaic of the developing learning community.

Now it is time to formally launch the camp. Lead facilitators Eduardo Mendonça and Silvia Giovannoni call the group together and offer warm, enthusiastic words of welcome. The two-hour opening group session is devoted to creating a context for learning and building a sense of community. Eduardo invites everyone to stand up and join in building a group rhythm, using their bodies as percussion instruments: "No experience is needed. All you have to do is follow me as we build this rhythm step by step." The young people quickly fall into sync with one another, smiling and laughing as they successfully achieve their first creative task as a whole group. After a few minutes the rhythm is firmly established. Eduardo affirms everyone, saying, "You all did such a great job that now we are going to bump it up to another level." Already, in the first few moments of the gathering, he is setting up a pattern of affirmation followed by creative challenge that will continue throughout the week.

Next, a young staff member and four youths tentatively step forward to sing a welcome song. We call this an invocation because it acknowledges the deeper purpose and possibility of coming together. It also demonstrates what it's like to take a creative risk, and how your offering doesn't need to be polished and perfect in order to be meaningful. The clapping and shouts of appreciation that ensue bolster the singers' confidence. Shyness falls away and they are all smiles.

The community-building session includes a variety of elements (which will be described in Chapter 4) and culminates in small-group performances that combine short dance movements with a cheer. Music and dance are ubiquitous in Brazilian culture, so the groups embrace this creative challenge with heightened enthusiasm. While it's obvious that this type of intentional, friendly community-building experience is brand new for the young participants, they are already beginning to feel at home. After the opening session, the staff is both relieved and proud of their accomplishment. They have met the underlying goals of a powerful beginning, and the air is electric with anticipation for what is to come next.

The following days are a whirlwind of whole-group interactive learning sessions, small-group workshops, reflection-group meetings and evening community arts activities. Hour by hour the atmosphere becomes richer and more delicious. On the second day, when people share their life stories through an activity called River of Life, the community bonds are already strong enough to hold the tears that accompany many of the stories. Young people begin to say things like "I have never felt safe enough to share what is really happening in my life until now" and "This is the first time I have taken the risk to talk about what is really in my heart, and I feel so much better." At the open mic several days later, the youth blow their own minds—as well as ours—with the risks they take dancing, playing music, singing, reading poems and telling stories to our warm and friendly community.

As with most camps, a few young people require more time and patience in order to relax into the embrace of this loving community. By the end though, the most challenged youth have moved from hovering on the edge of the action to being in the very center, with all of their enthusiasm. Staff members, some of whom had never worked with youth, are enthusiastically leading dance, writing and visual arts workshops and facilitating reflection sessions. On the last full day of camp, the youth lead all of the activities, including a community meeting, a whole-group learning session and a wide range of workshops. A deep sense of achievement and shared pride permeates the community. "Look at what we have created!"

And now it's time for the conversation to turn toward returning home and to ask the question, What meaning can each of us make of this experience in our lives outside of camp? After dinner on the final evening, a small group of campers and staff invite the entire community to join them in a closing ritual they have carefully designed. The 65 youth and adults form a circle on a candlelit patio. "I am leaving behind shyness," whispers 14-year-old Maria as she throws a slip of paper into a cauldron in the center of the circle. Picking up a decorated stone to take home as a memento, Maria then declares, "I am taking with me the courage to speak out." One by one, each youth and adult follows suit. The leaders then gather the slips of paper and toss them into a nearby fire pit, where they burn to ashes, the letting go made visible by the rising smoke.

When one of the adults steps forward to lead a final song, Tharles, a boy of about 16 taps him softly on the shoulder and says, "Excuse me, Rodrigo. I hope you don't mind, but we've planned something else for this moment." Tharles then stands in front of each adult, one after the other, and offers a personal message of affirmation and thanks. Finally he motions to the rest of the youth to join him in singing a song they had written for the staff in secret over the previous two days. "*Obrigado, Obrigado, Obrigado, Obrigado.*" (Thank you) They sing the refrain with gusto each time it comes around. "The words and melody brought tears to our eyes," says facilitator Silvia Giovannoni. "We were all bursting with pride over these kids we had come to love, and they were obviously proud of themselves."

The next morning everyone gathers in a circle to say final goodbyes, and then the youth reluctantly climb on the bus to return home. "If you don't hold a camp next year," calls one youth out the window, "we're going to hijack this bus and come back anyway." As they drive down the long driveway, we can hear the singing begin.

This camp felt special—as does every camp. Even though it was our first time running a camp in Brazil, and it was carried out by a group of people new to the Creative Community Model, it achieved all the aspects of a profound learning event. This demonstrates something we have experienced over and over again, in many different parts of the world: how deeply humans yearn to come together to connect and support each other in taking the next powerful steps to bring out their creative power. It's as if we are designed to be together in this way. As Luciana Andrade, director of a youth entrepreneurial program and a staff member at the camp said, "The camp made a huge difference in the young people's lives and in my own life. I believe the camp rescues the meaning of being human and living in a community."

 ## The Creative Community Model

The Agrifirma Brazil camp is based on the Creative Community Model, an approach to building transformative, intergenerational learning communities. The model, which we and our colleagues have developed over the past two decades, integrates creative process, the social application of the arts, group dynamics and interactive learning into a way of bringing people together that aims to move each person along his or her life

It takes a village to raise a child: The Creative Community Model

path. It is challenging to capture the entirety in words, because the model is based on a multi-dimensional experience influenced by the people who take part in any given program. What we can offer, however, is the structure, the underlying principles, and the role the facilitators play in leading programs and gatherings that elicit a kind of magic over and over again. While we will use the week-long youth camp as our primary example, in Chapter 3 you'll see how you can apply the principles and practices in a wide range of situations.

Underlying Principles

The quality and impact of your program is intimately connected to where you "come from"—the basic set of lenses through which you perceive and interact with people. Here's a good example of how perspective turned what could have been a shaming experience into a transformative one. Laura Ellen came to a Power of Hope camp in Canada seven years ago at her mother's insistence. "I did everything I could to avoid going, and I didn't want to be there!" she told us years later. "But the very first day, I had an experience that changed me forever." She and another new camper were watching some youth dance, and they started giggling when a developmentally delayed camper lay down on her back and twirled wildly around the floor. "One of the counselors came up to us and kindly asked, 'Why are you laughing? She simply wants to express her creativity,'" said Laura Ellen. "When she said that, something shifted in me. I realized that I wanted to feel free to express my creativity as well. In that moment, I decided to try everything at the camp, and that has had a lasting effect on my life. I'm now 22, and my choice of university, the experiences I've had, and my dreams and aspirations are completely different than if I had not gone to the camp. I would be living a much more constrained life."

The youth worker who spoke with Laura Ellen that first day of camp approached her kindly, believing in her goodness and the magnetic call of creativity, and that made all the difference. Here is the set of lenses or attitudes that are basic to the Creative Community Model.

Our lives have meaning: All life is interconnected, inherently meaningful and full of purpose. There is, as teacher and philosopher Parker Palmer says, a hidden wholeness in each of us waiting to emerge. This means that each of us is on Earth for a reason, and one of the purposes of life is to discover what that is.

We are all creative: Creativity is not found just in the chosen few who exhibit artistic talent. Creativity has to do with much more than the "arts"; it is a force that flows through each of us, allowing us to dream things up and make them happen. We can find, encourage and bring forward creativity in every single one of us.

We are good at heart: When we get to the core of each person we find compassion and love for the world. Humans are inherently loving, and under the right circumstances and the right influences, this inner goodness can emerge.

Life is an adventure to be lived, not a problem to be solved: Yes, we have challenges and so do most of the youth we work with, but we find that something quite different—and more creative—happens when we look at life from the vantage point of possibility rather than pathology.

The inner life is as vital as the outer life: We each have a life on the inside that is just as real as life outside of us. Our relationship to our inner self is as important as any relationship we have with other people. Part of the adventure of life is to come to know who we are on the inside.

Diversity is a resource: Nature thrives on complexity and diversity, and the same is true for the human community. Our differences in age, gender, race, culture and backgrounds provide a rich source of learning.

We all hold untapped potential: No matter what our life circumstances, we each have a vast capacity for growth. By virtue of our ability to imagine and to extend our caring for others, there are often more possibilities than we have considered.

Humans thrive within communities where they feel supported and seen: Just like a flower blossoms under the right conditions of soil, water and sun, human beings thrive when they feel safe, when they are witnessed and encouraged.

A healthy society requires intergenerational collaboration and wisdom exchange: Humanity is facing unprecedented challenges, and these cannot be solved by one generation alone. What is called for is a collective effort that spans generations.

We each have the power to make change: We are living in a time when, in order to thrive, we all must bring our skills and passions forward. The skills involved in creating positive change are required in the 21st century and are available to us all.

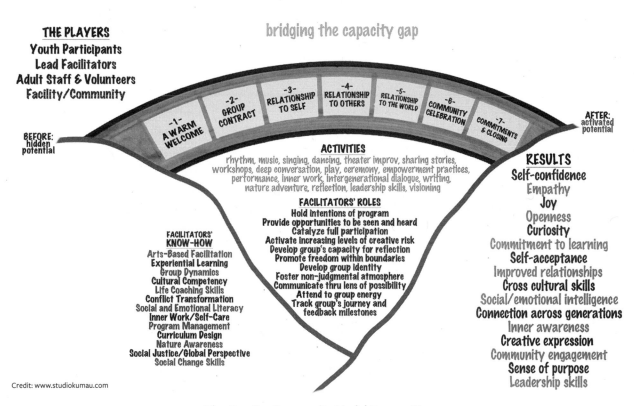

The Creative Community Model Process Map

Program Elements

Programs need a reliable structure in order to go deep—a skeleton that holds everything in place and guides the journey. The repetition of elements increases certainty; structure allows people to feel safe enough to delve deeper into their experience. We call these the elements of a program.

1. **A warm welcome:** preparing a beautiful, inviting space
2. **A creative invitation:** an activity that invites the imagination into the room
3. **Goals and agreements:** coming together on what we're here to do and how we can work together to optimize success
4. **Content activities:** interactive learning that addresses the program's theme
5. **Reflection:** articulating what we've learned and how we'll use it in our lives outside of the program
6. **Closing:** consciously acknowledging that the group energy is coming to an end

These elements provide the internal structure or framework for a program of any length, whether it's a week-long camp, a one-hour workshop or something in between. At a camp, for example, the structure provides the framework for the program as a whole as well as for each of the many events that happen within the camp, such as community meetings, small-group workshops and after-dinner reflection groups. Having a form that people can rely on sets the stage for freedom of expression and exploration.

The Nine Core Tasks of the Facilitator

You have your "come from" attitudes; you have your structure. What happens now depends on your facilitation. To achieve the benefits of the Creative Community Model, the facilitators attend to nine core tasks simultaneously. This may seem complicated at first, but the nine streams work together and support one another. While many other programs pay attention to some of these, the special alchemy of this model comes through integrating all nine.

MONDAY

7:30: Wake up

8-8:30: Breakfast

9-10:45: Whole group session

11-12:15: Workshop #1

1.
2.
3.
4.
5.
6.

12:15-1:30: Lunch

1:30-3:00: Workshop #2

1. NATURAL HIGH : Patty/Dave
2. ~~CLICK YOUR WE AM~~
3. BATIK : THADDEUS
4. FASHION FROM INSIDE OUT : LYNN
5. FREESTYLIN W/ RAY
6. ACROBALANCE : BROOK

3-3:15 Community meeting

3:15-5:45: Free time

45:30-5:45: Optional workshops

1. MASSAGE W/ DAVID
2. ART BARN
3. FASHION BARN
4.
5.

5:45: Gratitude circle

6-7:15: Dinner

7:15-8:00: Family Groups

8-10:30: EVENING Activity
   Theatre Improv!

11:00: Off to Bed

:30: Lights Out!

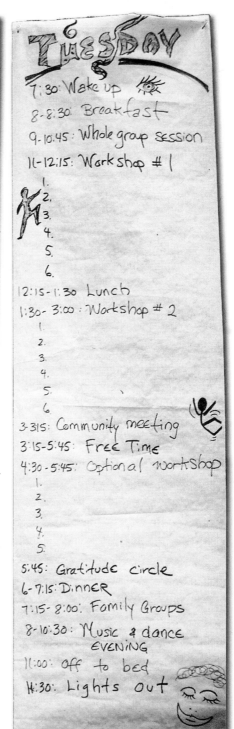

TUESDAY

7:30: Wake up

8-8:30: Breakfast

9-10:45: Whole group session

11-12:15: Workshop #1

1.
2.
3.
4.
5.
6.

12:15-1:30 Lunch

1:30-3:00: Workshop #2

1.
2.
3.
4.
5.
6.

3-3:15: Community meeting

3:15-5:45: Free Time

4:30-5:45: Optional workshop

1.
2.
3.
4.
5.

5:45: Gratitude circle

6-7:15: Dinner

7:15-8:00: Family Groups

8-10:30: Music & dance
   EVENING

11:00: Off to bed

11:30: Lights out

A camp workshop schedule waiting to be filled out.

Structure of a Typical Creative Community Camp

Here is the structure of a Creative Community camp. The structure sometimes varies slightly depending on the specific aims of our partner organizations. Each day follows a regular schedule. While the structure remains constant, what happens within it is ever changing. Following this exact schedule is not as important as having a flow that establishes a reliable rhythm to the days.

7:30 am: wake up

8–9: breakfast

9–10:30: community meeting and whole-group learning session

11–12:30: workshops led by staff and volunteers

12:30–1:30: lunch

1:30–3:00: workshops led by staff and volunteers

3:00–5:45: free time

5:45: gratitude circle

6–7:30: dinner

7:30–8:00: evening reflection groups

8–10: community event

General Themes of the Days

Over the course of the week our themes move from the inner life to our lives in the world.

Day 1: Community Building

Day 2: Setting Intentions

Day 3: Relationship to Self

Day 4: Relationship to Others

Day 5: Relationship to Nature

Day 6: Relationship to the World

Day 7: Youth Leadership

Evening Events

The themes of our evening programs move from community building to creative expression to reflection to saying goodbye.

Day 1: Community Building

Day 2: Theater Improvisation

Day 3: Music and Dance

Day 4: Personal Storytelling

Day 5: Free Evening

Day 6: Open Mic

Day 7: Closing Celebration

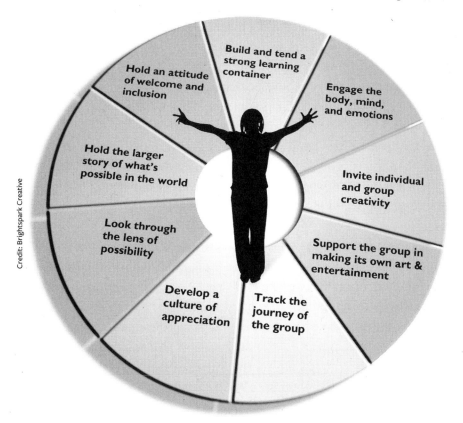

Credit: Brightspark Creative

The Nine Core Tasks of the Facilitator.

1. Hold an attitude of welcome and inclusion: "Let's only hear from youth who haven't yet spoken," says the facilitator. Inviting the quieter voices into a conversation is one way of attending to inclusion. Creative communities are all about participation, and it's the facilitator's role to invite everyone into the game. In multigenerational programs, the adults participate in all the activities right along with the youth while remaining conscious of not taking up too much space. There is no standing around the sidelines watching the young people do their thing. This creative engagement brings the adults alive and significantly shifts the dynamic between generations. As one adult volunteer said, "Creativity evens the playing field." Time and again we've seen young people light up when an adult is willing to take a big creative risk like making a stumbling attempt at freestyle rapping.

This spirit of inclusion calls for the facilitators to have a spacious, open attitude, ever scanning to invite in new voices and new forms of creative expression. It means welcoming conflict and diversity of opinion. It means looking for a place and a way for each individual to shine. And it never stops. Would those visitors who dropped in like to participate? Can the cooks take some time out to join a workshop? Would the maintenance team like to take a break and sing with the group? Can we find a role for a young man who sits quietly at the edge of the group? The more inclusive we are, the richer the experience is for all—and the benefits of inclusivity provide an important lesson for the youth.

2. Build and tend a strong learning container: "One of the best ways to build a community is to learn each other's names," says the facilitator introducing name games near the beginning of a program. She is actively building what's often called "the container," the invisible vessel within which a group creates a shared experience. The container for your program will be weak or strong depending on how well you construct and maintain it. The Creative Community Model calls for using a step-by-step process (described in Chapter 4) to build a strong and safe container.

Building a strong container also requires working with the staff and volunteers to understand risk management and boundary issues with youth, and making sure the young people know all the safety rules. Once the container is created, the facilitators need to tend it by noticing how each individual is thriving and how the group is doing as a whole. When the group hits rough waters, the lead facilitators have to rely on their faith in the process, holding to the structure yet at the same time responding to the needs of the group. As a facilitator you can sometimes find yourself saying to fellow staff and volunteers, "Don't worry. This is a perfectly natural part of the process," while beginning to wonder yourself if it's all going to be okay. This is a lonely position and provides a good rationale for working with a co-facilitator whenever possible. The more experience you have, however, the easier it becomes to trust the process.

3. Engage the body, mind and emotions in the learning process: "Okay! We have identified our community agreements, so let's seal the deal. I am

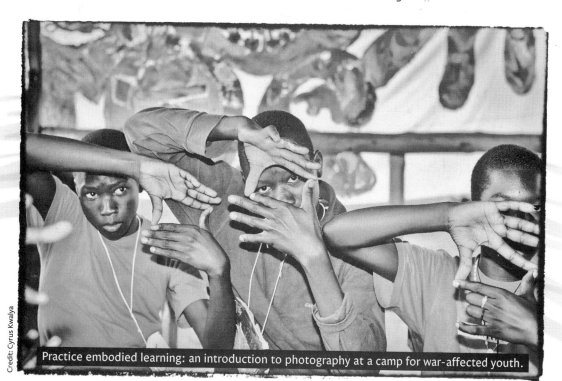

Credit: Cyrus Kwalya

Practice embodied learning: an introduction to photography at a camp for war-affected youth.

going to count to three, and on three I want everyone who can go along
with these agreements to jump toward the center of the circle all together
and shout out, 'yes' as loudly as you can!" The facilitator has just gone
through a process of identifying community agreements. Now he is providing a simple and direct way for participants to affirm their agreement
by bringing their bodies into the equation. Too many of us were taught
to sit still and learn, and we bring these stale habits into our groups. It is
your job as facilitator to attend to the energy of the group and find ways to
engage the "whole person" in the learning process all along the way. This
keeps everyone awake and involved, body and soul. The activities in this
book provide a myriad of ways to bring body, mind and emotions into
the process.

4. Consistently invite individual and group creativity: "Once you've told
us your name and where you're from, please mime something you like
to do," says the facilitator, starting a go-around of introductions. Adding

a low-stakes creative challenge like acting out something you like to do initiates a process of creative risk-taking. Providing opportunities to take incrementally more challenging creative risks over the course of a program is a cornerstone of the Creative Community Model. We start with easy risks such as making a colorful name tag or miming something you like to do, and then we turn up the heat slowly. Each creative risk we take builds our courage to take the next one, until before we know it we're singing solo for a group of 40 colleagues or comfortably speaking in front of an audience of 300.

Through this consistent process of taking creative risks and receiving support from the group, we watch youth after youth pop out of their shyness, and many never go back into their shells. It's as if you can see their self-confidence grow right before your eyes. The same occurs in adult trainings. In a program for educators in South Africa, for example, one especially quiet teacher began speaking up in the group while playing theater games. The headmaster of the school was happily surprised, especially when the teacher continued to participate more actively in staff meetings for months after the training.

Posing group creative challenges is another way to build personal confidence, collaboration skills and the ability to connect. When a group works together to make beauty, the members bond almost instantly in spite of their differences. Even the shyest participants will usually join in. At camps, the first of many group challenges comes at the end of the opening evening when the family groups (small reflections groups that meet daily throughout the week) each come up with a name and cheer to perform for the larger group. The results are fun, funny and heartwarming, and participants get a positive hit of appreciation for their offerings.

Weaving group creative challenges into a program design has the decided benefit of bringing people together across cultural differences. On the second day of a Creative Facilitation program in Santa Fe, New Mexico, three participants came up to us in tears, independent of one another, expressing essentially the same sentiment: "I've lived here for years and this is the first time I have experienced working together—Native Americans, Latinos, and whites—with respect and admiration. And having fun together." We see this same effect again and again.

5. Support the group in making its own art and entertainment: "For this week we all get to be creators of culture rather than passive consumers," has been our rallying cry since the very first camp. This means that the youth and adults make up everything from scratch. The staff paint colorful, hand-made signs for welcome, registration, daily agenda, workshop options, dishwashing schedules and any other logistical needs. The group provides all its own entertainment through song, dance, theater games and storytelling. The act of creating our own culture brings out the personality of each person and builds the group identity. It also proves that we are capable of entertaining ourselves without having to be perfect.

We recommend beginning your programs with empty walls—fresh canvases ready to be animated with the expressions of the group. When leading activities, start with a blank page rather than copied forms. If an exercise requires a chart, for example, ask participants to draw their own charts rather than handing out pre-drawn images to fill in. The results are always surprising, personal and imaginative. Over the course of the program, the art produced in plenary sessions and workshops covers the walls, reflecting the personality of the group.

6. Track the journey of the group: "What we are doing right now is really challenging," a facilitator tells the group when participants start to get fidgety during the opening session of a camp. "Getting a community started requires going over a certain amount of details, and I appreciate how you are hanging in there." Whether you have embarked on a seven-day residential camp experience or a two-hour workshop, you and your participants are on a learning journey together with a clear purpose. Your job as a facilitator is to hold the program goals and the roadmap of the process firmly in your consciousness and remind the group of where they are at key points along the way. This allows the participants to fully immerse themselves in the learning experience without getting lost.

Midway through a week-long camp experience, the leader might challenge the group by saying, "We only have a few days left together. Let's take a moment right now and think back to when we arrived. What intention did you set for yourself? Are you doing what you set out to do? What more do you want from this experience?" Tracking the journey assists participants in locating themselves within the full-on flow of the group's life together, helping the group and its individual members reflect on the experience and make more conscious choices for how they respond to opportunities for growth.

7. Develop a culture of appreciation: "I am noticing how well you are all listening right now, and that is really helping us get our camp going on a positive note. Thank you." The field of appreciative inquiry asserts that by paying attention to what *does* work (as in the case of the facilitator above) rather than what *doesn't* work we naturally move in the direction of improvement and greater integration. Cultures worldwide have taboos against appreciating oneself or another for fear of feeding the ego or spoiling the child. The tide seems to be turning on this, however, and we find appreciation to be powerful support for youth and adults alike.

The facilitators can set a tone by actively identifying strengths in individuals and the group as a whole. For example, "It took a lot of courage for you to stand up and say that in front of the whole group." Or "I really appreciate your ability to pay attention when we are talking." We similarly encourage all of the adults to identify strengths they see in the youth and in one another and feed them back to one another. You can consciously begin building a culture of appreciation during the community agreement process with agreements like "avoid put-downs of self or other."

8. Look through the lens of possibility: Educational philosopher Parker Palmer says that inside each of us is a "hidden wholeness." When we fully embrace this idea, we come to see one another as a bundle of possibilities to engage with rather than as a litany of problems to fix. It is easy to fall into bemoaning what's wrong, but it requires serious discipline to switch from problem to possibility.

When we hold this view of the youth at our programs, surprising things happen. For example, when Maria showed up at our camp one summer she had been living in a homeless shelter. Her first words were: "Get me the f--- out of here. I do not want to be around all these f---ing positive people." Rather than focus on her negativity, the facilitator paid attention to her strong presence and powerful voice.

While leading an opening activity, the facilitator approached Maria, who was skulking in the sidelines. "Maria," she said, "I'm having a hard time being heard. If I whisper the instructions to you, could you call them out so everyone can hear?" Maria did so, and by the end of the activity her attitude had completely shifted. After that she saw herself as a leader at the camp, and so did the others. Given her background, gaining the admiration of youth from so many sectors of society was a new and important experience. Maria attended camp multiple times and became devoted to the program. Even though initial indications suggested that things might not go well with Maria, the facilitator gambled on the side of possibility and it paid off.

We also use the lens of possibility in how we react to situations as they occur in the real-life adventure of building a community. When we run into the bumps and bruises that come in community living, we ask the youth to focus on what is possible among us as a group and how we might work together to get there. Even distressing situations provide powerful opportunities to move beyond our habitual ways of responding. If some money is stolen at camp, for example, rather than lay down the law, we might inquire with the group, "How might we handle this differently?"

At a girls' empowerment weekend, for example, it came out that a small group of students had been harassing some of the other participants. To address the situation, the facilitator called an impromptu community meeting and began with the question, "What have we been doing so far that has been achieving our goal of building a positive community of girls and women?" One of the girls who had been causing the trouble called out, "I haven't felt like pulling out a knife and stabbing anyone this whole weekend." A youth worker immediately cut in with, "You can't say something like that here!" But the facilitator stood up for the girl: "Yes, she can. She's being honest." That proved to be a magical moment. Once the young women realized they could say whatever was on their minds, as long as they were being honest, everyone relaxed. Feelings were expressed and they all came together around the aim of working together during the last six hours of the program to make new headway with their goal of building a positive community.

9. Hold the larger story of what's possible in the world: "This world we live in—yes we know there are huge problems," says a camp facilitator. "It can even look quite hopeless, and yet at the same time there is so much that we don't know. There is so much mystery, so much beauty, so much joy, so much possibility." We find that young people thrive in a community where adults aren't afraid to admit to the magnitude of the challenges we are facing in the world and yet choose to live vital, positive lives, appreciating the mystery, the challenge and the adventure of it all.

Standing in possibility rather than cynicism empowers participants to believe in their own capacity to impact their world. With this in mind, it's the facilitator's job to remind the young people that the underlying purpose of the gathering is not to create a safe and blissful bubble, but rather for them to be able to return to the larger world more capable of living the lives they want and playing their part in moving toward a more just, loving and sustainable world. Holding this perspective will inform how facilitators guide a reflection process, present creative challenges to the group and relate to group members, acknowledging their inherent capacity to make an impact in the world. Holding the larger story of what is possible in our world infuses the whole learning experience with a deeper, more compelling purpose.

 ## Ready, Set, Create…

Building a creative community is both an art and a science, and it most certainly is an adventure. Let's move on to see ways to take this model out of the camp structure and apply the principles and practices in a wide range of situations.

The Creative Spark

Although the Creative Community Model emerged from our work with week-long youth camps, the principles and practices are applicable in almost any kind of gathering or learning program. In this chapter we'll take you to programs using the model in a wide range of venues from classrooms to business training sessions, from community events to parties.

 ## Adding an Arts Stream to Conferences

The five-day national gathering of the Earth Service Corps, a teen environmental organization sponsored by the YMCA, brought together a diverse group of 125 participants from all parts of the US, and it had a big agenda to cover. We were invited to design and facilitate the conference. The conveners were a bit nervous about letting us integrate the arts into the plan, for fear of losing focus on the business at hand, but it all worked out beautifully.

With the help of a small team of teaching artists, we developed a design that lightly wove creative expression throughout the entire conference. We opened the conference with the arts-infused community-building process outlined in Chapter 4. Each day began with a 45-minute "Get Creative" session in which people chose workshops in theater, visual arts, percussion or creative writing. One evening our drama specialist led a whole-group session on playing theater games to build community, and on the last night the whole group came together in an artful closing ritual designed by a committee of participants.

From the first evening, the conference was energetic and joyous. The morning "Get Creative" sessions set a lively, improvisational tone, and the group continued to demonstrate the power inherent in an arts-based approach. Here are two examples. One morning the Earth Service Corps executive director came to us and said, "I've always felt too shy to talk to big groups, but after drumming for the last hour, I feel so energized that I think I can do it." She proceeded to step onto the floor and deliver an inspiring and motivating call to action. This made a difference for the organization as a whole and proved to be a big step for her as a leader.

On the final afternoon of the conference, a few people called together a group to explore issues around racism and cultural disconnect in the environmental movement. Nearly a third of the conference joined in. The conversation went deep and continued through free time to dinner. There were lots of stories and lots of tears, and by the end, people felt that a miracle had occurred. How was it possible for such a diverse group to wade into the waters of racism and oppression, hear one another's stories without shame and defensiveness, and sit so tenderly with the pain of each other's experience?

We learned two important lessons at this conference. First, spending time being creative together at a conference—even one on a theme such as science or activism—activates learning and motivates people to return to the work at hand more energized and open. And second, people are more courageous about having difficult conversations when a strong community has been developed through taking creative risks together.

Even if you are not in the position to design a conference from whole cloth, you can make a significant impact on a gathering by adding a few arts elements to the process. Some years ago Peggy was invited to lead workshops on creative facilitation at a conference for environmentalists, policy makers, college professors and nature educators working on projects to save the Columbia River Watershed in the US Pacific Northwest. When she offered to add a light touch of arts into the conference process itself, the conveners readily accepted. Peggy started things off on a creative note by setting out art supplies and encouraging people to decorate their name tags as they arrived. To the surprise of some of the organizers, people happily absorbed themselves in the task. She then covered the front wall of the main conference room with a large hand-drawn outline of the Columbia River as it makes its way from the mountains of British Columbia to Oregon's Pacific coast. Over the course of the weekend, participants represented their projects along the river, using words, images and color. A vibrant map of their work emerged, providing a powerful image of their shared efforts to regenerate and preserve this magnificent ecosystem.

On the last morning of the conference, Peggy invited the entire assembly to form into groups of six to explore the wisdom of the animals in their region. She asked each group to choose an animal or plant and find a way to share that being's wisdom with the rest of the conference. Group after group entered the stage wearing colorful scarves, playing hand-held percussion instruments and making forest sounds. "I am eagle," said one group, facing the audience. "As you plan your activities to care for our forest, fly high, look far and wide and take the long view." This time of "embodied learning" added levity and energy to what was to be a long morning of speeches. The light touch of arts facilitation throughout the event brought together people from diverse sectors in the movement to care for the Columbia River watershed, and charged the conference with energy and enthusiasm.

Peggy's husband, Rick Ingrasci, similarly added creativity elements to a think-tank event he has hosted at the Hollyhock Center in British Columbia for over 25 years. Designed as a time for leaders in their respective fields to step off the podium and share their newest thinking with colleagues in a convivial and relaxed atmosphere, the Hollyhock Summer Gathering now looks a bit like a Creative Community camp for adults. The conference is filled with stimulating and far-ranging conversation as well as lots of opportunities for creative exploration and expression: decorating name tags, singing, theater improvisation and storytelling. The height of the conference is the open mic, which according to Rick plays a key role in the event. "The open mic seems to serendipitously pull together the major themes, values and learning that emerge at the

A father and son look at "graphic facilitation" of the Hollyhock Summer Gathering.

Credit: fbistudios.com

gathering as the participants creatively express what has had meaning for them." Rick now also runs a winter gathering at the Whidbey Institute on Whidbey Island each February. It's a winning format for bringing people together to address local and global concerns.

✋ Building Connected, Collaborative Teams

Business schools are increasingly recognizing the need for creativity training. At the School of Inspired Leadership (SOIL), a graduate-level business school near Delhi, India, Charlie accomplished this through a team-building training event based on the Creative Community Model. The first group of 30 spanned a wide age range and included esteemed professors, now teaching after successful careers in the business world, along with young staff members who had come of age in an India very different from that of their elders.

Over the course of the two days, participants learned ways to build more connected, innovative teams and increase the creativity of others through using arts activities based on creative writing, storytelling, music, dance, movement and theater. At one point Charlie watched in delight as several of the older professors danced across the room with colorful scarves to illustrate a group poem they had written. As the younger staff witnessed this, their bemused expressions told him they were truly seeing their elders in a new light.

This training was a creative stretch for all concerned—with lasting results. As one member of the group said, "I did things I could never see myself doing. The level of liberation I experienced will stay with me for a long time." Another said, "It was amazing to experience how seemingly simple techniques can be used to unleash creativity in our day-to-day work with industry." Months after the training, team members reported that the training had created a lasting shift in relationships and had significantly bridged the gap between the older and younger staff members.

Charlie similarly developed a two-day creativity-based team-building initiative for students in the Hult Business School's Master of Social Entrepreneurship and Master of Marketing programs in London. The students work in teams throughout the year, so his aim was to help students get to know one another, develop trust and build a supportive learning community. This cohort comprised students from all over the world; several were living in a new country for the first time.

The event included a number of collaborative challenges in which, for example, small groups worked together to perform group poems. Open-ended, creative challenge in an affirmative, judgment-free zone can build a deep sense of cohesion in a group. By the end of the first day of training, a very positive sense of community had developed. People who typically sat quietly on the sidelines were jumping in freely. Comments like, "We are all the same but so different, and it is comforting" and "I have never felt so at home in a group so quickly.… I am so excited about the year ahead," told him that something special was happening for this group as they embarked on their year together.

Through applying these principles in numerous university settings, we have learned to trust that "something special" happens when people find the safety and the tools to claim more and more of their creative selves. For instance, in the Hult event one seemingly shy young woman from Jordan later shared: "I was feeling unconnected to the people I was surrounded with here at school. After this PYE program I've got the strength I need to feel comfortable sharing with my classmates. I am amazed to be feeling this way!"

Transforming the Classroom

Artists, facilitators and elementary school students in Vancouver, BC, are demonstrating the effectiveness of using the multi-arts to cultivate an understanding of themselves and each other. Human EYES is an inter-generational and intercultural storytelling project that engages students in exploring the diversity of perspectives and experiences within their classrooms and their own ancestry. Spearheaded by Deblekha Guin, executive director of the Access to Media Society, and PYE facilitators Rup

Human EYES students play non-verbal freeze tag.

Credit: Human EYES

Sidhu and Sara Kendall, the program uses rhythm, beat boxing, theater, song, music, spoken word, photography, sewing and video animation to create a dynamic and learning journey. "The minute Rup, Peggy, and Ella stepped into the room, the class was blown away," said Daniele Carrara, a teacher at Hastings Elementary School. "Right away they had the students sitting in a circle making rhythm and music—totally engaged."

Among many activities, the students used a version of the "My Life As a Stream" activity as a metaphorical "way in" to interviewing and retelling the stories of their elders through collage and animation. (See page 241.) "Oftentimes we don't think to ask the people around us questions about their lives," said Daniele. "This program gave my students a reason to open up that line of communication with their elders, and the stories that came forward were truly incredible."[13]

"This is one of the most effective interdisciplinary programs I've ever been a part of in connecting youth with each other and their own personal ancestry," said Rup. "I attribute this to the combination of caring facilitators, youth hungry for connection and the multi-arts approach, which gives everyone a place to shine." The videos and pictures of Human EYES demonstrate many of the activities in this book—and show how they can be used in the classroom to develop empathy, emotional intelligence and an understanding of social justice issues. For more information about Access to Media's work, visit www.accesstomedia.org.

Jackie Amatucci is an example of the increasing number of public school teachers who use the Creative Community Model practices to shift the culture in their classrooms. She had been teaching language arts in public schools for 20 years when she first came to a PYE Creative Facilitation workshop. "During the training, I had a major 'aha,'" she recalled. "I realized for the first time that I am, in fact, creative." With that new identity, she decided to implement some of the training activities in her classroom. She soon discovered that by making small changes that required very little time, she could have a huge impact on her students' performance.

"I began to view each classroom period as a mini-learning event that requires all of the Creative Community program elements from opening to closing," said Jackie. "I began my early morning class with an opening metaphor activity I call 'Taking the Temperature of the Class.' I go around the room and ask everyone to rate how they feel on a scale of one to ten, one being 'I'm too tired to be here,' and ten being 'Ready to go.' I then acknowledge each student's offering without judgment. Once we've gone around, everyone is more awake and ready to learn." After doing this for a few days, one of the students spontaneously began adding all of the numbers and coming up with a daily average that he charted on the wall to show how the class was feeling over the course of a week. "This is the kind of thing I see happen spontaneously when I welcome imagination into the room."

She also began to take control of the end of the class period. "The students would always get fidgety at the close of class, and when I let the bell be the closing, it left everyone feeling jagged." She came up with different ways of closing the class, such as going around the room asking each student to say one word for how he was feeling as the class ended. She'd then give them the final few minutes of class time to get their things together and prepare to leave. "Taking control of the closing allowed all of us to leave the class with a feeling of calm."

Jackie also started integrating arts-based activities, such as making group poems, into her literature and language classes (see page 197). "We wrote the poems and posted them all over our classroom and in the hallway right outside our door. The students took great pride in their work." Bringing the arts into her classroom had multiple benefits, said Jackie. "Once I realized I could be a creative artist in my own classroom, I found a new joy for teaching, and the students began to excel in new ways." And she was able to do all of this without even asking for permission. "I just slipped it in. I now believe that we can all be stealth change agents in our own classrooms."

 ## Youth Workers Training Teachers

Here's how teaching artists in a Ugandan organization used the model to affect their local school system. In Movement, our partner organization in Kampala, provides art classes and camps for primary and secondary school students from orphanages. Time and again the local teachers would ask the In Movement staff why their students were so much more enthusiastic about the arts camps than they were about school. Finally, In Movement decided to offer training for the teachers to demonstrate their approach.

Friendly trainers and colorful welcome signs greeted the 30 teachers, and the workshop followed a typical day at an In Movement youth camp, based on the Creative Community Model structure. "By the end of the day, the teachers had become very self-reflective and vulnerable in their sharing," said In Movement advisor Justin Silbaugh. "There were many tears during the closing as the teachers talked about how they could see that some of their practices were actually harming their youth." Several days later one of the teachers reported that he had taken a new tack with a student who had been continually late for school. Instead of punishing the child, he took the time to have a conversation with him. As he listened he learned about the home situation that was preventing the student from getting to school on time. The teacher then called the family, and together they solved the problem.

Through training teachers in six countries, we have come to expect such epiphanies as participants reclaim their own creative lives and

Young Women Empowered participants enjoy a talk at their career day.

Credit: Y-WE

witness how youth thrive when they feel safe and their imaginations are engaged. Said one teacher in India, "Before this camp, I never knew what these children were capable of. My teaching will never be the same."

 ## Empowering Young Women

For the past three years, an innovative group of youth workers, teaching artists and mentors in Seattle, has been running a creative leadership program for teen women, based on the Creative Community Model. Called Young Women Empowered, the program serves girls from a wide range of communities, many from immigrant families. "We include creativity in every aspect of our program," said cofounder and program director Jamie-Rose Edwards. "Studies show that girls get quiet as they reach adolescence. Creative expression helps them come out of their shells, develop confidence and find their voices—and even gain the courage to speak in front of a large group."

"Oftentimes when youth workers send young women to the program, they say things like, 'I hope you won't be disappointed, because my girls won't do any of that creative stuff,'" said Jamie-Rose. "But we never see that. Everyone who comes loves to dance, make art and play theater games. It's as if they were just waiting for the chance."

Using the arts also helps the mentors and young women develop rapport and enter into deep discussions about issues they face every day.

"People are always surprised by how comfortable they feel, even when they are joining in for the first day and don't know anyone," said Leslie Cotter, cofounder. To learn more, see www.youngwomenempowered.org.

 ## Fostering Youth/Adult Dialogue

Adults often tell us that they yearn to know people from younger generations in their community. We developed a format for intergenerational dialogues in our own town, and several years ago it was taken up by a group of youth and adults after a tragedy occurred on Vashon Island, a community near Seattle. A heated exchange between a 16-year-old and her dad resulted in the man killing his daughter. As the shock and grief subsided, a group of community members decided it was time to do something to change the dynamic between teens and adults in their town.

More than 50 teens and 50 adults attended the first event. They followed a basic format that included building community through making creative name tags, doing a group rhythm activity, sharing goals and agreements, playing name games and then the storytelling game Yes, and… (see page 216).

The adults and youth then divided into separate groups for an exercise called Fishbowl. Each group came up with a list of questions they were sincerely curious about. Then the whole assembly reconvened, with the youth sitting in the center of the circle. The adults posted their questions on a flip chart, and for 20 minutes the youth responded to the questions that appealed to them. Then they switched roles. The adults sat in the center of the circle and responded to questions posted by the youth.

A Dialogue in Kampala, Uganda, brings youth and adults together to discuss living with HIV/AIDS.

The Fishbowl questions in a community dialogue vary widely depending on the theme of the conversation and who is in the room. Some questions are disarmingly simple. "What are you afraid of?" asked one island teen, saying she felt like adults avoided her as she walked down the streets in her community. A middle-aged man shared a similar experience of feeling invisible to teens and asked, "What to do you think or feel when you see someone like me?"

At the end of the Fishbowl, the facilitators engaged the entire group in discussion. Finally they asked everyone to identify action steps they could take to improve the relationship between youth and adults in their community. They closed the event with a time to share thanks and sing a song.

The positive impact of this community dialogue was immediately evident. The group continued holding these gatherings for over seven years and developed other initiatives as well, such as a series of intergenerational potluck dinners to provide a forum for more informal discussion, and a film series with topics of interest to both teens and adults. Attendance at local youth art and performance events increased dramatically as a multitude of new relationships were formed.

One young woman shared, "Very rarely are youth given the opportunity to interact with adults on the same level. Speaking as a youth, I can tell you that it is positively intoxicating." An adult reported, "One of the things that made the Vashon Island dialogues really deep and energizing was the opportunity to get creative together, because when that happens, people show up as who they really are and trust gets established quickly. I've never seen anything like it." After several years of participating and finally leading the dialogues, another young person said, "The interesting thing that I learned is that the issues of adults and the issues of youth are exactly the same. They are just packaged differently."

We have used this Creative Community dialogue process in several communities around the world, and the results are equally impressive. In Uganda, for example, we held a dialogue between teens living with HIV/AIDS and adults in leadership positions in NGOs, health organizations and local churches. The adults were surprised by the depth and clarity of the youth, and gained new perspective on the real needs of the teens they were serving.

Hosting Parties with Punch

Parties? Really? Yes, a party—like any other human gathering—is an opportunity to connect. You can use the arts-based activities in this book to turn your parties into truly memorable occasions where people have a lot of fun and really connect with one another. Of course, you are *not* going to want your guests to feel like they are at a workshop, so you likely won't include goals and agreements. Here are some ideas:

Write pass-around poems: In groups of six or seven, ask everyone to write pass-around poems (see page 199). One person from each group then gets to share a poem with the whole group. If it's a special occasion, such as a birthday, you can use metaphors representing the celebrated person as starter phrases for the poems.

Play theater games: This can be a big stretch for some people, so you need to start with low-risk games and give people the chance to opt out entirely. The results are fun, funny and memorable. Inevitably people get to see new aspects of their friends.

Make blessing cards: At the beginning of a New Year's Eve party one year we asked each of our guests to write a blessing on a card and then add design using oil pastels, feathers, ribbons and/or collage. We placed the cards in a basket, and at midnight we held a short ritual in which each person stated an intention for the coming year and pulled a card randomly out of the basket. While everyone enjoyed receiving the cards, we later realized that making the cards had had it's own effect. As people wrote blessings it was as if they were blessing themselves. This cast a warm glow over the entire party.

Tell a group story using Yes, and …: At the 70th birthday party of a close friend, 30 of us used the game Yes, and… to weave an imaginary story of his life from birth to the present (see page 216). As the narrative drew to a close, he looked at us incredulously. "How did you know?" he asked. It turns out our story uncannily followed the actual events of his life.

He was so moved, he said it was one of the best birthday parties he had ever had.

People enjoy being recognized and honored, particularly during life transitions. And most of us yearn to connect at a deeper level. Parties are an ideal place for this to happen.

Making It Your Own

In this chapter you've seen several ways to use the ideas and activities in this book to bring joy, meaning, and a deeper sense of connection to gatherings and learning events for youth or adults. We hope you feel inspired and challenged to bring your creative self to more and more areas of your life and work. But please be forewarned: working in this way can become addictive!

six elements of the community experience

Powerful Beginnings: Building a Community

Fourteen-year-old Brendan arrived at his first Power of Hope conference in an angry mood, but that soon changed. "My mom forced me to come here," he later confessed, "but after I arrived, I started having the feeling that this might be good." He liked the way the entrance hall to the public high school had been decorated to feel friendly. "This place seemed really cool. I met all kinds of people as soon as I got there, and I found myself wondering why I hadn't wanted to come."

Anvesh, an MBA student at the SOIL business school near Delhi, India, was similarly out of sorts when he arrived at our Creative Facilitation workshop. How was he was going to survive a program where he was expected to step out of the box? he wondered. As soon as the workshop started, though, his mood began to shift. "I somehow felt welcome in spite of my depressed state of mind," he said. Anvesh has a keen interest in group process and wondered how we had made it possible for him to move out of his negative state of mind so quickly.

Whether your participants are angry and upset when they arrive or happy and excited, you can be sure their emotions are heightened. Think for a moment about what it's like for you when you enter a new situation—a group, a conference or a classroom. Depending on the circumstances, you might feel uncertain or maybe happy to be there. You might be asking yourself questions like, Are these people going to like me? Am I going to like them? Am I going to enjoy being here? Is this worth my time? Emotions run the gamut.

Time and again people tell us they are surprised by how quickly they settle into Creative Community programs. We credit this to the attention we pay to the beginning. We intentionally build a safe and supportive creative community by developing the social connective tissue that binds people together and gives them the courage to be themselves. When that invisible glue is absent, people feel stiff, uncomfortable and disengaged, but when it's there, the flow takes over.

The good news is that with a little knowledge and practice, you can consciously create that comfortable, at-home feeling in your group. To achieve this, however, *you must* dedicate time to community building during the first segment of your program. It doesn't just happen on its own. The amount of time you need depends on the duration of your program. For example, community building takes three to four hours at a week-long camp, but only an hour and a half for a two-day training. For a two-hour workshop you might compress it to fifteen minutes. If you make the mistake of bypassing building your community, however, and instead rush to get into the "real" stuff of your program, you'll spend the rest of the time making up for it. By the end of a successful opening process, a positive group identity will have begun to form. Most participants will be relaxed and engaged and infused with a common sense of purpose.

Community Building in 11 Steps

Here is an 11-step process for building a creative learning community, with ideas on how to operationalize each step. As you become familiar with the activities and their purposes, you'll likely discover many others you can use to achieve the same results. The challenge is to provide multiple opportunities to take creative risks by weaving arts-based activities into all aspects of your opening, stepping up the level of risk bit by bit as you move along.

	Goal		How to Get There
1	Welcome the whole person.	→	Create a warm and welcoming space with colorful signs and a friendly greeting.
2	Invite the imagination.	→	Decorate name tags or make them from scratch.
3	Engage the body.	→	Build a group rhythm.
4	Acknowledge a larger purpose.	→	Share a poem, performance or song that sets a meaningful tone for the program.
5	Establish your credibility with the group.	→	Deliver a short, compelling and vulnerable personal introduction.
6	Bring every voice into the room.	→	Invite participants to do personal introductions or, with large groups of over 40, do a poll of who is here.
7	Learn names.	→	Play creative name games.
8	Clarify the purpose and potential of the experience.	→	Present the program goals with talking points.
9	Share the responsibility for maintaining a positive group experience.	→	Develop and agree upon a set of community agreements.
10	Develop deeper bonds.	→	Play games that allow participants to practice self-disclosure.
11	Build group cohesion.	→	Address a creative challenge in small groups with an opportunity to perform for the larger group.

1. Welcome the Whole Person

People arrive in a new program with their senses heightened, ready to notice and interpret the smallest details of their experience. This means you can accomplish a lot through a positive initial encounter. How you set up your room and how you greet your participants really matters.

Take the time to make your workshop space as warm and welcoming as possible. If necessary, clean the room and move out any excess furniture

Beautiful hand-made signs provide a warm welcome.

Credit: Jackie Amatucci

to make a large open space. Whether you are in a funky, cluttered space or a bland conference room, do the best you can to spiff it up. Finally, set up your room with a circle of chairs and a flip chart and markers to signal to your participants that this will be an interactive, collaborative experience.

When people arrive, take the time to introduce yourself and chat a bit. This both helps them feel comfortable and eases your own pre-program jitters. A warm welcome can make a difference at the beginning of a school class as well. After attending our Heart of Facilitation program in Washington State, one teacher said. "I used to spend the time between classes sitting at my desk with my back to the door catching up on my email. Now, I stand at the door and greet each student individually as they enter the room. My students are much more attentive as a result."

2. Invite the Imagination

The sooner you can get people involved in a creative activity, the quicker your community will begin to take form. At our trainings we ask everyone to make *a creative name tag* as soon as they've registered. This activity is both starter yeast for the imagination and a gentle icebreaker. It's so much easier to ask someone to pass the scissors than it is to embark on a deep conversation. While most people jump right into making their name tags, some get that deer in the headlights look. Gently encourage the more reluctant artists by saying things like, "Let yourself be inspired by other people. There's no harm in copying," or "Feathers are the secret ingredient for great name tags. Add some feathers, and it's guaranteed to look great." This is a chance to let people know that they won't be judged here. This workshop is going to be fun and supportive.

If you don't have time to make name tags from scratch, ask people to add a bit of color and design to their pre-made tag. The color on the name tags radiates creativity. If your workshop is part of a larger conference, your participants' name tags will stand out and spread a meme of creativity.

At longer programs, such as camps or conferences, you might have time for a more involved opening arts activity such as I-AM posters. Youth and adults thoroughly enjoy making these personal posters. Make a gallery of the completed I-AM posters to help participants get to know each other.

A Recipe for Participation

One of the most common questions we hear in training events is, How do I get youth to participate? Here is a model of group formation that offers some insight. It's called the IPC model and it goes like this:

Imagination⤵
　　　⤷Participation⤵
　　　　　⤷Commitment

I. **Imagination:** When you engage people in an activity that activates their imaginations, you are giving them the message that their whole selves are welcome here, including their personalities, their quirkiness and their ideas. This leads to...

P. **Participation:** When people's imaginations are engaged, they are more inclined to participate. This in turn leads to...

C. **Commitment:** When people participate with engaged imaginations, they tend to connect more deeply with others and become committed to the activity and group.

Keep IPC in mind throughout the course of your program. Always begin with an activity that ignites the imagination, and whenever the energy in your group falls flat, reactivate the IPC model with an activity that restarts the imagination, such as one of the theater games in Chapter 12.

Credit: charlessteinbergphotography.com

Making an artful name tag provides a chance to take a creative risk.

3. Engage the Body

Once your group members assemble in a circle, give them a warm welcome and then lead an activity that gets their bodies moving. We've been using one particular group rhythm activity for over 18 years in all kinds of settings and with all age groups. This activity never fails to delight. Building a rhythm together eases anxiety, activates the right brain and brings a group into sync. While the rhythm appears challenging at first, 95 percent of people learn it quickly with joy and a sense of accomplishment. (For a demo see www.pyeglobal.org/rhythm/.)

We launch into the rhythm by saying something like this:

Before we get into what this program is all about, please join me in building a group rhythm. Let's imagine that we're walking together as we embark on this creative journey. No previous experience is required to build this rhythm. Just watch me and do what I do.

Opening Arts Activities

Creative Name Tags: Set up a large table with a buffet of colorful art supplies: tissue paper, glitter (a huge favorite), colorful bits of wrapping paper, oil pastels, markers, feathers and natural objects. If possible, provide card stock for the name tags themselves and string for hanging the tags like necklaces. Ask people to make fun, bright, creative name tags, whatever that means for them. Wherever we go in the world, people love making name tags. Even in areas of extreme poverty, group leaders find materials to use, such as shells, twigs and chicken feathers.

I-AM Posters: Set up an art table with 18" × 24" poster paper, crayons, oil pastels and markers, plus magazines, scissors and glue for making collages. Take digital pictures of participants as they arrive, and print them on a portable printer. Have the photos ready at the art table as soon as possible. After people have settled into their accommodations point them in the direction of the art table.

At youth camps, we ask each participant to make a personal poster that features a photo of himself or herself and offers some personal information, such as:

1. My name
2. Where I live
3. Something I love about where I live *or* something I love to do
4. My favorite food or music
5. One of the hardest things I've ever had to do *or* a challenge I've overcome

This final question is a gentle invitation for self-disclosure. Don't worry if some youth don't respond to it. Encourage everyone to use more images than words on the poster, because we express so much about ourselves through image. Support reluctant artists by telling them the drawing on the I-AM poster can be completely freeform. Stick figures are also just fine.

I-AM posters are a big hit at adult conferences as well. In addition to basic information such as name and where you're from, tailor the questions to fit the conference. Examples include:

1. Something you might be surprised to know about me
2. Something I'm passionate about
3. Something I'm proud of
4. Three words that represent topics I'd like to discuss with people

Once everyone is walking in place say, "I want you to clap on the 'one' of a four-beat count—and clap 2, 3, 4, clap, 2, 3, 4." You then start a group body rhythm using handclaps and light percussive slaps on the chest and legs. Once everyone is doing the rhythm, stop and ask for a volunteer to lead half of the group: "Who thinks you can lead the group if I get you started?" There is always at least one person willing to step forward. The volunteer then leads half the group in the rhythm and the facilitator brings in the other half of the group midway through the rhythm, creating a new, more complicated and interesting rendition in a matter of seconds. All this occurs in just five to seven minutes.

Your group has been together for only a few minutes and yet they have already risen to a creative challenge and surmounted it as one body. They have created beauty—the sound of the rhythm. They are loosening their bodies, and they have come into sync with one another. It's a winner. This early experience of group success sets the foundation for a safe, creative community.

4. Acknowledge a Larger Purpose

When PYE facilitator Leslie Cotter led a workshop for the staff of a school in Johannesburg, South Africa, she decided to take a risk. "I don't think of myself as a singer," she said, "but I decided that if I was going to ask these people to take creative risks all day, I should do so as well." She sang a short peace song that her 12-year-old daughter had learned at school. "The results were infectious," she said. "The content of the song set a context for the importance of the work we were doing together, and the fact that I took such a risk opened the door for everyone else to do the same."

Starting your program with a poem, a spoken word piece, a song or a short skit sets a powerful context for learning. We call this an invocation because it invokes a mood that says "It's important that we are together, and we are going to take this time seriously." We often invite a volunteer from the group to offer an invocation, and we've rarely been disappointed. If you treat the invocation as a special opportunity, someone will come forth with a meaningful offering. At one of our early camps, a young Coast Salish First Nations woman surprised us with a haunting lullaby from her tradition to "invite the spirit of peace to the gathering." At an adult conference a 16-year-old visitor recited a poem she had written a few years earlier at a Power of Hope camp to remind everyone to be creative and playful.

At youth programs the invocation gives young people a chance to stand up in front of their peers and take the risk of sharing something meaningful. At a media literacy weekend for teen girls, for example, three young women took turns reading US poet laureate Maya Angelou's poem "Phenomenal Women." You could hear a pin drop as they recited the final refrain in unison three times: "Phenomenal woman, that's me." We were barely ten minutes into the program, and yet it felt like we'd been together for a day.

Tips for Designing an Invocation

- Keep it short—between two and five minutes.
- Invite participation from the group. We often ask early arrivals to work with a staff member to prepare an invocation.
- Choose an offering that connects to the larger purpose of the event. Using Maya Angelou's poem to kick off a girl's conference on media literacy is a good example.
- Feel free to include full-group participation through movement, song or call-and-response.
- Keep it meaningful but light. You don't want to start with something too intense or obscure.
- Credit and explain cultural sources if using songs or traditions from a specific culture. *We strongly advise using material from your own culture.*

Examples of Invocations

- **A poem related to the theme:** Participants read poems written by themselves or others. Two good source books are *Earth Prayers from Around the World* and *Life Prayers from Around the World*, by Elizabeth Roberts and Elias Amidon.
- **Spoken word pieces:** Returning camp participants write and perform short spoken word pieces that give a preview of what people can expect at camp.

- **Percussion and song**: A group of adults and youth teach a song accompanied by drumming.
- **Short theatrical performance**: A group of returning youth and staff create a short impromptu performance that includes dance, spoken word and music.

5. Establish Your Credibility with the Group

Now it's time for the group to learn something about you. This is your opportunity to develop personal credibility and to model speaking with authenticity and vulnerability. A short, well-crafted introduction can let your group know that they can trust you, that you have the background for leading this group and, most of all, that you believe in *them*. In the book *Primal Leadership: Learning to Lead with Emotional Intelligence*, Daniel Goleman[14] says that the first task of a leader is to create a sense of emotional resonance with the group. Through a well-executed two- to four-minute self-introduction you can accomplish all of this, plus more.

We developed a simple format for a personal introduction several years ago when our young Power of Hope staff members were leading 50-minute arts/empowerment sessions in Seattle high schools. They had to build instant rapport with up to 40 students, most of whom had no idea why these people were even in their classroom. Carl, a young percussionist with a quiet presence, was pleasantly surprised by the impact of his introduction the first time he used it. "I was very nervous, but I did it," he said. "And then—I couldn't believe it—they gave me a standing ovation!" Anyone who has worked in high school classrooms in the US knows this was no small feat.

The Power-Packed Personal Introduction

Here's the basic format for a winning introduction.

    Part 1: Your name

    Part 2: The organization you represent and a one-sentence description of its work.

    Part 3: The role you will play with this group today.

    Part 4: A short story from your life that demonstrates your passion for leading this group. It could be something about how you were transformed by the subject at hand. Or it could be a story drawn from your work leading this theme with other people. The operative word here is *short*—it should be no longer ten sentences.

Part 5: Something you believe about your participants. This is where you get to share your vision of what's possible for your group and express your excitement for the task at hand.

Parts 1, 2 and 3 are easy. They lay out the basics of who you are and what your role is with the group. Knowing this basic information helps set your participants at ease. Parts 4 and 5 are more challenging. You can feel quite vulnerable sharing your passion for the work and your vision of what's possible. Delivering these parts, however, is what produces the emotional resonance. While at first you may feel awkward following this formula, it works like a charm. Once you have the elements down, you'll be able to deliver a compelling and spontaneous introduction every time.

A Sample Introduction

1. Hi, my name is Josiah.
2. I am from an organization called PYE—Partners for Youth Empowerment. We provide arts/empowerment workshops for young people all over the world.
3. I will be the leader of your workshop on creative writing today.
4. When I was in high school I went through a very hard time. There were problems in my family, and I was depressed. One of my teachers suggested I join an after-school creative writing club. We learned easy techniques to get the flow going, and once I started writing I could hardly stop. Suddenly I had an outlet for all the feelings that were bottled up in me, and to my surprise, I started to feel better. I've continued the practice of creative writing through my life and it keeps me sane and happy. So I know how powerful writing can be.
5. [*Looking directly at your group*] Now, some of you might wonder whether you can write. Actually writing is as simple as telling a story and putting it down on paper, and I know that each one of you can do it. If you can phone your friend and tell him what happened last weekend, you can tell stories. If you can tell your parents or your brother or sister

about what happened at school today, you can tell stories. I know that each of you has important things to say, so I can hardly wait to see what we do together. Let's get going!

Take your time in preparing parts 4 and 5. Part 4 requires you to look inside yourself to discover why you are passionate about the subject at hand and to find a way to communicate that to your group. Remember to keep your personal story short—a little bit of self-disclosure goes a long way. Participants want a flavor of who you are and what your life is about, but they don't want the whole saga.

Part 5 requires very direct communication and can be challenging even for those with a direct communication style. When you say to your group "I believe in you," you may feel very vulnerable. We encourage you to give it a try, though. When you let people know the possibility you see in them, you will gain their rapt attention.

Practice makes perfect. In our training programs, participants write their introductions and practice delivering them in pairs and then in small groups. When an introduction hits the mark, the whole group can feel the emotional resonance. Though practicing with peers can be awkward and embarrassing, go for it. You'll notice the benefits the next time you stand up in front of a group.

6. Bring Every Voice Into the Room

Group development experts tell us that one of the best ways to ensure a high level of participation is to get every voice into the room early on. The longer your participants sit and listen in silence, the farther their attention can drift. A good way to quickly activate all of the voices is to poll your group using a process called Who's Here? The facilitators ask a series of questions, and participants raise their hands, stand or clap if the question applies to them. "Who's here from [various places you know people are from]?" Be sure to cover all of the geographic areas represented in the room so that everyone gets to say "yes" to something. You can also ask questions like:

• Who thinks you came from the farthest today?
• The closest?

- Who has been to camp (or this program) before?
- Who is new?
- Who knows more than ten people here?
- Who came alone and didn't know anyone before you got here? That takes a lot of courage. Let's look around and make sure we pay attention to these people.
- Who came because someone said, "You have to go to this program whether you like it or not!"
- Who is a little nervous?
- Who is excited to be here?

You can really work with Who's Here to build your group, pointing to values around inclusion, acknowledging people's feelings of resistance and fear, and ending with a show of expectation and excitement.

A round of personal introductions—used in place of or in addition to Who's Here—also brings every voice into the room. Here are some approaches to use depending on the size of your group.

Personal Introductions with a Creative Twist

For a group of 10 to 30 people, you can make introductions fun and energizing by asking participants to answer a series of short questions and then take a small creative risk. In our two-day trainings we usually use something like, What's your name? Where are you from? What kind of work do you do? What's one thing you'd like to gain from this program?

And here's the kicker. Once a person has delivered his introduction, he is to mime—act out silently—something he loves to do. This can be something as simple as reading a book or as complex as parachuting from an airplane. Groups take as much delight in witnessing the simpler mimes as they do the more complex. When the group guesses correctly, you'll often hear a collective "ah" of delight and the "mimer" receives a powerful dose of recognition and appreciation. It's a subtle but powerful community builder—giving each individual a jolt of self-confidence while at the same time providing a positive experience for the group. You can feel the energy build as you go around the circle.

Longer Introductions

Here are two ideas to use with groups of up to 15:

- Ask participants ahead of time to each bring along a small object of personal significance. They share those objects and their meaning as part of their introductions.
- Pass around a bag filled with small objects such as animal statues. Each person randomly picks an object from the bag and then talks about what that piece tells her about what she has to learn in this workshop.

Speedy Introductions

If your group is too large for extended personal introductions, here is a quick alternative that involves little more than three words from each person. You pass a microphone around and participants stand up one at a time and say their name, where they are from, and three words that represent their interests and values. To set up a pattern of brevity, you need to start with a few people who are primed to introduce themselves quickly and succinctly. You can accomplish well over 100 of these short introductions in less than ten minutes without feeling rushed. It's hard to believe three words can make much difference, but we've used this quick go around with groups as large as 120 with great effect.

7. Learn Names

Learning names is one of the best ways to build intimacy in a group, and this starts with you as the facilitator. People love to be addressed by name, and calling people by name inspires trust and gives you credibility. Neither of us consider ourselves very good at remembering names, but we know that we can do it if we make it a priority. The first step is to simply decide you're going to learn the names of everyone in your group, no matter what it takes. Then experiment to find memory processes that will work for you. A reasonable goal is to know the names of all of your participants by the end of the first half day of your program—no matter what it takes.

Strategies for Learning Names

Here are some suggestions for cracking the code:

- Review your participant list prior to the program and take note of any relevant data. For example, someone might live near you or may work for an organization you know. Associative thinking is a powerful memory aid.
- Informally introduce yourself to participants as they arrive. If you really pay attention, you'll likely know half the names of the people in a 30-person workshop before you officially begin the program.
- Lead your group in name games and jump in yourself.
- During whole-group discussions, ask people to say their names before they state their ideas.
- Call people by name whenever you have the chance. If you get a name wrong, don't worry. You are modeling taking a risk, and you can model self-acceptance when you get it wrong.
- While participants are busy with activities in small groups, scan the room to see if you know all the names. Have your master list available to help you.
- Encourage adult staff and volunteers to learn everyone's name as well and to call people by name.
- Make a contest out of who knows the most names by the second day of the program.

Helping Participants Learn Names

To build a strong community, it's also important for participants to learn each other's names. We talk with the group about the importance of learning names, and we give people permission to ask each other's names— even up to the last minute of the program. A fun way to normalize asking for names is by setting up a role-play with two participants. "Hi. Excuse me. What is your name?" "I'm Emma." "Thanks Emma, I'm Jamal."

8. Clarify the Purpose and Potential of the Experience

It's now time to bring everyone together around the purpose of the program. Why are we here? And, equally important, Why should we care? You can accomplish this by sharing the goals of the program and talking about why each of these goals might matter in the lives of your participants.

Name Games

Playing name games is the altogether best way to help people learn each other's names. These games also get everyone moving and provide opportunities to take creative risks. Be sure to use games that employ known memory aids such as rhythm, repetition and associative thinking.

Walk Into the Circle

Here's a game we have used with great success in many parts of the world. It gives each person the chance to take a creative risk for just a moment and receive a heap of praise in return. Begin with everyone standing in a circle.

(Groups of eight to ten are good.) Decide who will go first (A).

- A walks into the center of the circle doing a special walk. She could be hopping, skipping, dragging her feet. She can choose any style as long as everyone else in the group will be able to copy her.
- Once in the center, she looks around the group and says loudly, "Hi, my name is [her name]." She then goes back out to the circle, using her special walk.
- A stays on the perimeter of the circle and the rest of the group moves to the center of the circle copying A's special walk. Once

"You're special!" Playing the Walk into the Circle name game.

in the center they all turn to A, point to her, and say in unison "Hi, [A's name]. You're special!"

- The whole group then moves back to the perimeter of the circle, using A's walk.
- The person to A's left then does his own special walk into the circle and you continue the process until you've gone all the way around the circle.

Yes, we know the "You're special" part sounds cheesy, but much to our own surprise, this game is a winner and it quickly gets everyone into play mode. We've used it with youth and adults. We usually warn participants ahead of time that they are going to have to let go of their cool persona for this one.

The Patterned Name Game

This is our favorite game for learning a lot of names quickly. The game works in a pattern and employs memory boosters such as rhythm, repetition and associative thinking. Once you learn the pattern, you can come up with your own versions of the game. Begin with eight to ten people standing in a circle. Choose a person (A) to go first. Get everyone started doing the following four-beat rhythm: slap thighs, clap hands, click fingers on right hand, click fingers on left hand.

- Once the rhythm is established, A says her name on the finger clicks. The whole group repeats her name on the next set of finger clicks.

- Then B (to A's left) says his name on the finger clicks.
- Everyone repeats B's name.
- On the next clicks everyone then says A's name, and then B's name.
- C then says her name on the finger clicks. The group repeat's C's name then goes back and says A's name, B's name, and C's name.
- D then says his name and on around the circle you go, each time going all the way back to A and repeating the names one after the other on the finger clicks.
- Once you have completed the circle, you can continue with the rhythm and say each name one time on the finger clicks going in the reverse direction. Then ask everyone to change places in the circle and see if they can say each name one time in the new order.

Here are some other versions of the game. In both cases you follow the pattern of copying and repeating outlined above.

- Instead of using a rhythm, each player says his name and makes a dramatic gesture. The group copies the name and the gesture and continues the pattern around the circle.
- Each player says her name preceded by an adjective that starts with the same sound as her name while adding a gesture. For example, dynamic Dia or amiable Amina.

Good program design is founded on well-crafted, compelling learning goals. These inform your choice of activities. Begin your planning process by articulating your goals, and then choose your sequence of activities as a means of achieving those goals. After your planning is complete, you should be able to tie each activity back into one of the goals. We then recommend rewriting your goals in simple, direct language to appeal to your participants.

The underlying purpose of presenting the goals is to get everyone excited about the journey ahead. And here is the cardinal rule: After you deliver a goal, you don't tell people *what they are going to do* in the program. Rather you tell them *why they should care.* What benefits will they receive by achieving these goals? How will this learning improve their lives? When you deliver the goals you're actually selling the program to your participants, and if you succeed, you will have them sitting on the edge of their seats eager to start.

A Basic Format
- State the goal.
- Talk about how reaching this will positively affect your participants.
- Restate the goal.

To develop your talking points, you'll need to deeply consider the relevance of your goals for your participants. This in turn sets you up to be a far better facilitator or guide of the process. We'll demonstrate here with the first goal of Creative Community camps:

To expand our creativity
Our first goal is to expand our creativity. This means that we believe each and every one of you is creative—whether you believe it or not. A lot of people think that only the people whose CDs we buy or whose movies we go to are the creative ones. Creativity is actually about thinking things up and making them happen. Each of us has a powerful imagination, and the more we bring it out, the more power we have—the more we can make things happen in the world, the more we can create the kind of world we want to live in. So this is our first goal: to expand our creativity.

Once your participants see that creativity is about more than drawing pictures or singing a song—it's actually about having power and effectiveness in the world—they are more likely to be interested in doing all kinds of activities that will move them in that direction.

Things to Keep in Mind When Designing Goals for Your Program

1. Use simple, street-level language. Avoid jargon.
2. Begin each goal with an action verb such as *discover, increase* or *explore.*
3. Keep your goals open ended, so people are moving along a learning continuum.
4. Include only one goal in each statement. (The tendency is to string several together.)
5. Keep your total number of goals to a minimum. We have five goals for our week-long programs. For a shorter program you might only have two.

9. Share the Responsibility for the Experience

Once you have everyone on board with the goals, the question becomes, What can we do as a community to optimize meeting these lofty goals? We call these community agreements. There are a variety of ways you can work with your group to establish agreements, but the operative idea is that these are agreements—not rules set down by the management! The more everyone buys into these shared agreements, the better the experience will be for all involved. Occasionally, challenging behaviors arise at our camps, but we have come to almost take for granted a high level of buy-in and positive behavior on everyone's part. This comes in large part from a well-led agreement process.

Our preference is to start with a set of agreements that we find helpful in building a creative community. We then ask the group for additional suggestions with a question like, "What else do we need in order to have a supportive creative community over the next week [or other time frame] in order to have a great time and surprise ourselves by how far we come in just that time?"

We are ever surprised by how involved youth get in setting agreements. In our second year of Power of Hope camp, when it came time to suggest agreements, one of our returning students raised his hand and called out, "Let's not make the adults have to be like police." When we heard that, we knew we were in for a very good week!

Our Agreements
1. Avoid put-downs of yourself or other people.
2. Be willing to try new things.
3. Listen well.
4. Participate fully.
5. Be respectful of others, yourself and this place.

At youth programs, for the safety of both the youth and the organization, we also add some non-negotiable agreements—and we present them as such. These include no drugs or alcohol, no coupling/no sex and no violence.

Building clear community agreements creates safety. Clear boundaries let participants know what they can count on from one another and the community. Clear agreements also give the facilitator something to fall back on when negative behavior does occur. "We all agreed to this. What's up?" is a far better conversation starter than an authoritarian command. You deliver the agreements the same way you do goals. State the agreement. Then talk about the "why" of the agreement and state it once more.

10. Develop Deeper Bonds

You've taken some creative risks, learned some names and shared the goals and agreements. By now, you should be able to feel a web of connection forming. Now it's time to get to know one other at a deeper level by connecting one on one. Our all-time favorite activity at this juncture is called Milling. We use it with youth and adult groups.

Milling, an activity that comes from the theater world, involves participants walking randomly around the room and then stopping, finding a partner and answering prescribed questions. We'd seen this activity done in light, fun and frenetic ways, but when PYE facilitator Hanif Fazal first came to a Power of Hope camp, he demonstrated the full potential of this activity to increase self-awareness, social and emotional literacy and so much more.

Getting Your Group's Attention

"Something extraordinary happened in my classroom this week," a middle school science teacher told us at one training session. "Usually I yell at my class to get them quiet, but this week I decided to try that clapping thing you taught us last month. I didn't really think it would work, but it did. I did it, and then there was total silence. I was stunned." (See "If you can hear me, clap once," below.) There's nothing more jarring than an adult yelling over a crowd of youth to get them to be quiet. (Maybe letting out a loud piercing whistle is worse!) It's actually possible to lead an entire youth program without ever raising your voice, but you need to have some strategies for getting the group to come to attention. Here are a few techniques we use:

If you can hear me clap once: When you want the group to get quiet, say in a loud voice: "If you can hear me, clap once." Clap. Then say, "If you can hear me, clap two times." (This time more people will catch on.) Clap, Clap. Once you say, "If you can hear me, clap three times," you are likely to have everyone's attention. Be sure to thank your group and then move on.

Raise your hand, close your mouth: Imagine you have one end of a string attached to your chin and you are holding the other end in your hand. When you raise that hand, the string pulls your mouth closed. Playfully demonstrate this to your group and then ask them to practice the mechanism. Then say, "When I want everyone to get quiet, I'll raise my hand, and my mouth will close. When you see me or any other person with hand raised, please join in, and we'll all get quiet."

Make up your own: Groups often come up with their own signals. Here's one we particularly like. The facilitator says: "And a hush fell over the crowd." Everyone responds by saying together, "Hushshshshshshshshsh."

Once you have taught a technique, try it out with the group by asking them to make as much noise as they can. Then try the signal and see how fast they can respond. "Aw, come on, I'm sure you can get louder than that—and you can also get quiet faster. Let's try it again." Playing with opposite energies makes it fun and gets everyone on board.

Getting to know each other through milling at a Cape Town training.

Credit: PYE Global

Ask your group to stand up and begin to move around the room. Challenge participants to spread themselves out to fill the entire space. A way to do this is to say:

Keep moving into empty spaces. Don't bump into anyone, and don't let anyone bump into you. Change directions so you're not all walking around in a big circle.

Once the people get moving you can ask them to begin to notice their feelings:

Notice how you are feeling. Are you nervous? Are you excited? Take some deep breaths. Feel your feet on the ground. Allow yourself to relax. Don't look at anyone as you pass. Simply walk around the room filling the empty spaces.

Now see if you make eye contact with other people as you walk by. Try to stay in a quiet place. Just keep walking and nodding to people in a silent hello. Now, when you are ready, connect with someone you don't know very well and stand back to back, with your elbows intertwined. In a moment, we'll ask you to turn around and share your name, where you are from and answer the following questions. [Give them the questions.] Once you have answered the questions turn back to back again.

When the majority of participants have finished answering the questions, ask everyone to begin milling again. You continue the process, with each set of questions getting deeper and more heartfelt. Slowly build up the size of the groups so you move from pairs to fours and then to sixes. Just as you gradually raise the level of challenge in taking creative risks, you incrementally increase the depth of these questions. A sequence might go like this:

1. What's your favorite food and something you love to do?
2. What's something you love about where you live and something you'd like to change?
3. What is something people might be surprised to know about you?
4. What is something you are passionate about?
5. Who is someone you love and why?
6. If you were standing in front of a microphone and the whole world was listening, what would you say?
7. What's a big dream you have for your life?

You can design the milling activity to address particular goals. Here are some examples:

1. **Build the imagination:** Come up with inventive ways for people to move through the room between times of partnering. For example, say:

   Imagine you are skating on ice. Imagine you are walking through a room full of thick clouds. Imagine you are late for a bus. Imagine you just got an A on a test. Imagine you are six years old and you are sneaking into the kitchen at night to snatch some cookies.

2. **Develop visioning capacity:** For your last question, asked in groups of six, invite people to imagine they are standing in a chamber where

dreams come true. "Now, we want each of you to share with your group a big dream you have for your life, and say it as if it is already happening."

3. **Develop comfort in speaking in front of a large group**: After the first few rounds of sharing, ask for volunteers to share with the whole group. This gets particularly interesting around topics such as something people would be surprised to know about you, someone you love and why, what you'd want the whole world to hear, or a big dream you have for yourself.

Leading milling is a great way to increase your ability as a facilitator because it provides experience working with the group energy as you move participants around the room, use images and sequence questions that will prepare your group to embark on the theme of the program.

A family group at a camp rises to a creative challenge using a theater game to introduce themselves.

Credit: Sara Dent, Power of Hope Canada

11. Build Group Cohesion

You can end your community-building process on a high note by issuing a performance challenge to be accomplished in small groups. At camps we break into family groups—pre-determined reflection groups that meet together for 30 to 45 minutes after dinner each evening. The family group members introduce themselves to one another and share their hopes and fears for the week. They are then presented with the creative challenge of coming up with a name and a cheer to represent their group. The community-building session culminates in each group presenting its name and cheer to the whole group. Every one has a chance to be on stage—for just a moment—and receive a rousing ovation from their peers.

The Beginnings

If you can implement the ideas from only one chapter in this book, this would be the one to pay attention to. If you do, we're convinced that you will see a dramatic shift in the quality and depth of any program you choose to lead.

5

Theme-Based Sessions: Bringing Learning Alive

"What's this?" asks the facilitator Rafael, drawing a picture of a box with antennae on the top. The youth immediately identify it as a radio. "Right on, and what are the frequencies on the radio?" AM and FM. "Right again! What's the difference between AM programs and FM programs?" The youth get right into talking about radio.

Rafael goes on to say, "For the purposes of this activity, we're going to imagine that AM and FM stand for two kinds of conversations we have in our heads. AM stands for 'against me' conversations. Those are the conversations we have with ourselves where we're putting ourselves down. FM stands for 'for me' conversations or 'forward moving' conversations. Those are the times we're telling ourselves things that help us move forward toward our goals and dreams. The good news is that we have the power to flip from the AM channel to the FM channel any time we want."

Using the metaphor of a radio to address the issue of self-talk resonates with young people all over the world. On this day, the session is with youth living with HIV/AIDS. They have had a lot of practice living on the AM side of the dial since many of them experience severe shunning on a daily basis. For at least one camper, named Oscar, the session was the most significant learning of his five-day experience. Charlie recently reconnected with Oscar years later while working together at a program in northern Uganda. When asked what he most remembered about the camp, Oscar said, "The whole idea of AM/FM had a big effect on me. I realized that I could not change everyone in society and how they think of people with HIV/AIDS, but I could change how I treated myself. I learned that I did not have to live the rest of my life feeling negative about myself. I became my own best friend." All of this from one metaphor presented and applied in a group learning session. A powerful group learning session can literally save lives!

Each morning at our youth camps the entire group gathers for a community meeting and a whole-group learning session on a theme. We call these plenaries. An ideal length of time for a plenary is 60 to 90 minutes, although they can be as short as half an hour. Integrating the arts into these sessions transforms them from boring, sit-in-your-chair lectures to engaging learning adventures.

A typical session includes an opening activity, a few goals for the session, special agreements if needed, one or two main activities with reflection and a closing. A well-led session will begin on a light note and get deeper as it goes along, giving participants the chance to reflect and speak from their hearts. What follows are five sample sessions that are favorites at our camps.

Setting Personal Goals: The Intention Tree

This activity belongs near the beginning of a program. We use it on the second day—the first morning of camp. The youth and adults identify personal goals for their week. They then proclaim their intention to their new community and ask for support.

Opening: A song or poem

Goal: To learn how identifying intentions helps us reach our goals

Activity 1—Defining intentions: Begin a discussion on the power of intention with a series of questions:
- What is an intention?
- How does intention work?

- Does anyone have an example of a time you made an intention and then it happened?
- What's the value of making intentions?
- What happens when we don't make them?

Challenge participants to make it personal:

> This week is a special time for all of us, so we're going to spend time this morning making some personal intentions. Think about what you most want to achieve in these next seven days. What would make this experience a real win for you?

In groups of five or six, each with a mentor, ask everyone to come up with a few goals for their time at camp.

> Your goals need to be a stretch for you but achievable. They need to be specific enough that you will know whether you achieved them. A goal like, "Be nice to everyone" is too broad. A clearer goal might be, "I intend to meet two new people everyday."

Activity 2—Setting intentions: Invite participants to share their goals in the small groups and then choose one to focus on for this activity. They turn it into an intention by fitting it into the following phrase: "This week I intend to _____, and therefore I will _____." So perhaps it is "This week I intend to

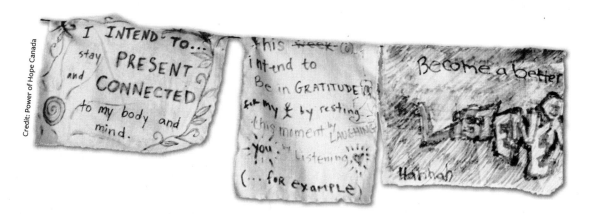

Canadian camp participants draw their intentions on small flags.

overcome my shyness, and therefore I will sit at the dinner table with new people every night." Using paper and crayons or oil pastels, each person then makes an art piece with her intention on it to hang from an intention tree.

Activity 3—Holding the ceremony: The intention tree ceremony accomplishes many things that are important in the beginning of a program, and we find that the youth and adults enjoy this and take it seriously even after coming to the camp several years in a row. Everyone gets to:
- focus on a personal goal
- take the risk of stating it publicly
- stand up and speak in front of the entire group—just for a moment
- ask for and receive support
- take charge of his own learning and his own experience

In preparation, set up a large branch at the front of the room. This is the intention tree. Participants share their art pieces and intentions with their small group members. You then form an audience, facing the tree. One group at a time stands near the tree. One by one, the group members go to the tree, stand facing the audience and say: "Hi, my name is _____. I come from _____. This week I intend _____ and therefore I will _____. Will you support me?" The group responds by saying in chorus, "We support you [name]." The person then hangs her intention on the tree and returns to her seat.

 Some goals are very simple: "Make new friends." Others are more esoteric: "Let go of all resistance and feel at one with everyone." Still others are practical: "Come up with an offering for the open mic and actually do it in spite of my fear." The depth of the goal doesn't matter as much as the act of creating and sharing it.

Activity 4—Singing: It's great to end this session with a rousing group song to "invest all of our intentions with power!"

Closing: Place the artful intention tree in a corner of the room to remind the group of their intentions over the course of the week.

**Becoming Our Own Best Friend:
The AM/FM Conversation**

Some of the most profound learning comes through exploring our relationship to ourselves. We are ever surprised by how eagerly teens delve into this territory. One of our favorite activities is the AM/FM activity mentioned at the beginning of this chapter. We learned this metaphor from PYE facilitator Hanif Fazal. Here is how we put it to work in a plenary session:

Opening: A short group warm-up, perhaps a theater game

Goal: To become aware that the way we talk to ourselves affects us and to learn how to change the channel from negative to positive.

Activity 1—Introducing AM/FM: Begin by drawing a picture of a radio on a flip chart and then engage participants in a conversation with questions such as:
- What is this?
- What are the two different types of bandwidth you can tune into to find programs?
- What kinds of things do you hear on AM?
- What kinds of things do you hear on FM?

Follow up with some instruction:

> For the purposes of this activity, let's imagine the radio is like our minds and AM and FM represent the kinds of conversations we have with ourselves. Let's imagine that the AM stations represent the "Against Me" conversations and the FM stations represent the "For Me" or "Forward Moving" conversations.
>
> Who can give me an example of an AM statement you might make to yourself?
>
> Let's hear an FM statement.
>
> And what do you do if you want to switch from AM to FM? You change the channel.

Activity 2—Transforming AM to FM: Ask everyone to draw a line down the center of a blank piece of paper. On the left side, they list four or five AM statements they tell themselves. Now, on the right-hand side, they write FM statements that counteract each of the AM statements

In groups of four or five, each including at least one adult, ask participants to share both their AM and FM statements. Then debrief in the whole group.

Activity 3—Practicing talking in FM: Each person then gets to talk about himself to his small group for two minutes, completing the statement, "If you really knew me, you would know that…" The person has to speak in the FM channel the entire time, and everyone in the group listens without comment. Follow this with both a small- and whole-group debrief.

Closing: Stand in one big circle and go around, with each person stating one FM statement she would like to say to herself more often.

 ## Envisioning the Future: Dream Trees

Here is an exciting and motivating way for participants to explore their hopes and dreams. The sequence is inspired by Dave Ellis's Falling Awake Life Coaching training.[15] You begin with a brainstorm session based on the question, What do I want? Then participants draw trees that hold their dreams.

Opening: A song or theater game.

Goal: To explore our hopes and dreams for our lives.

Activity 1—Brainstorming desires: Ask participants to make a brainstorm list of everything they can imagine wanting in life.

Please think about this question: What do you want? We want you to make a big brainstorm list of everything you can imagine wanting in your life. Your list can include selfish things and altruistic things. Material things, like a smart phone or a car. Things you want in your relationships, like a boyfriend or a girlfriend or more time with Dad; ways you'd like to be, like loving and courageous; qualities you want in your life, like a deeper relationship with spirit; ways you'd like to help out the world, like alleviate hunger; and things you'd like to see in the world, like peace, justice or an end to hunger. You don't have to know how you will get these things. You don't even have to be sure you're motivated to get these things. This is just a way to turn on the flow. Just keep making a long, long list of things you want.

After everyone has a list of several items, ask for volunteers to share something from their lists with the group.

Who has something to share? So, you want a better relationship with your sister. Great. Now if any of you wants a better relationship with your own sister, add it to your list. Or if that makes you think of something else—like, I want a better relationship with my mom—write that down. Let yourself be inspired by each other. Feel free to steal each other's ideas and make them your own.

You can really have fun with this and build a positive energy. Hearing each other's ideas sparks the process and pulls in the less engaged youth.

Activity 2—Drawing dream trees: After everyone has generated a long list, hand out 18" × 24" paper and oil pastels. Ask each person to draw an image of a tree and place his wants and desires on it. Encourage participants to use both words and images. Share the pictures in groups of six to eight, with an adult in each group. You can then tack the trees on a wall to form a forest of dreams.

Activity 3—Developing a multiple-action plan: If time permits, ask participants to each choose one dream and then brainstorm a list of things they can do to achieve that goal. Share in small groups.

Closing: Stand in a large circle and go around, with each person sharing one dream.

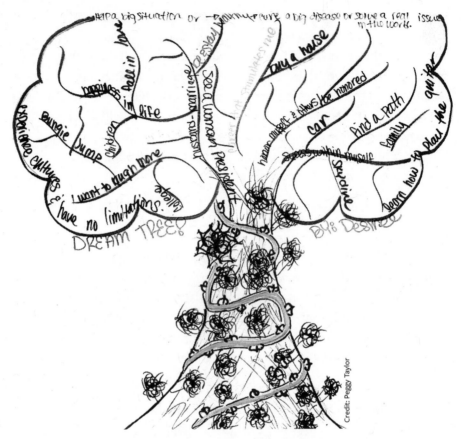

A 16-year-old expresses her hopes and dreams on a dream tree.

🖐 Befriending Nature: Outdoor Activities

The main goal of this plenary is to serve as a "match-maker" between nature and youth by showing them, through their own experience, that connecting with nature is safe, fun and basic to our humanity. The hope is that as a result of this experience they'll *want* to spend more time in nature and develop life-long habits of nature connection. The intention, in a phrase, is *to inspire and initiate youth into meaningful relationship with nature.* This plenary is designed and written by Evan McGown, a nature educator and PYE facilitator. He is co-author of *Coyote's Guide to Connecting with Nature,*[16] an all-around great resource for all kinds of nature activities.

Activity 1—Setting the context: Begin by asking the group to play a game with you.

> Okay, everybody. Will you play a little game with me? It's called List the Logos. Raise your hand if you can think of a logo of a company or corporation, and we'll see how many we can list.

Play with the group, encouraging them to remember logos, corporate colors, marketing jingles. Praise them:

> Okay, wow, that's quite a list. You all have incredible memories!

Put up a new flip chart page and deliver a new challenge:

> Okay, now let's make a list of all the plants you know—wild plants that just grow outside without any help. Okay, yeah, grass, that's a plant. Can you describe a leaf of grass to me?

Work with them on building this list, asking what the various plants look like, etc. Then compare the two lists. Invariably the list of logos is longer.

> What does it mean that we know more corporate logos than plants?

This leads into a discussion about nature and being in nature and why it might be important to have a relationship with nature. (This activity was inspired by the Adbusters Teacher's Media Kit: www.adbusters.org.)

> Now, we are going to do some experiential activities that will range from being still and tapping into peace to downright fun and play. Along the way, you will get to connect with nature in a fun way, to plug back into the mother Earth, our home, the original classroom and ultimate teacher of all our ancestors that recently we have forgotten to listen to. See what parts of nature you connect with most easily. That's your starting place. See what you're curious about and follow that.

Guide participants outside for the following activities. If you have a large group, you may want to break into smaller ones. Have pre-selected leaders who are trained and ready to lead the various activities.

Nature is our teacher.

Credit: Sara Dent, Power of Hope Canada

Activity 2—Playing You're Only Safe If…: This is a simple and fun game. Identify one person to be "it." This person is the tagger. The game leader shouts out something like, "You are only safe if you are touching a blade of grass!" Everyone has to run to the safe item while the tagger tries to tag a new person to be "it." To reach safety the players will have to figure out what a blade of grass—or whatever is called out—looks like. They will ask each other and start learning to look around and see differences between the various kinds of trees and plants. Keep calling things out every few minutes, "You're only safe if you're touching a tree with needles for leaves (a pine tree)" or "…if you're touching a dandelion plant" or "…a plant with purple flowers." Or whatever. You can make it fresh and fun by throwing in a few "non-nature" things such as one of the other facilitators (who will then be swarmed by everyone).

When folks get tired, have them all come back together and slump into a group on the ground to rest. Ask what they liked about the game. Did they learn any new plants or trees or start to "see" things they hadn't noticed before?

Activity 3—Meeting a tree: Participants pair up with partners. One person is blindfolded (bandanas work great for this) while the other leads her to a nearby tree. The blindfolded person gets to know that tree as well as she can through touch, smell, etc. The partner then leads her back to the starting place. She takes off her blindfold and goes to find her tree. Then the partners switch roles. You can debrief about what they paid attention to, as well as the social dynamic of trusting the person leading you, etc. This is a fun one—and the senses get really engaged.

Activity 4—Imitating animals: The goal of this activity is to get people to walk slowly and pay attention to the world, rather than staring at the ground. Start with everyone standing in a big circle. Ask,

> Has anyone ever taught you how to walk in the most optimal way possible—how to use your human body for basic motion? What kinds of walks are there?

Demonstrate the "Busy City Strut" of a business person rushing to an appointment, staring at the ground, talking on his cell phone, oblivious to the world around him. Ask someone to demonstrate another style of walking they see people doing. After each demonstration ask,

> What did you notice about this walk? What is good about it? Bad about it?
>
> If you're in nature, with birds and animals around, what is the best way to walk in order to actually see them? Yes, a slower and more mindful walk will help. Try walking with your head up so you can still see the world around you, and use your feet as "eyes" by dangling one foot in front of you and feeling the ground before you step. When you find a good spot, shift your weight forward. You can look up the whole time and not worry about stepping on something or tripping. You are in total control, like a martial artist.

What animals might you imitate to walk in a sneaking and quiet way? Martial arts and yoga imitate animals to optimize the use of the human animal. Start thinking of imitating an animal whenever you need to do something.

Activity 5—Sense meditation, gratitude and sit spot: Ask your participants if they ever go and just sit in nature.

> Do you remember doing it when you were younger? It's pretty natural for us to do. I like to think of us like house cats. It's natural to go outside and just sit still, watching things for a while, sneaking around a bit, interacting with the birds, maybe hunting for something that intrigues us, finding mysteries.

From here, send them out to pick individual private places in nature to sit for just a few minutes. Give them directions:

> Keep your senses open and aware. Stand up and walk in your animal walk to a place that "calls you"—a place of your own. This is to be done in silence and on your own. This is about you and nature.
>
> Once you find a place, sit down and find one thing around you that you feel grateful for. Then think of one thing in your life in general you feel thankful for. You can even speak it out loud. If you want, you can ask a question about your life that you would like an answer to.
>
> After that, all you have to do is sit and use your senses to notice what the world around you is doing and saying—maybe something will even happen that gives you a clue about your question.

After 10 to 20 minutes, call them back, ideally with an animal sound, such as a crow call. Choose the timing based on your judgment of how well primed they are and how much solo time they can endure. Sit in a circle on the ground and ask them a few questions: How was that for you? What happened? Allow any stories to come out and ask them questions in response. Reflect your enthusiasm and excitement for what they're experiencing in their relationship to nature. You can also say:

Many people think nature is the greatest teacher—we only have to learn how to listen. Did you feel as though anything out there had something to teach you?

Closing: If you have multiple groups, call everyone back together and open up a general discussion:

Is your relationship with nature any different from when we started this morning? What do you want moving forward?

Close by reminding them of the importance of nature:

Nature is a resource you can always turn to, and connecting with nature is a life-long and endless journey. You can keep strengthening your senses and whole brain and body to be more natural until you die. Nature is the ultimate classroom for us human beings, and it feels good for a reason. We hold our sessions out in nature for a reason. Nature is crucial to our humanity.

There are many beautiful poems about nature you can end with. One great example is "The Peace of Wild Things" by Wendell Berry.

 ## Taking Action in the World: The Great Turning

On the second last day of camp we take up the question, How can I use my creativity to make a difference in the world?

We take a lot of inspiration from our friend and colleague Joanna Macy, an author and facilitator who has worked with communities all over the world. Joanna describes the times we are living in as the Great Turning and says that the essential adventure of our time is living through the shift from an era of unsustainable industrial growth to one of life-sustaining civilization.

She believes that we have the technical know how, the communication tools and the material resources to grow enough food, meet our basic energy needs and maintain clean air and water. Future generations will look back to this time as a turning point—a time when society began to make a conscious shift toward a life-sustaining culture.

Youth at a Canadian camp list their concerns.

Credit: Sara Dent, Power of Hope Canada

Opening: A good opening quote for this plenary comes from the anthropologist Margaret Mead: "Never doubt that a small group of thoughtful, committed citizens can change the world. Indeed, it is the only thing that ever has."

Goal: To help participants locate themselves within the burgeoning movements for change occurring all over the planet, to support them in exploring their own calling and envision their next steps in the adventure of life.

Activity 1—Presenting the Great Turning: We begin by sharing our core belief that "the happier life is the engaged life" and that we are each here on Earth for a reason. We each have a part to play in the monumental but exciting challenge of healing our world. We convey a sense that the situation confronting humanity is indeed serious, and that working for solutions leads to a happier life that is rewarding regardless of the final outcome. We state that this session will focus on our relationship to the wider world. We then briefly describe Joanna and her work and share her ideas about the Great Turning.

We often use the metaphor we shared in the introduction of this book to bring the concept of the Great Turning alive:

> It's as if all of us are travelers on a massive, smog-belching, ironclad cargo ship that is heavy in the water and charging ahead in the wrong direction. What's more, only a fraction of the wisdom, compassion and energy of the passengers is being called upon. And we collectively have been given a challenge. Somehow we have to find a way to change direction while transforming this hulking mess into an elegant sailing vessel, equipped with the most innovative and nature-friendly technology imaginable. And each member of the crew on this *new* vessel gets to contribute the best of what she has to offer.

This metaphor aptly describes our real-life adventure—serious, fraught, sometimes exhilarating and potentially full of joy, with room for everyone who wants to play.

We then go on to say,

> Three dimensions of change are needed to accomplish the new shift in direction at the same time as we design a new vessel to carry us. Let's see where you might fit into the picture.

1. Carrying out holding actions: These are the actions required to slow the damage to the Earth and its beings. The youth then give examples of holding actions such as:
- protecting the Amazon and other remaining ancient forests
- protecting the oceans and their creatures
- eliminating the use of plastic bags

2. Creating new, life-affirming alternatives: This means looking for the structural causes of our problems and spreading new solutions.

> It is not enough to simply prevent further harm to the Earth and her people. We need to understand how the system currently operates, and come up with new ways of living, and new ways of solving our problems.

When we ask for examples of this, we hear things like:
- advocating for bike paths and public transportation
- changing the educational system so that young people are using their creativity to tackle real-world problems
- spreading new, non-polluting technologies for growing food
- developing shared gardens and cohousing communities

3. Producing a shift in consciousness: This third dimension is equally important.

> We can't stop further damage and create new life-affirming structures unless we change our values and our perceptions of reality. The world we create together reflects our beliefs and values, and if we do not shift our consciousness toward viewing the Earth and all her beings as beautiful, whole and sacred, we will end up right where we are today. Nothing will ultimately change for the better.

Though this dimension can sometimes be a little more challenging for youth to grasp, we still ask for a few examples of actions we can take in this regard. We often hear things like:
- honoring the wisdom of native peoples
- confronting the spread of materialism in the media and in our lives
- challenging stereotypes of people different from ourselves
- developing ourselves through contemplation and being quiet in nature

We end this introduction to the Great Turning by emphasizing that all three dimensions are equally important and that they are interrelated. While we each likely focus on one, we can participate in all three.

Activity 2—Engaging with the Great Turning: The next part of this plenary employs personal storytelling. We use three small containers such as hats (one for each dimension of the Great Turning) and pass out pens and paper. Then we ask participants to think about what they have done so far in their lives to care for the world, and what they have seen other people around them do. They write these actions and practices on separate slips of paper and drop them into the specific hat that represents: a) carrying out holding actions; b) creating new structures/alternatives; or c) shifting consciousness. This takes five to ten minutes.

We pull several slips from each hat and ask the participants who placed them there to stand and talk about the actions they took, what happened, and how they felt. We welcome the cheering and clapping that happens with each sharing. This cultivates the habit of celebrating the good work people are doing on behalf of all. This sharing should take about 20 minutes and cover all three dimensions. Youth and adults can take part in this storytelling, but youth should have the most time to talk.

We write all the projects on flip charts under the three categories. As time gets tight, we ask people to name their project in a sentence, and we add it to the list. We now have a map of all of the actions and desired actions that exist in this one small group of people.

Activity 3—Taking next steps: We then gather the group in circles of five, with one adult in each circle, and ask participants to orally respond to the question, Which dimension of the Great Turning do you feel most called to and what is a possible next step? We give 15 minutes for this small-circle sharing and then bring everyone back into a large circle. We then go around the circle, with each person sharing one thing he is inspired to do in the next six months.

Closing: A rousing way to close this plenary is by singing a song from a liberation movement such as the US civil rights movement. One of our favorites is "Ain't Gonna Let Nobody Turn Me Around." Here are the words:

Ain't gonna let nobody turn me around
Turn me around, turn me around

Ain't gonna let nobody turn me around
I'm gonna keep on a walkin', keep on a talkin'
Marching up to freedom land.

This is a zipper song, meaning you replace the word "nobody" with words like fear, cynicism, racism or sexism to form new verses. You can hear Sweet Honey in the Rock sing this on Youtube.

 ## Making It Up As You Go

Hopefully the plenaries described above have given you a feel for how to put the elements together to create a transformative learning event. As you gain experience, you'll be able to breathe life into all kinds of curricula by integrating the arts and experiential learning. This is where facilitation gets fun and creative.

Engaged Reflection: Making Sense of It All

"Raise your hand if you think you'll be able to hear this when it hits the floor," says Akim Funk Buddha, a Zimbabwean performance artist holding a sheet of paper high over his head. Eighty hands shoot up. "Okay, close your eyes and let's see. Raise your hand when you hear it land." The paper floats to the floor and lands with a soft clunk. Hands fly up. "Okay," he teases as he tears the paper and holds half of it in the air. "How about now?" All hands go up again as it connects with the floor. "And now?" tearing the paper in half again. The youth are entranced as he continues to hold up smaller bits until the paper gets so small it floats to the floor with barely a whisper. Youth crane their necks toward the sound and raise their hands tentatively, unsure whether they've heard it or not. And finally, it's quiet.

"Now try this," he says, crouching in the center of the room. "Close your eyes and listen. How many sounds can you hear within this room? Raise your hand if you can hear three distinct sounds." A sprinkling of hands go up. "Two sounds." More hands go up. "One." The rest of the hands shoot up. And what did they hear? The quiet clanking of a pipe, clothes rustling, a stomach gurgling, quiet breathing. "Okay," he says. "Now close your eyes again. What can you hear outside of this building?"

A bird sings. An airplane flies overhead. Wind blows in the trees. "Now bring your attention back inside the room. What do you hear?" As he guides our attention back and forth, our ears attune to subtle sounds emerging from the silence. The youth identify more and more sounds. And in the room, tranquility sets in.

While on the surface Akim is leading a series of fun and entertaining games, at a deeper level he is consciously preparing this gangly group of young people at a Power of Hope camp to be able to enter into what could be called the heart of learning: the ability to reflect. Reflection allows us to turn experience into learning by looking inside, exploring our attitudes and beliefs, and making new choices about how we want to be. Unconscious attitudes and beliefs hold the stories of our lives in place. Reflection makes learning conscious so that we can transform experience into tangible change. As such, it is the cornerstone of personal empowerment.

Groups of young people are frequently told to be quiet, but rarely are they shown how to do so. Our favorite way to teach the art of silence is through play, as modeled by Akim. The young people get so involved that at first they aren't aware they're learning to be quiet. When they finally experience silence as a group, it feels good. Very good. Playing listening games raises the group's capacity to pay attention, and this makes a huge difference in the quality of any program. We find that if we don't spend at least a short time playing with silence at the beginning of a program, everyone has a much harder time focusing.

Self-reflection is an essential skill for all of us, but particularly for teenagers. "Adolescents experience a profound cognitive shift that allows them to experience transcendence for the first time," says Dr. Sharon Parks, a Harvard-trained psychologist and educator whose work focuses on human development and the formation of leadership and ethics. "Suddenly they are able to reflect on their lives and ask the larger questions like, 'Who am I?' and 'Why do people suffer.' And they are able to see themselves as others see them." While transcendence can be a positive experience, this heightened sensitivity also makes teens susceptible to alienation and despair.

According to Dr. Parks, youth are at risk in two specific ways when adults do not recognize and nurture their inner lives. First, their increased vulnerability to despair can fuel depression and deep loneliness. And second, their inner development—building the capacity to make meaning, form values and develop motivation—can be stymied. For this reason, we approach reflection—commonly accepted as an important phase of the learning cycle—as a multi-dimensional set of skills that move from the inside out. Whether working with youth or adult groups, the capacity to move inward and then back out brings depth and meaning to the learning process.

Preparation for Success

Reflection is a commonly accepted part of the learning cycle, but too often it's conducted as a boring afterthought. How can we make reflection as exciting and as much of an adventure as the activities themselves? Though reflection comes after activity, the effectiveness of the process depends on how you set up your program in the first place. If you prepare your group for learning through having clear goals, agreements and creative warm-up games, you are far more likely to have lively and deep reflection.

Here are some guidelines for enlivening reflection:
- Make reflection fun.
- Use the arts and mix the media.
- Find ways to turn reflection into a creative performance.
- Be excited about it yourself.
- See is as a natural, essential part of your program.
- Use it as a way for people to speak from their hearts through art or conversation.

A Culture of Reflection

Rather than set aside reflection as an independent activity, find ways to integrate it naturally into all aspects of your program. You can do this by asking provocative questions along the way as you and your group learn together. In our camps we weave reflection throughout the day.
- **Daily community meetings:** We spend 10 to 15 minutes each morning reflecting as a whole group on how our community is doing.

We always start by asking, "What is working?" Then we move to, "How might we improve?" We close the meeting with affirmation. By starting with the positive, the group relaxes and opens up and moves more easily into what needs changing or improving.

- **Morning plenaries:** These sessions provide opportunities for reflecting individually, in pairs, in small groups, and as a whole group. The small groups are where the action really is in terms of deep conversation, self-disclosure and the bonding that results. Whenever possible we ask an adult to join each small group to model deeper reflection and support the youth in making the most of the activity.
- **Small-group workshops:** We generally end these sessions with a look at what we have discovered or learned.
- **Gratitude circles:** We hold a 15-minute gratitude circle before dinner, where the whole community reflects on the day and shares thanks for kind actions small and large.

Instilling an attitude of gratitude: daily thanks circle at camp.

- **Family group meetings:** After dinner each night, the entire camp meets in small groups for 30 to 45 minutes of reflection. (See Structured Reflection Groups, page 112.)

This all adds up to teaching the habit of reflection as a normal part of everyday life.

 ## Tips on Leading Reflection

Leading reflection is the essential art of facilitation. Here are some tips to keep in mind when you are debriefing and leading group conversations.

Be curious: Skilled facilitators exhibit a curiosity and interest, even fascination, with what emerges from the group. When you are truly interested in what evolves, you'll know just where to guide the conversation. The facilitator's job is to hold an overall context for the conversation yet allow the content and wisdom to come from the group. Holding an overall context means you keep the conversation in the general territory you intend but you don't manipulate the group into saying what you want them to say. If you use the debrief as a way of getting your own point across, you'll miss the wisdom that comes from the group, and your participants will feel manipulated.

Ask powerful questions: What did you notice? What actually happened? How did you go about getting what you needed? Where else does that happen in your life? What meaning did you make of that? What does that belief cost you? What is the benefit? How else might you look at that? How might you use this new awareness in your life?

In our advanced facilitation courses we challenge people to lead entire conversations by simply asking questions. The facilitator can make one short opening statement and then has to move to questions. The participants often revolt at first, thinking it's an unnatural way to hold a conversation, and yet, if you listen carefully, skilled facilitators often carry on conversations with groups for extended periods through just asking questions. The purpose is to hold a debriefing conversation that is as free as possible from your own lecturing.

Use both closed- and open-ended questions: Closed-ended questions can be answered in one word, often yes or no. For example, Did you like that movie? The question will generate more conversation if you turn it into an open-ended question, one that can't be answered in one word: What did you think of that movie? Closed- and open-ended questions each have a role in facilitation. Closed-ended questions bring in participation, providing a quick way to get every voice in the room. Open-ended questions lead to deeper exploration.

Avoid asking Why?: Questions that begin with "why" imply judgment and tend to close people down. When you ask why, you are asking people to explain themselves or account for their opinions. More powerful questions begin with what, where, when, and how.

Ask only one question at a time: Too often facilitators will bunch a few questions together. For example: "How was that activity for you, and who found the beginning challenging?" This leaves people confused. If no one is responding to your question, check to see if you've asked more than one. You need to pick your questions apart and ask them one at a time.

Don't rush: When you don't get an immediate response to a question, it might be because your participants are thinking. New facilitators often jump into the silence after a question and disrupt the flow. Even if you're uncomfortable with the silence, sit with it for a time and give the group a chance to respond. If the silence continues for a very long you might rephrase your question: "Let me ask this in a slightly different way…"

 ## Goals and Agreements As Tools for Reflection

No matter the length of your program, your goals and agreements provide a powerful compass for reflection. We'll start by looking at how you might use a goal as the basis for reflection. "Learning from people different from ourselves" is a goal in many of our camps. In a morning community meeting the facilitators might ask, "How are we doing on our goal of learning from people different from ourselves?" This naturally leads to a facilitated conversation with questions such as:

- What have you done so far to reach for that goal?
- How did it go?
- What benefits came from that?
- How else might you find ways to learn from people different from yourself here at camp?
- What gets in the way of reaching out to people different than ourselves?
- What's the downside of always hanging out with people similar to ourselves?
- What might we do together to achieve that goal?

You can similarly use community agreements as a reflective device.

- How are we doing on our agreement about avoiding put-downs?
- Who has had some success?
- How does it feel when you try something new knowing that you're not going to be put down?
- And what about that little voice in our heads that puts ourselves down? How are you doing with that?
- What strategies are you using to quiet that inner judge?
- How is it working for you?
- Can you imagine doing that after leaving camp?
- What would it take?

You can also use personal goals that participants make for themselves (such as through an activity like the intention tree) as tools for reflection (see page 88). Say, for example, "Raise your hand if you've made progress toward that goal you made for yourself." And the conversation moves from there.

At the end of your program you can also revisit your goals to reflect on all that participants have learned. In this way, goals and agreements serve as a compass throughout the program. Again, you can use this technique no matter how short your program.

Getting Mindful

Five teens are lying on blankets in the darkened living room of an old farmhouse at an early Power of Hope camp.

"Become aware of your feet. Now tense your feet and let them go," intones youth worker Lucia Ramirez. "Now become aware of your knees." The youths' bodies visibly shrink toward the floor as she takes them through a relaxing scan from toes to head. She then asks them to watch their breath as it comes in an out of their bodies, teaching them a non-religious form of meditation called mindfulness.

"Wow," said one youth afterward. "What was that? I felt like I lost part of my brain!" "How come no one ever taught us this before?" asked another. When we asked one group of campers what they wanted more of the next summer, they responded in chorus: "Meditation." We were surprised, and to this day, whenever we offer mindfulness training at youth programs, we are surprised to see the room fill to the brim with eager participants. In her attempt to help a wakeful group of teens settle down for sleep, Lucia inadvertently started a long tradition of learning self-regulation skills and mindfulness meditation at Power of Hope camps.

We learned early on that, in an arts-rich supportive environment, young people will follow their higher instincts, and we trusted their desire to learn self-regulation skills such as relaxation and centering. They need to know how to get centered and how to take care of themselves in our revved up society, and few people are teaching them this.

There is now a growing body of research that suggests that the self-regulation skills learned through mindfulness practice are stronger predictors of success than cognitive skills. These include executive function (the ability to plan and make things happen), focusing (following through in spite of frustration), mindfulness (the ability to focus on the present) and metacognition (the ability to think about thinking). Mindfulness programs, such as Mind Up, started by US actor Goldie Hawn, are making their way into schools, serving kindergarten children through high school students.[17]

 ## Structured Reflection Groups

If you are running a multi-day camp or conference, setting up reflection groups that meet regularly throughout the program can provide intimacy and consistency. At our camps, we call these "family groups." They meet after dinner each evening for 45 minutes of reflection; they also—based on a schedule—take responsibility for camp tasks such as washing dishes.

Concerned that youth from chaotic home situations might not like the term "family groups," we thought of changing them to core groups or base camps. But it turns out that the campers love the concept of family. They affectionately refer to their group leaders as Mom and Dad or Uncle and Aunt, and their fellow youth as siblings. We organize the groups with an eye for including a range of ages and cultural diversity in each one. Thus the campers get to know people they might not otherwise spend time with. The structure also keeps everyone from getting lost in the larger group.

The family groups use a circle process in which each person has time to time to talk about a high point and low point of the day. Participants then answer an additional reflection question that ties into the flow of the program. For example, early on in the week the question might be, "What are you learning about how you make friends?" or "What makes it easy to take a creative risk? What gets in the way?" Later in the week, the question might be, "You have two days left at camp—what is a big goal you have for yourself in the next few days?" On the last evening it might be, "What are three things you can do to make the transition home easier for you?" or "What's one thing you've learned at camp? How will you put that into practice at home?"

For years we've used a bead process in the family groups. Each group receives hemp strings to form necklaces, a big bag of beads that includes different-colored beads for each day of the week, and another big bunch of random beads we call "special beads." Each night participants receive a bead when they answer their family group question. The special beads are for bestowing on anyone at camp in appreciation of something specific the person has done. Over the week, the necklaces grow into a memento of the camp experience. Time and again we run into young people well into college and beyond, still wearing a string of family beads hanging around their necks.

✋ Reflection Activities

With some creativity and enthusiasm for the task, you can seamlessly weave reflection into a program of any size. Here are a few activities to get you started.

Circle process

This is a useful method for reflecting in small groups. One person speaks at a time, with no interruptions. Using a talking object, such as a stone, for the speaker to hold can be helpful. The circle process slows things down and gives a chance to people who need a longer time to put their thoughts to words or who are less likely to speak up in a group. When the space is opened in a circle process, just about everyone has something to say, and interestingly, the biggest gems often come from the quieter youth. You can start the circle process with a core question as in a family group; you can use the format to reflect on a shared activity; or you can use the process to do personal check-ins or check-outs at the beginning or end of a program.

Youth workers in Colombia learn to use drawing as a method for reflection.

Credit: Sara Kendall

Art

Free writing and drawing assist the reflection process in a number of ways. Before jumping into a group conversation, ask participants to free write on the theme (see "Timed Free Writing," page 192). This will get their thoughts and emotions flowing, and the conversation itself will begin on a deeper, more reflective note. You can also offer the option of drawing a picture or doing freeform drawing prior to a conversation. Ask, "When you think of this theme, what thoughts and feelings occur? Express those feelings with color and form." You might not even choose to have participants share the free writing or pictures. The act of making art in itself stimulates the right brain and deepens the conversation.

Similarly, you can use free writing or drawing at the end of your day or of your program. One camp facilitator instituted the practice of journal writing for ten minutes every night as a cool-down after participating in stimulating evening arts activities. "We all came to relish that quiet time to reflect in a personal way after a whirlwind of activities," wrote one volunteer. "The daily journal writing somehow brought us back to ourselves and prepared us for a more restful sleep."

Dekaaz

Musician and facilitator Rachel Bagby has created an elegant group reflection tool—a new poetic form called dekaaz. Consisting of three lines with just ten syllables, it's a simple, fun and powerful form for distilling and sharing insight. Dekaaz can consolidate a vast amount of experience into a tiny poem, and the brevity offers a democratic way for many voices to be heard in a relatively short amount of time. A dekaaz is constructed like this:

- two syllables in the first line
- three syllables in the second line
- five syllables in the third line

Flowers
Are Earth's way
Of laughing out loud
— Jeff Vander Clute, executive director, New Stories

Your muse
might approach
like a hungry doe.

Dear You,
Keep asking
Love, Copernicus!

— Holly Thomas, a senior writer at Microsoft

Rachel says a ten-syllable poem doesn't officially become a dekaaz until you speak it out loud to another living being. Thus, the dekaaz process is innately interactive. We have used dekaaz with youth and adults. At adult conferences we introduce dekaaz in the opening. Then we leave time for people to write and read their dekaaz after every presentation as a way to share, synthesize, question and reflect on what they've heard. The dekaazes become deeper and more profound as the conference moves on. To learn more about dekaaz and Rachel Bagby's Dekaaz Facilitation Training see: www.dekaaz.com.

Slideshow

Here's a theater game that makes reflection lots of fun. In groups, participants make a list of important moments in their experience together. (They may have been together for a day-long workshop, a week-long camp or even a year-long program.) They then find a way to illustrate each event by creating a "slide" using body postures and facial expressions and then freezing in place. Each small group prepares a short slide show for the larger group, with one person calling out the caption for each slide. This creates a powerful memory for the players and the audience—and it usually evokes lots of laughter.

Learning/intention statements

Here is a personal inquiry tool we learned from Dave Ellis of the Falling Awake coaching and leadership training. To turn learning into action, ask participants to write a series of statements based on the following format:

One thing I learned (or relearned) is _____
and therefore I will (or I intend to) _____.

After participants have written several statements, ask for volunteers to share one each with the whole group. We've used this with youth as well as adults. It's one of our favorite ways to end a program. Ellis's book *Falling Awake, Creating the Life of Your Dreams* is chock-full of useful empowerment activities to use solo or with groups.

 ## Creative Reporting

You've just had a stimulating time discussing an issue or doing an activity in a small group, and now you're back together with the whole group. The facilitator asks a volunteer from each small group to report to the larger group on the salient points from the small-group discussion. As reporter after reporter drones on, heads nod, people check their cell phones for messages.

Sound familiar? This common practice of reporting back from small groups is rarely energizing or even listened to, and yet facilitators do it almost by rote. Group reports can be a lot more interesting and illuminating if you inject creativity into the process. Here are some ideas:

- Each group reports the three top ideas that came up in their group, sharing each idea in one short phrase of eight words or less.
- Each group makes a frozen sculpture that represents the content of their conversation. One by one the participants call out one word or a short phrase that represents their piece of the sculpture (see page 230).
- Each group comes up with a group poem that represents their learning. They then read their poems to the whole group.
- Each group draws a picture that represents the ideas in their conversation and shares it with the larger group.

Over the years, we have learned to be quite daring in what we ask of people. For example, once when we were facilitating a session about youth and adult connection at a primarily academic conference, we came up with the idea of asking the small groups to do reports tightly structured around a theater activity. Can we really ask them to do this? we wondered. Oh, why not! After the groups set themselves to the task, one person came and asked, "Do we have to stick with the instructions?" "Of course not," we said. What followed was a series of mini-performances that were funny, sad, poignant and highly creative. And the energy of the conference picked up dramatically.

The Gift of Reflection

Reflect, reflect, reflect! It's our gift as humans, and it's one key to creating a more positive future. As author Margaret Wheatley wrote, "Without reflection, we go blindly on our way, creating more unintended consequences, and failing to achieve anything useful."[18] Reflection isn't encouraged and rarely taught, so be patient. For many people it will be a new skill.

7

Community Arts Happenings: Becoming Creators of Culture

Sixty-some people are arranged flower-like, lying on their backs, heads to the center of a large room. The lights are low; breath softly whooshes in and out as the young participants follow instructions for deep relaxation. Once deep silence prevails, a young woman enters from the side singing "MLK," a lullaby written by the band U2, in a soft soprano. "Sleep, sleep tonight. May your dreams be realized." A second teen enters from the other side and takes over singing in a mellow alto. A third silently moves into the room and sings the song in a tenor. As they drift in and out of the relaxing bodies, they intertwine their melodies to form a haunting harmony. When the singing ends, the young participants silently leave for bed, tear stained cheeks on flushed faces, looking more like five-year-olds than sophisticated adolescents.

The singing of the lullaby is the culmination of a music-and-dance evening at a week-long Power of Hope camp in Canada. In this mid-week event, the community shares songs and dances, working themselves into a joyful frenzy. The sweet close of the evening touches us to the quick. How is such beauty possible? we sometimes ask ourselves.

Not so long ago, most humans lived in participatory cultures where they sang and danced, made music and art, and told stories as part of their everyday lives. In the late 1900s piano manufacturing was one of the largest industries in North America, and group singing in homes, schools and public places was common. In a very short time, people in many parts of the world have moved from being active participants of culture to passive consumers. We listen to other people's music and watch other people's stories. We even spend hours watching other people's experiences through reality TV. And in the process, something precious has been lost. A shift back to a more participatory culture is not only possible, however; people are ready for it, and young people are proving eager to take the lead.

At Creative Community camps, we spend most evenings engaged in some form of collective art-making conjured entirely from the imaginations and energies of all who are gathered. As a rule, we do not invite extra talented guests in to provide "entertainment," and we rarely use recorded music. We learn how amazingly entertaining we can be for each other, and we take great delight in each other's brilliance. It's heartening to witness young people waking up to this. It's not uncommon to hear a camper say "I just realized that I haven't watched TV all week and I have never laughed so hard—or cried for that matter. I never knew how entertaining we all could be!"

Providing our own entertainment turns out to be about more than just having fun together and laughing with wild abandon. It's about recovering something profound, about being a human being in community. The vast majority of the young people attending camps in North America have never experienced the joyful intensity of singing the kind of songs that send shivers of good feeling throughout the body. Few have danced in large circles or long lines of people and really let themselves unabashedly move their bodies without fear of being uncool. Whether it is a hilarious night of theater games or a mind-blowing open-mic talent show, these collective creative happenings leave an indelible imprint and boost our gratitude for being born human.

You don't have to run a camp to join in the game of becoming creators of culture. Each of the community arts events we describe in this chapter is transportable to other settings: conferences, schools and communities.

Community Building through Theater Improvisation

Magdalena Gomez is a performance poet, playwright and arts educator living in western Massachusetts. Years ago she joined us as the theater specialist at the week-long gathering we led for the Earth Service Corps, a national youth environmental organization run by YMCAs across the US. An evening session she led using theater games to build community has influenced our work ever since.

The evening of theater games began with a dance circle in which every last one of us got to lead for just a few moments (see page 261). Magdalena slowly turned up the creative heat as she led us through a series of basic theater games that involved the whole group, smaller circles of eight or ten, and pairs. Occasionally she invited participants to come up in small ensembles and perform for the entire conference. Over the course of the evening, through shrieks of laughter and hushed attention, individual personalities started to pop out and shine, taking our community of 125 to a new level of connection.

Theater improvisation evenings have now become standard fare at all of our camps. We also lead them in other venues, such as adult conferences and university classrooms, whenever we have the chance. It is fun, and the results are rewarding. No matter what the venue, people welcome the opportunity to get silly and play—often to their own surprise. Lead the session well and laughter will break out early on. Bodies loosen up and people begin to exhibit that shimmering joy Rollo May talks about.

A few years ago, Peggy led theater games on the Saturday night of a conference for NGO leaders and local philanthropists. The purpose was to spark the overall creativity in the group. Money had been put on the table at the start of the conference, and the NGOs had to come up with collaborative projects they would pitch the following day. "The improv session had a galvanizing effect on everyone," said one of the conference organizers Libba Pinchot. "People woke up on Sunday morning bursting with a whole new level of creative energy, and their project ideas literally flew together. It was interesting to observe how their style of collaboration was so directly influenced by their experience in the improv session."

Theater games are fun, bonding and inherently funny.

Credit: Autumn Preble

To lead a successful evening of theater games, you need to be clear about your purpose. You are not running an acting training class—rather you are using theater activities to build the web of community and ignite the creative energy in your group. Leading theater requires a certain level of facilitation skill to manage the group energy and deliver directions quickly and clearly, but you don't have to have a theater background. In fact, professionals can be at a disadvantage if they let their acting ability set too high a bar for the participants when they demonstrate activities. Nothing will shut down a group quicker than a perfect demonstration!

Steps for Leading a Theater Improvisation Evening

Here is a step-by-step process for leading a session of theater games. You'll find full instructions for the games in Chapter 12. Once you understand the basic structure and flow, you can substitute games at will.

Defuse the critic: Many people—youth and adults alike—are terrified of acting, but they usually relax once they realize that theater improvisation is a series of games with easy-to-follow rules. Start by assuring everyone that this is going to be easier than they might think. "No need to run out of the room. You'll be safe here!" Don't underestimate the fear, and yet don't overcompensate. If you don't have a theater background, you might share your own experience in learning about improvisation: "I used to be terrified when the words 'theater games' were even mentioned. So I've learned to lead the games in a way that makes them easy to play—even if you're really nervous about it." If you do have a theater background, make your demonstrations low key—so people can see themselves doing this. Anything else you can say to normalize improvisation also helps: "Theater improvisation is just the way young children play together—making things up as they go. We've all done it, and we can do it again."

Share some quick agreements: Laying out a few group agreements puts people's minds at ease and helps them jump in more fully. The most important agreement is this: "For the next hour and a half we're going to ask you to avoid put-downs of yourself or others." You might ask people to invite their inner critics to take a walk outside during the session. Another helpful agreement is to play full on: "Just throw yourself at it. This evening is not about being good. It's just about participating." With youth, it's a good idea to include an agreement to keep things clean and safe. We often challenge young people by saying it's all too easy to fall into sex and violence in scenes because we are surrounded by those images in the media. "Let's really call on our imaginations to do something different. Something more creative." During your session, you might have to gently remind your group of this challenge.

Teach signals for getting quiet: When you're playing theater games with a large group, chaos will reign unless you have some techniques for getting the group quiet. There's nothing more annoying than a facilitator yelling over the crowd and spending too much time trying to create order. You'll save everyone the frustration by explaining this ahead of time and sharing ways for the group to get quiet (see page 81).

Start with a focusing game: A good one for this purpose is called Count to Seven. Begin by asking the group if they think they can count from one to seven. Of course, the answer is yes. But here's the catch. They have to count to seven as a group, with each number named by a different person and with the numbers said in the proper sequence.

> When I say, "Go," one person in the group has to say one, another has to say two and so on until you get to seven. You have to accomplish this as a group, with no pre-planning and no signaling. If two people speak at the same time, you go back to one and start all over again. This is a chance to practice tuning in to each other.

After a predictably bumpy start, you can ask the group for suggestions on how they might achieve this task: listen more, go more slowly, etc. Sometimes facilitators suggest that participants close their eyes. If your group tries repeatedly without success, finally say, "Okay, this time, only people who haven't spoken at all yet can speak." With a smaller field of players, they are more likely to succeed, and here is the point: you want them to succeed at this activity. Some facilitators like to play on the success and raise the ante to 10 or 15. Our suggestion is keep it to seven. Set your group up for a big success and move on.

Play imagination games: Play two or three games in groups of eight or ten. Good starter games are This is Not A... and What are You Doing? (see page 209) because they engage the body and the imagination, and they are fairly low risk. People will ease into the process, and before they know it, they'll relax and start laughing. Introduce the games through modeling, and encourage people to put their bodies and voices into the action. As the activity moves around the circles, encourage people to put even more sound and movement into their demonstrations. When working with youth, keep your ears open to hear whether the group is keeping it clean. It might be good to challenge the group again to keep it safe and clean.

Use imaginative ways to move to new groups: When you want to change the groups between activities, say things like, "When I say 'go,' everyone tiptoe in silence into new groups of eight as if you were sneaking cookies in the night as a child, or everyone run as if you are rushing to catch a bus." This makes moving to new groups fun and easy and cuts way down on the chaos. A lot of talking between activities dissipates the energy.

Play miming games: A good next step is games like Pass the Ball and Magic Clay (see page 211). These games move participants into the non-verbal realm of body and sensation. People gain a felt sense of how their minds affect their bodies, and they develop skills for more challenging theater games. As you conduct Pass the Ball, play with the groups as if they are small musical ensembles. Encourage them to get into the images. Magic clay is best done in smaller groups of four or five because it takes some time for each player to form the "clay" into an object and demonstrate using it.

Tell stories: Now that participants are relaxed and tuned into their bodies and senses, you can move into storytelling. One of our all-time favorite games is Yes, and… (see page 216). This storytelling game ignites the imagination and demonstrates the power of saying yes to other people's ideas. We recommend playing this game in groups of three or four.

Take it on stage: After playing Yes, and… in small groups, invite four or five people (from different groups) to play the game on stage for the rest of the participants. This is fun for the audience and provides an extra challenge to those who are ready to take it on.

By now, more of your participants will be ready to take a small risk on stage. A good follow-up for Yes, and… is Conducted Story, in which people stand in a line and take turns telling a story whenever the conductor points to them. Sensitivity Line and Sensitivity Line with Stories are good follow-up activities, giving people a chance to tell an extended story extemporaneously to the group. All three of these games require such careful listening that it diverts the participants' attention from being on stage, thus helping them be present even while standing in front of a group.

Close with calm: Close your session with an activity that brings the whole group back together and calms the energy. You could do a Yes, and… story around the entire group (if it's not too large) or a dance circle with quiet music (see page 261) or simply stand in a circle and take a few deep breaths together.

Reflection During Theater Improvisation

If you are introducing the use of theater games as a means for building community, you might want to do some quick debriefing along the way. Good questions include the following:

- What have you noticed about the group?
- Has your feeling state or physical state changed since we started playing these games? If so, how?
- Has your attitude toward your fellow participants changed? If so, how?
- What have you noticed about your imagination?
- How might you incorporate games like this in your workplace?

Three Program Plans for Theater Improvisation Evenings

Plan #1: Storytelling Focus

- Count to Seven
- This Is Not a…
- What Are You Doing?
- Pass the Ball
- Magic Clay

- Yes, and…
- Conducted Story
- Sensitivity Line
- Sensitivity Line with Stories
- Closing

Plan #2: Improvisation Focus

- Magic Word
- This Is Not a…
- What Are You Doing?
- Magic Clay

- Non-verbal Freeze Tag
- Improvisation Carousel
- Verbal Freeze Tag
- Closing

Plan #3: Focus on Team Building

- Magic Word
- This Is Not a…
- What Are You Doing?
- Pass the Ball
- Magic Clay

- Yes, and…
- Conducted Story
- Make an Object
- Closing

An Evening of Music and Dance

Nawal is a Somali immigrant who loves to dance. In her high school north of Seattle, she worked with youth from diverse cultures to put on an annual Unity Festival where they would share music, dance and fashions from their home countries. When she first moved to a new school south of Seattle, she found the cultural climate quite divisive, with students sticking with people from their own country or race.

"There are a lot of Somali and Liberian students in my new school," she said. "In the annual multicultural assembly, they would usually showcase a dance from one of those countries and call that the whole continent." When she suggested they represent all of Africa by mixing dances from lots of African countries into one performance piece, she was met with resistance.

"Some people said they couldn't learn dances from other countries, but at the end of the day we choreographed a piece that included dances from lots of countries, including the US. We ended with American Hip Hop because, after all, this is where we live." The audience loved the performance, and Nawal's leadership in developing a more inclusive offering made a difference in her school.

"It showed people that you can learn something new if you put your mind to it, and we actually all became tighter and closer," she said. Music and dance are universal languages that unify us beyond our boundaries of culture and age.

Creative Community camps are filled with dance, music and song. Enthusiasm builds incrementally, and by the end of the week we hear reports of youth singing and dancing in the streets and on the public transportation as they wend their way home. Music-and-dance night usually takes place on the third evening of camp. It gives people the opportunity to share parts of their own culture, to take leadership and to step into one another's shoes for just a moment. Here is how to design a rousing participatory song-and-dance night for your school, community or other venue.

Just as with community building through theater, develop a plan that begins with a low level of creative risk. Let the intensity build slowly,

Getting into the groove at a song-and-dance night.

Credit: Sara Dent, Power of Hope Canada

reach a peak and then cool down to quiet and relaxation. Some of our deepest moments at camp emerge at the end of a song-and-dance night when people have thrown themselves into the action and are now calm and quiet.

A good place to start your evening is with some easy-to-learn songs or a dance circle. Songs, well led, will bring your group into harmony and get every voice into the game. Many people are completely new to harmonic singing. The vibrational experience is extremely pleasurable, and the beauty melts their hearts and minds.

When introducing singing, be sure to mention that everyone has a beautiful, unique voice—whether they believe it or not—and that this is the time to just let it out. Even the most self-conscious singers will fall into the groove when surrounded by people singing the same part. Once you get going, invite people to open their ears to see if they can hear the other parts while singing their own.

A dance circle is always a winning way to bring everyone into the action (see page 261). We structure the dance circle so that everyone gets to lead for a moment. Choose rhythmic, danceable music. It's a bonus if you find lyrics that support the theme of your overall program. The important thing is to make everyone feel comfortable by acknowledging how the "non-dancers" might feel and modeling some very simple options for them to use when it's their turn to lead.

If your music-and-dance evening is at a camp or conference, put out a call ahead of time for leadership from the group. Dance evenings at camps have included such diverse offerings as salsa and Irish step dance, South African gumboot dance and soul trains, electric slide and square dance. Suddenly youth who wouldn't have been caught dead square dancing in the school gymnasium are doing so with gusto. If a group member volunteers to teach a dance step, be sure he—and you—are clear on the instructions. It's not fun for the group to get bogged down with overly complicated or unclear instructions.

The end of a dance-and-music night presents a great opportunity to introduce young people to self-care practices such as the relaxation, affirmation and visualization methods that are taught in mind-body programs, integrative health clinics and yoga classes. Our facilitators often lead relaxing, self-affirming guided visualizations in which they invite participants to appreciate their bodies, their relationships and their lives. These visualizations usually begin with a progressive relaxation exercise, starting with the feet and moving upward. Other adults often improvise a bed of relaxing music to hold the experience. It's beautiful to see the young people let go of the tension in their faces and morph back into young children.

Sample Plan for a Music-and-Dance Evening

1. Dance circle to very upbeat music
2. Two or three group songs
3. A session of cultural dance, led by youth or adults
4. An extended soul train, with music provided by a group of youth and adults
5. Drum circle

6. Drum circle with dance
7. Two energetic songs
8. One quieter song
9. Dance circle to soft, quiet mood music

 ## The Very Open Mic

The open mic is the high point of Creative Community camps. This new version of a talent show is more about sharing your heart and soul with the community than flaunting your talent. In fact, we prefer the name open mic because it signals that the stage is open to everyone, no matter what their level of expertise. Performers just need to be authentic and willing to take a creative risk.

While some conveners might be inclined to manage the quality of their open mic, we find that something quite miraculous happens when you open the stage without vetting performances ahead of time. You are saying, "We trust that you have things to say and that you will do so in a respectful way." Once you establish a safe atmosphere, people will get up and share themselves in the most touching ways.

This story from a large conference funded by a government agency is a perfect example. The conveners had a rule against opening up the stage in their dining room for people to perform, because they were concerned that someone might jump on the stage and say something that would get the organization in hot water politically. During lunch one day, however, they took a risk and invited people to the stage, making a disclaimer that they hadn't reviewed anyone's offerings and asking people to be sensitive. At first, members of various teams got up and sang ditties in appreciation of a team member, receiving embarrassed titters in the audience. Before long, however, people started to share poems they had written. And finally, something completely unexpected happened. A burly young man stepped up to the podium and said, "I want you to know that I've never stood up in front of an audience ever—and certainly not in front of 800 people. But my dad died in this town last year. I haven't been back since, and I want to sing a song to honor him." The clear tones of a love song wafted to the very corners of the cavernous room. Eyes brimmed with tears. If we don't

Credit: Sara Dent, Power of Hope Canada

The audience plays a vital role at the open-mic night.

have the courage to open the stage to our community in full trust, we'll never know what we might have missed.

It takes a leap of faith to host your first open mic. When we facilitate conferences for outside groups and suggest having an open mic on a Saturday night, we are inevitably met with, "But what if no one is willing to perform?" "Don't worry," we say. "They will." So far in all these years, we have not been disappointed. If, however, you are worried that people won't sign up to perform, or if you have a particularly introverted group, there are some ways to stir the pot. If your open mic is part of a larger program that includes arts-based workshops, the workshop leaders can organize their participants to present a short performance together: dancing, singing, playing drums or doing theater skits. This gives lots of youth the chance to participate and experience the thrill of performing. The workshop leaders can also keep their eyes out for individuals who might like to perform, and then provide them with the necessary support. Family group leaders at camps also encourage their group members to perform and sometimes come up with a special family-group performance. If you don't have workshop leaders to prime the pump, nudge people to take a risk. Also be ready with some group activities, such as theater or storytelling games to get the action started.

Setting the Stage

Here are some suggestions for making an open-mic night a treat for everyone involved.

Use agreements rather than previews: We don't require previews of performances. Rather we trust people to abide by community agreements such as keeping things clean—in the case of youth programs. At the same time, we encourage a broad bandwidth of expression as long as it is authentic. Only on very rare occasions have we had to ask performers to exhibit restraint. And the young people seem honored by our trust in them.

Permit one short performance per person: Ask people to perform solo only one time and to keep it to three minutes or less. This means only one song or a few short poems. No encores are allowed, no matter how much the audience begs for them. This opens the mic to as many people as possible and avoids grandstanding by a few. We usually invite people to participate in as many group performances as they like, as long as they are not the leading voice in them.

Select MCs carefully: The MCs play a vital role in setting the tone for the open mic. We invite two or three older teens to be the MCs at camps; at adult events we choose people who have some facilitation skills. The MCs need to understand that it is their job to keep things moving and to energize an atmosphere of affirmation and support for each performer. Becoming an MC is one more opportunity for a young person to step up and develop a leadership skill. We usually have two or three adult volunteers serve as support, helping with setup, sound and lighting and troubleshooting any issues that come up.

Keep things moving: Once the show begins, the MCs can keep the momentum going by asking people to get on deck to prepare while the performer ahead of them is on stage. It's also a good idea to let performers know ahead of time that you will give them a signal if they are going over time. This prevents the embarrassment of having to pull out the hook unexpectedly.

Educate your audience: At the start of the open mic it's helpful for the MCs to talk about the audience role as a supportive presence. Statue improvisation is a useful tool for playfully making your point:

> When we say "Go," everyone take a pose as if you are totally bored and distracted. Imagine how it feels to be on stage facing this kind of audience. Now, take a pose as if you are riveted by the performance. This is your job as an audience.

Remind the audience that the open mic is not about being an expert. The important thing is to just get up on stage and share.

Give visual artists their due: If you have an art barn or arts and crafts workshops, invite the visual artists to develop a short performance piece to show off their work. It can be as simple as a movable art show in which the artists parade around the room and across the stage exhibiting their work. This gives your visual artists a chance to have that same hit of energy that others receive when they are on stage.

Chicken in: Leave a few slots on the program for people to "chicken in." Anyone who has not previously signed up can spontaneously take the stage at this point. Some people will work up their courage as the show progresses and be disappointed if they don't have a chance to perform. This is their chance.

Include a quiet zone: Plan your evening with neighbors in mind. If you need to dampen the noise midway through the show, save your quieter performances for the second half. You can also switch from clapping to hand waving or spirit fingers (holding up hands and wiggling fingers) to express delight and appreciation.

End with calm: There are many wonderful ways to end an open mic on a quiet note. Singing a soothing song or taking a few deep breaths together are two possibilities.

 ## An Evening of Storytelling

An evening of personal storytelling is fun and inspirational and adds warmth to an event. We particularly like to lead storytelling at adult conferences because it really opens hearts. As with facilitating any art form, it's important to begin with warm-ups so that everyone feels comfortable participating. A few low-risk theater games will get people in the mood, and before you know it, everyone is ready to tell a story.

The most important principle to keep in mind in leading a storytelling evening is participation. The evening is far more fun and satisfying if everyone has a chance to tell at least one story. To accommodate this, we suggest having people tell stories in small groups before opening up the stage for individuals to tell a story to the whole group.

Structuring Your Evening

Here is a format for a storytelling evening that we've used numerous times with great success. You can suggest a theme for the stories or leave it open ended.

Setup: Place a special chair at the front of the room and dress it up with colorful scarves or cloth. If you are in a large room, you may need a hand-held mic. This is the *story chair*.

Opening: Talk about the purpose and format of the evening, and then lead people through two or three theater games to warm up the storytelling voice. Good activities include Yes, and… and What Are You Doing? If you have time for only one activity, Yes, and… is a must (see page 216).

Group stories: Ask people to form circles of four. Provide a theme, such as a breakthrough, a challenge faced, a transformation or leave it open ended. Time the groups, giving each person three minutes to tell a story.

Follow each story with appreciations (see "The Three-Minute Story," page 240).

The story chair: Now invite people to form an audience facing the story chair, and choose a theme for stories or leave it open. Invite individuals to sit in the chair and tell their stories—keeping them under five minutes. Let them know that you will be timing them and that you will give them a 30-second warning. The individual storytelling can go on as time permits.

Closing: A group song, such as the interfaith peace chant, caps the evening off quite nicely (see page 253).

 ## Daunting but Rewarding

Look for an opportunity to set up your first community arts event. We know it might feel scary, but experience tells us that people want this. Get some fellow social artists together and give it a whirl. Remember, if you don't, you'll never know what you're missing.

8

Conscious Closing: Optimizing the Learning

"The closing ritual will now begin," called out a young woman draped in festive scarves, standing on a chair in the middle of a meadow. Reading from a document, she proclaimed, "We have come from far and wide. Some from as far as New York City. Others from the neighborhood here at Chinook. We are officially beginning a ritual to celebrate our time together...."

Forming two lines, we walk beneath a flower-laden arch and then skip up a short hill to the fire circle. Members of the welcome committee tuck flowers in our hair and usher us to our seats. The next hour and a half is an emotional roller coaster. We share highlights of the week—the good, the bad and the funny. We sing songs. We give thanks for all who made this time together possible, and finally, one at a time, we step forward and throw a twig into the fire to "let go" of a habit we want to leave behind. We then reach into a basket full of painted oyster shells tied in ferns to choose a gift to take home. Inside each shell is a secret blessing—such as "May you live every day in joy"—to remind us of our camp community when life gets hard. The ceremony complete, everyone streams down the hill to the main hall to party!

A closing ceremony such as this, rich in arts and symbolic meaning, goes a long way toward easing the transition from an intense learning

The stage is set: young people thrive on ritual.

Credit: Sara Dent, Power of Hope Canada

experience to life back home. Not only does it provide closure for the group, it opens the door for creativity and surprise.

✋ Closing with Intention

The closing of a program is as important as the opening. You have brought people together, created a strong container, worked together within that container, and now it is time to depart. An intentional closing is needed, no matter the length of your program. Otherwise participants leave feeling jangled and disconnected.

A one-hour workshop requires a very short closing, such as asking each person to share one word for how they are feeling as the program draws to a close. For a day-long training you might use a slightly longer process, like asking each person share one thing she has learned.

Multi-day programs, however, require extra attention, especially when you are working with young people. At our week-long camps, a group of the youth and adults design a special closing ceremony that can take up to two hours on the final evening of camp.

Closing a longer program generally requires more than the ceremony alone. We view closure as a process with four key elements: preparing for re-entry, identifying the learning, exploring next steps and saying good-bye. These elements intertwine during the last day and a half of a week-long program. In this chapter we'll look at these various aspects of closure and share arts-based activities that aid the process. These activities are equally useful with adult groups.

 ## Preparing for Re-entry

"This was the most powerful week of my life" and "For the first time in my life, I could be myself" are typical comments we hear from young people who attend our camps. While a fair share of the youth are returning to challenging home situations, facing the end of such a powerful experience can be fraught with anxiety and sadness even for those returning to supportive families. As the final day of camp approaches, we often see youth reverting to the behaviors and defenses they arrived with. It's as if they are putting the clothes they wore when they came to camp back on as a defense against what they might face when they return home. The adults at camp usually look forward to their family group meeting on the last evening as a culmination of the intimacy that has developed over the week, and they are sometimes disappointed by how easily distractible the youth are as they inwardly process the end of camp. This is a perfectly natural and healthy response on the part of the youth as they prepare themselves for leaving.

Sometimes offering a gentle acknowledgment that endings are hard and giving encouragement to choose a positive way of completing the program helps young participants put into practice more of who they want to be. Fundamental to the re-entry process is learning to say good-bye in ways that complete the experience and acknowledge and celebrate what we are taking forward in our lives.

Giving the Re-entry Talk

Think for a moment about how you deal with goodbyes. Do you avoid them? Face them directly? Do you express your emotions? Saying goodbye is a part of life, and how we choose to do it has a positive or negative effect on all of our relationships. Therefore, calling the group's attention to how we say goodbye can be the catalyst for an important life lesson. On the last full day of camp, the facilitators set the context for coming to the end of camp by framing the challenge of re-entry. We talk with the group about what it means to leave the temporary community that we've co-created and re-enter our communities of families and friends back home.

The facilitator might say something like:

> Tomorrow afternoon we will say goodbye to one another. Our time together as this particular community in this particular place will come to an end; we all will travel back to our homes and communities.

Participants might say things like "We are going stay here forever" or simply "No!" The facilitator then acknowledges the wave of emotion and reaction from the group.

The facilitator continues:

> My guess is that this is not the first time each of us has had to say goodbye to a friend, a family member or a group of friends. Seems like endings are just a part of life. That means we all know something about how to do this. So the challenge for us now is to say goodbye in a good way, in a way that honors what has happened for us here, that acknowledges the friendships we've made, that celebrates the good times we've had, and the hard times as well. Do you think we can do this? Do you think we can end this camp as well as we began it, as well as we have done all week? I know we can. So here is what I want to know: think back on other times you have said goodbye. How did it go? I am going to divide this flip chart into two columns. I want you to call out ways of saying goodbye that leave you in a good place and ways of saying goodbye that haven't worked so well, that you wish you could have done differently.

The facilitator then starts fielding comments and lists behaviors in the appropriate columns. We often end up with a list like this:

Things that work well	Things that don't work so well
Sharing your feelings	Stuffing your feelings
Talking about anything left hanging/unfinished	Avoiding talking about the hard stuff—and the good stuff
Telling people what they mean to you	Letting something important go left unsaid
Not being afraid of emotion	Being afraid to cry
Realizing that tears are okay	Pretending you don't care
	Reverting to your old style

Envisioning the return

The other key part of the re-entry discussion focuses on what it might be like to be back home. Imagining what we may encounter and exploring ways to respond in advance of being in the situation can help avoid unnecessary difficulties and hard-to-handle feelings. We often use a simple diagram to frame up the challenge of re-entry.

Drawing two circles on a flip chart, the facilitator says,

When we leave an experience like this it feels like the world is divided in two—those who have been to camp this week and those who haven't. Our job when we get home is to bring these two circles together. How can we do that?

The facilitator then deepens the context by saying something like:

It is safe to say that we have all had an important and deep experience this week. We return home with a lot to share, but here is the tricky thing: there is no way to give someone else an experience; the only way for them to have had this experience is for them to have been here. So what do we do?

It would not be uncommon at this point for someone to call out, "We show them!"

The facilitator:

Brilliant! That's exactly right! People will get a sense of this experience from how you act, from what you do, and how you are. Here is a really great thing to keep in mind. All the while you have been here at camp having your experience, people in your life back home have been having their experience too. Life has been going on. Here is one of the best things you can do. When you get home, rather than gushing with a lot of words about what happened (because, let's face it, unless they were here, some of the stuff we did would sound pretty weird, right?), what if you said, "Hey, I have missed you, tell me all about your week," and then do what? That's right! Just listen. It's that simple. What happens when people feel listened to? They feel good and they feel connected to you. So we can give those listening muscles we developed a real workout when we return home. Also, when you listen to people, you get all sorts of information, and that will help you re-acclimate to being home. It's a win-win!

This practice of listening to the people in your life when you return home has worked so well for participants that we make sure we include it in all our re-entry talks.

The facilitators can then explore with the group other strategies for easing the transition to home. They might ask, "What are some other things you can do or keep in mind when we re-enter?" We usually hear ideas like

- Remember to take time for yourself; find a quiet place—perhaps a place in nature—where you can relax and reflect.
- Don't be too hard on yourself—this is challenging.
- Take your time. You don't have to tell everyone everything that happened all at once.
- Continue doing creative activities such as journaling and drawing.
- Stay in touch with each other and plan to get together. Remember, this is the end of camp, but it does not have to be end of friendships that have begun here.

From what we hear, the re-entry process strikes a chord with the youth, as evidenced by this story: "I was quite worried when I left my son at camp," one mother told us months after her son had returned home. She had insisted he go, and had to practically peel him from the car to get him into the bus heading for camp. His final words to her: "I hate you." But when she picked him up after camp, she was in for a surprise. "He jumped into my arms and said, 'Mom, I love you. Thank you so much for sending me here.' He then completely surprised me by saying, 'Before I tell you about camp, I want to hear all about your week at home.'" She told us that he listened intently to her talk about her week. "And believe me," she said, "this was a new experience." We just had to smile.

 ## Identifying the Learning

Our overall goal in an immersive learning program is for each person to move along her own learning trajectory and emerge happier, more whole and cognizant of at least some of what she has learned. We say "some" be-cause the learning will keep coming, and new insights will often emerge well after the end of an intense experience. If we have been practicing reflection during the week, it's quite easy for participants to identify some of their key learning when camp is about to close. We begin exploring this in the last day and a half of camp.

Free writing, poetry, drawing, collage and theater provide excellent tools for final reflection. To facilitate this process, we use simple, direct open-ended statements as starter phrases. Participants can use these phrases to begin a free write or respond with drawing. They can use them to inspire small reminder cards (art cards, page 178) or respond through making body postures (page 229). You could also use the starter phrases for building a "statue" as described on page 230.

- One thing I learned about myself this week is…
- One thing I learned about other people is…
- One thing I've learned that could make a significant difference in my life is…
- When I think back on the week, one thing I am most proud of is…
- One thing that surprised me most this week is…

- One thing I discovered that can help me make a difference in my community is...

Exploring Next Steps

Once we become aware of what we've learned, how do we make it operative in our lives? We encourage participants to think as specifically and descriptively as possible about how they want their lives to be different, what more they want for themselves and how they might go about making it happen. Here are several activities that support this process:

Key Questions

As above, you can work with key questions using a myriad of art forms:
- What can be different in your life as a result of what you know now?
- What are two or three beginning steps you could take to make this happen?
- Who do you know who would understand what you want to make happen?
- What can you do on your own to move forward with what you want?
- What kind of support do you want from the people in your life?
- Imagine yourself six months from now. If you apply what you've learned, what is different?

Through open inquiry, participants will come up with plans that are specific to their own situations. At a camp with war-affected youth in northern Uganda, for example, the youth said one of their biggest takeaways was the importance of sharing what's hurting on the inside. They left camp determined to start reflection groups in their schools.

The Bull's Eye Action Plan

This process offers an effective way to harness one's energies to achieve a goal. On a large piece of paper, draw a form similar to the one pictured here.

A clear goal: Come up with a clear goal. The goal needs to be something important for you, achievable and attractive to you. For example, I want to

The kind of support I need from my family, friends and peers.
The skills and resources I already have that will help me achieve the goal.
OBJECTIVES
GOAL
The habits of thought or action that I need to change. The lifestyle changes I need to make.
The skills and resources I still need to develop.
Credit: Brightspark Creative

The bull's eye action plan.

become a better piano player. You write the goal in the center circle. This is the bull's eye; it is where you aim the arrow of your intention.

Multiple objectives: In the next circle, surrounding the goal, write your objectives—the small and big things you can do to achieve your goal. For example, practice for at least 15 minutes every day; play music with a friend; find a music teacher; take a music theory class at school; play for my family.

Forces for and against: The larger circle surrounding the objectives is divided into four quadrants.

> **Quadrant #1: The skills and resources I already have that will help me achieve the goal.** This is a great place to start, because when we fill in this quadrant we often realize that we are already well on our way to achieving our goal. This recognition helps build momentum for change.

Quadrant #2: The skills and resources I still need to develop. This quadrant helps us get specific and practical.

Quadrant #3: The kind of support I need from my family, friends and peers. Reflecting on this enables us to see that we do not create change in a vacuum. This helps us determine what we can ask other people for.

Quadrant #4: The habits of thought or action that I need to change. The lifestyle changes I need to make. This quadrant brings us back to ourselves and helps us to recognize there are steps that only we can take in support of what we really want in life.

We used to give participants a handout to fill in with pencil, but eventually we moved to asking people to draw the chart for themselves. The results were beautiful, motivational art pieces they could post on their walls at home. This activity can go very deep. We remember one young woman, for example, who identified her goal of joining the police force. Upon reflection, she realized she could not do this without going into drug rehab. Just after camp, she explored options for treatment and committed to a program a week later.

Letter from the Future

Here is a common writing activity that engages the unconscious to imagine a possible future. We use this with youth and adults with equal success. Sometimes the results are quite surprising and can even motivate significant change. A man in one of our short training programs actually quit his job after doing this activity. "I realized that the future I thought I was headed for was not what I really wanted, so I quit my job and followed my dream of becoming a metal sculptor," he told us. Youth often report that their futures unfold seamlessly after doing this activity. "I saw myself three years from now entering college. I'm now doing all of the things I need to do to get there," a 15-year-old girl said.

Ask people to imagine a time in the future. It could be at the end of a current project, the close of the school year, two years in the future, or even more. Their hopes for the future have unfolded perfectly—in fact things have gone even better than they expected. You now invite them to imagine that they are writing a letter to a trusted friend or relative—someone who loves to hear about their successes. In the letter they tell the person about their success in detail. Give them five to seven minutes to write the letter, describing what has happened between now and then. Encourage participants to include sensory detail in the letter. What does this success feel like? What are you doing? Who is with you? What are your relationships like? After writing the letter, give participants the opportunity to read their letters to at least one other person. If there is time, open the floor for reading to the entire group.

This is an excellent activity to do with a team working on a project. After writing about how well the project turned out, they can harvest the ideas that appear in the letters and turn them into action plans.

Saying Goodbye

Humans through the ages have thrived on fanfare and celebration. Closings are the perfect time for this. In our camp programs the last evening is devoted to a closing ceremony designed by a small group of youth and adults. This provides yet another opportunity for youth to take leadership and for creative collaboration across generations. Youth, and humans in

Preparing seed balls to give as gifts during the closing ritual.

Credit: Sara Dent, Power of Hope Canada

general, have a natural affinity for ritual, and it is always moving to see what the team comes up with and how deeply the young people honor the significance of the closing ceremony. It is important that youth and adults other than the lead facilitators lead the closing ritual. This demonstrates that the participants have taken full ownership of the community life.

We provide the team designing the ceremony with a basic structure and a suggested time frame. The group then decides on the flow and content of the ritual. An important element of the closing ceremony is an opportunity for each person to state, to the whole group, something he is leaving behind—something he no longer wants in his life—and something he is taking away from the experience to help create the life he wants. Youth and adults end this experience and move forward in their lives knowing there is a whole community of people who believe in them and wish them well.

Holding a Closing Ritual

Closing ceremonies are open to the creativity of the group. We've seen fairly short but deeply moving rituals as well as ornate affairs that include fire dances and parades. Our advice is to keep it fairly simple and not too long, and ask the youth to lead as much as possible.

- **Opening:** It can be a statement or a poem.
- **Opening song:** Choose something that speaks to the significance of the moment.
- **Gratitude:** Give thanks for everything that made this program possible—both seen and unseen. This gives everyone the chance to see the large web of support that makes an event like this possible. This can include short phrases as well as a few longer testimonials about how people have been moved by the experience.
- **Leaving and taking:** Provide an activity that includes symbolically leaving behind a habit or attitude that no longer serves and taking home one that improves one's life. It's useful to symbolize this by throwing sticks or slips of paper into a fire, and taking home a gift made by someone in the group. Ideas include cards or shells with inscribed blessings, painted stones or bracelets.
- **Closing song.**

We usually end our closing rituals with a party or an informal gathering so everyone can shake off the emotional energy and say goodbyes one on one.

Closing the Circle

"Emeralds for the staff." "Slugs for the rain!" "Emeralds for all the creativity that was expressed here." "Slugs for waking up at 7:30 each day!" "Emeralds for friendship!" "Slugs for having to leave." On the very last morning, the group convenes in a circle for a final goodbye, arms draped over one another's shoulders. The Emeralds and Slugs game is a way to playfully acknowledge the good parts of the week as well as the less pleasant parts.

The closing circle marks the final moments of your time together as a group. It is time for a final song, final expressions of gratitude, and announcements of upcoming opportunities to get together. Various activities, such as a spiral dance and songs that involve the whole group moving together, are particularly appropriate for the closing circle. The important thing is to acknowledge that you are symbolically breaking the circle, and everyone is now moving on. Here is one of our favorite short closings, created by Torkin Wakefield, founder of the Bead for Life poverty eradication program in Uganda:

> Let's all imagine that we are a pod of whales. We have been swimming together, and soon we will be moving in our separate directions. Let's hold hands, and we'll take three big breaths together. On the third breath we'll all reach down and move toward the center of the circle and end with a loud whoop, taking all that we have learned out into the world!

 ## Ending for the Beginning

As the old saying goes, "All's well that ends well." We would amend that to say "All's well that begins and ends well." In fact, a powerful and intentional closing to any event sets the stage for a new beginning as the cycle of living and learning continues.

9

Empowering Performance: Getting Our Voices into the World

Several years ago we were invited to bring young people from our program to meet with visitors from a foundation that had given our organization significant support. We told them that the youth wanted to put together a short presentation about their hopes for the future. When the day came, the young people had to travel over an hour and a half after school. They arrived tired and haggard, with no interest in putting together a performance. We were met with choruses of "Do we really have to do this?" "We just want to hang out." We talked it over with them as we ate dinner, all the while asking ourselves, What have we got ourselves into? We had set up this expectation, but we certainly didn't want to force these kids to do something they didn't want to do.

We finally retreated to a corner to strategize. In the meantime, our very upbeat colleague Gina Sala joined the youth. "Hey, everyone. Let's try out that song we wrote at the environmental summit last week." The youth were energized in a flash. They sang the song, and they were ready to go. Everyone sat down and did a free write exercise starting with "The world I want to live in…" We then created a presentation that included readings from those writings interspersed with singing the song. "Let's walk in doing a body rhythm," suggested one of the boys as we were ready to go into the hall to join the adults.

We are strong advocates of performance as a way for young people to get their voices out into the world. It's powerful on so many levels—and it's always a high-wire act. When you produce a short ad hoc performance everyone, including you, steps into a real-life adventure. No one really knows exactly what will happen—and that's what makes it powerful for everyone involved: the adult team, the youth and the audience.

The young people marched into the hall performing a clapping rhythm, immediately engaging the attention of the 20 adults who had been meeting for the afternoon. Our little troupe placed themselves in a line facing the adults and broke into song. One at a time, the youth shared short sections from their free writing, expressing their visions for the world they want for their grandchildren. And then the magic began.

One of the young women issued a playful challenge to the adults. "You want to try?" she asked. We all stood in a circle and sang the song. Then one of the adults made a courageous attempt at speaking her dreams for the future in a spontaneous poem to a beat. The song picked up again, and then another gave it a try. By the time we had worked our way around the circle, at least five of these people had walked right to their creative edge and jumped in. By the time we sat down for a group conversation the ice was well broken.

A lively conversation ensued. At one point a 15-year-old boy whose family had immigrated to the US from Eretria said, scanning the group, "Some of you look old enough to have been alive during the civil rights movement. Can you tell us what Dr. King was like?" Two women jumped in to tell their stories. One was an African American woman who had worked very closely with Dr. King. "I've stopped talking with young people about my experiences. I wasn't sure they'd be interested," she said afterward. "I now see how important it is to do this." The other, a white woman, shared her story of going to the South with her husband and twin babies to work in the civil rights movement—a choice that resulted in being shunned by their families. In a flash, these older women became heroes in the eyes of the young teens.

As we were about to end the meeting, a young man asked, "Can we sing that song we do at camp where we touch each other's hearts?" To be honest, it seemed like a risk, but how could we say no? We taught the group *Hava Nashira*, a two-part Hebrew song that means "Let us sing, sing Halleluiah." Everyone began milling around the room singing the song, stopping in front of one other, looking into each other's eyes. Before you knew it, people were gently hugging.

The biggest surprise of all came as the young people were climbing into the car to go home. "Do you know what was happening at the end there when we were hugging?" said one youth. "These people were whispering beautiful things in our ears like 'You are amazing' and 'I'm so proud to meet you.'" The young people left that evening with a new sense of the importance of their own thoughts and feelings, and the adults with a new appreciation for this generation of teenagers.

Although that event was out of the ordinary, given the spontaneous group experience that evolved, we find that when young people share their thoughts and feelings with adults through performance, the results are always powerful for both the youth and the audience. Youth voice performances at once break down the walls between generations and build up the confidence and sense of efficacy of the youth. Paradoxically, we

Credit: Jennifer Tai

Young Women Empowered participants engage with an audience of 300 at their international dinner.

find that adults are ever eager to hear the thoughts and feelings of youth, and the young people are happily surprised by the response they receive.

Youth performance in this context also has a restorative and energizing effect on the adult community. Our communities suffer for the lack of the visionary, passionate and creative voice of young people. Adults who welcome and really hear the voices of young people are usually deeply moved and find their faith in the future renewed. Over and over again we hear people saying things like "I didn't realize that teenagers feel so deeply about these issues" or "I did not know that teens were capable of such depth" or "I never thought about or understood how young people feel about this issue."

 ## For Adults Too!

This chapter is not about youth performance alone. Short, message-oriented performances can make an impact in business, organizational and community settings as well. If you are willing to put yourself on the creative edge with a group, you can offer a powerful and motivating performance that encourages deeper exploration of a theme. The performance will surprise and delight people and set a creative tone for your event. As you read this chapter, think about the many settings, including public meetings, that could be energized by an ad hoc performance.

 ## The Anatomy of a Performance

The key to developing winning performances is to use improvisational theater structures as vehicles for the thoughts and feelings of the performers. Sequence these using a basic performance format and you can create a powerful five to ten minute offering in under an hour. When people come up to us excitedly after a performance asking, "How long did it take to put this together? How many hours did you practice?" we have to laugh, knowing how quick it really was.

The Basic Formula
- Begin by articulating a clear and inspiring purpose for the performance. For example, "With this short performance that we'll create together,

we have a chance to turn people on to the fact that we have deep concerns about what kind of environment our children will inherit."

- Then come up with a clear structure that includes a variety of art forms. The participants funnel their own thoughts, ideas and creative expression through the structure. When working with a large group to produce a quick performance, create small groups based on whatever art forms you want to use: visuals arts, dance, theater, spoken word, song or percussion.
- With the help of a teaching artist or other adult, each group comes up with a short performance offering.
- You then put all of the individual pieces together into one integrated performance.

Elements of a Performance

These components will create a winning performance every time.

Strong beginning: How you start makes all the difference. Find a way to grab the attention of your audience. For example, the performance group might enter the stage singing a song or doing a body rhythm. Or they may all step onto a darkened stage in silence and come alive as the lights come on. Percussion and fanfare also come in handy at the beginning.

Dance and/or theater piece: A good follow-up is a short dance routine or theater piece that speaks to the theme.

Spoken word pieces: Five or six people share short spoken word pieces that address the theme. This is the heart of your performance because it's where people can share stories and visions of the future most directly.

Song: Choose a song that someone knows, or invite a small group to write one for the occasion. It helps if the song is short and repetitive. We often use the song in conjunction with the spoken word pieces, singing the song as a refrain between each piece.

Strong ending: Find a way to end with energy and drama. An example would be singing a rousing song and then ending with raised arms.

Two Examples of Performances

Here are the outlines of two youth performances we did in Seattle. One was the culmination of a weekend arts-based environmental program called Dance the Salmon Home. The second came at the end of a day-long program for teen girls at an annual women's conference called Women of Wisdom.

Performance	Street performance about saving salmon, put on at the Fremont Sunday Market in Seattle.	Performance celebrating young women's power, put on at the beginning of a concert for 800 people at the Women of Wisdom conference in Seattle.
Opening	Everyone walked into the market in a big parade. The centerpiece was a giant salmon—made Chinese dragon style—draped over eight people. Others held beautifully painted salmon signs. People walked to a clapping rhythm accompanied by drummers' rhythm.	Two processions came in on the right and left sides of the auditorium. Leading each procession were young women carrying large pictures they had created to represent the strengths of women.
Dance or theater	Once this ragtag crew was in the market, a crowd quickly formed into an audience. Several young men threw down mats and began break dancing.	Six of the young women broke off from the procession, walked down the center aisle and broke into a short hip hop dance.
Theater	A group of youth did a short theater piece that highlighted environmental choices people can make to save the salmon.	Six other girls moved to the front of the stage and performed a quick theater piece called "Real Girls," in which they refuted common stereotypes of girls.
Spoken word and song	Four youths shared short spoken work pieces about the world they want for their grandchildren.	Five young women shared stories from their lives that spoke to the theme of "What I want you to know about what it's like to be a young woman growing up in the world today."
Closing	The troupe reassembled as a parade and walked to a new performance site.	The young performers walked back off the stage in two lines at the right and left of the auditorium.

Tried-and-True Performance Devices

Here are a handful of performance structures you can use in developing a performance in a limited amount of time.

Sensitivity Line with Stories on a Theme

You can use this activity in a variety of ways to provide a structure for personal storytelling or spoken word pieces. The players begin by standing in a straight line, with their backs to the audience. They turn, one at a time, to face the audience, either randomly or sequentially, and deliver several lines of a story or other content. This is a very pleasing and sturdy performance structure that looks accomplished and well thought through. You will get a clearer idea of how to use this structure in performance by experimenting with the Sensitivity Line game described on page 219.

Group Tableau

This tool from Augusto Boal's work (see Group Sculptures, page 230) is a dynamic way of opening up the many facets of an issue. Rather than

Credit: LIFEbeat

A LIFEbeat camp open mic: performing together bonds a group.

forming into a group statue, the player's face the stage and create a picture for the audience, using their bodies and one word or a short phrase. Each person takes a physical position to represent one aspect of the issue and freezes. As she takes her pose, she calls out a phrase that represents the issue. Or each person might strike a pose to represent an emotion that relates to the issue. This is relatively low risk for the players, and the overall effect is powerful. If your performance addresses an issue or a problem, it is often effective to include two tableaux, one that addresses the problem and the other that represents solutions.

Spoken Word with Musical Background

Free writing is one of the most effective tools for generating potent content for performances (see page 193). Begin the free writing with a sentence-completion exercise that relates to the theme. Writing non-stop will generate lots of material that can be shaped and edited into a short performance poem. Often the first draft is ready for delivery with just a little bit of editing. Delivering the poem to a quiet, live music background adds mystery and a sense of professionalism. Keep the music simple so that it doesn't distract from the power of the words. Supporting the spoken word presentation with soft piano or guitar chords is very evocative and not too difficult to pull off—and it makes the spoken word performer feel and sound like a star!

Rap

Hip hop is a powerful force in youth culture. Young people readily respond to it, and adults do as well—when they can hear and understand the words. A lot of the professional rap music reinforces negative stereotypes, but there is a decidedly positive and uplifting stream in this worldwide cultural phenomenon. Youth can rap about any subject—think of it as poetry delivered in a rhythmic way over a propulsive beat. It is good to draw on the natural talent and enthusiasm that youth have for this art form and to expose adults to a positive expression of youth culture that originated in the intense inner-city neighborhoods of North America.

Beat Boxing

Another skill from hip hop culture, beat boxing was invented by urban youth who did not have the resources to buy electronic drum machines. Instead they produced complex rhythms and sounds using their mouth and voices. Beat boxing sounds amazing, and chances are you know a young person who is skilled at this. A beat boxer can provide the rhythm for rap poetry, and it always ignites the audience.

Percussion

Rhythm is your friend in creating performances, whether it is generated through body rhythm, beat boxing or percussion instruments. Hand-held rhythm instruments such as shakers, bongos or tambourines are often easy to come by. If they are not available, you can use a wide variety of found objects, such as sticks, cardboard boxes, plastic bottles and metal or plastic pipes. An empty plastic water bottle filled with rice or seeds becomes a shaker. The rattle of a shaker used to accentuate and animate a flow of words adds snap to a presentation.

Group Body Rhythms

Group rhythms such as those on our website[19] are great performance devices. Walking in with a large group doing a body rhythm bonds and focuses the performers and dazzles the audience. If you have seen the musical *Stomp*, you have an idea of how impactful body rhythm can be in performance. Learning even a few body rhythms is a great investment to your performance portfolio!

Song

Singing adds an emotional depth to a performance. When creating a performance, it is useful to ask, What songs do we know that speak to this theme? You can also put a melody to original lyrics and create a song specifically for the performance. A free writing activity may produce several phrases that catch the ear of the group and speak to the core message. Be on the lookout for these written phrases or words that people are just happy to repeat. Here's an example: "We are the future, the future of this world." The quick song or refrain can be repeated at different points of the performance to create a bridge between sections. If the performers are just learning the song and are feeling unsure of the words, you might want to write the lyrics on a large piece of paper and hang it so that they can see it. Engaging the audience in singing all or part of a song can be another effective part of the performance.

✋ Things to Keep in Mind

Keep it short: A 5- to 10-minute performance is plenty long. Focus and impact are more important than length. If you stretch it out, the performance can lose energy.

Use a multi-arts approach: Weaving together several art forms gives a performance energy and depth. By using a variety of art forms, you can also ensure that everyone can find a place in the performance.

A young woman speaks to an audience of 850 for the first time.

Credit: Josie Nickum

Give everyone a part to play: Find a role for everyone without forcing anyone too far out of his comfort zone. Stage-shy youth are often quite happy to carry banners on stage and hold them up as a backdrop. They then get to enjoy the energy of being seen and heard along with everyone else. Be careful, though. Never coerce a youth into being on stage if he is adamantly against it. You might find another role for him, such as recording or timing the performance.

Weave in personal story: Story is what connects us and brings issues home. The story could be sourced from one person, or you could include short vignettes from several or all of the performance-group members. Personal story comes most directly through spoken word pieces.

Draw on the strengths in your group: Notice who has some developed artistic skills such as playing a musical instrument, singing or dancing. Individual offerings can also add energy to a performance.

Identify a clear core message: Clarity about the message you want to get across will guide you in shaping the performance and will empower the performers with a powerful, unifying intention.

Identify the call to positive action: If you are seeking to mobilize the audience in some way, identify ways they could take action, and weave that into the performance.

Act like you mean it: Acknowledge to your group that this performance is not going to be perfect, but encourage them to act "as if" they know exactly what they are doing. "Act as if you have been practicing for the past six months and this is your big debut," we often say. Or "Act as if you know exactly what you are doing, and if the audience doesn't get it, it becomes their problem, not yours."

Warm up your group: Just as athletes warm up before a practice, we all need to warm up before engaging in a creative endeavor like designing a performance. Games such as What are You Doing? This is Not a Pen, or Yes, and… (see page 216) will prepare your group to delve into a creative process together. Creative writing activities also get people's imaginations fired up and often generate material for a performance.

A Few More Examples

Performances don't have to be complicated. Here are a few examples of very simple performances that had a powerful effect.

A Quick Stomp

At the end of the first day of a youth conference in Portland, Oregon, the entire group of 100 stepped onto the stage at the opening evening of an adjoining adult conference. They entered doing a body rhythm.

One young person stepped forward, welcomed the adults and challenged them to learn the body rhythm. He then led the rhythm step by step, with the chorus of youth on stage demonstrating. This quick "performance" galvanized the group of youth and introduced the adults to the youth conference.

Report from Camp

A group of youth and adults who were interested in starting up a Creative Community camp program in Eugene, Oregon, attended a Power of Hope camp. Upon returning, the youth put together a storytelling performance to share stories of the camp with the board members of the Oregon Country Fair, a large local NGO. They used the Sensitivity Line with Stories (see page 219) as their basic format. Six youths stood in a line with their backs to the audience. One at a time they turned and told stories of their experiences at the camp. "How long did it take to put that performance together?" asked an impressed board member. "Uh, ten minutes," admitted one of the youth. "It was all improv." Not surprisingly, the organization committed to leading an annual camp called "Culture Jam" and has been doing so for over ten years.

Why It Matters

Performance, no matter how ragtag it might be, is essential to growing a world in which everyone is a change maker. Youth and adults get to practice stepping up and stepping out, taking a big creative risk to be heard. Through this we get to develop the muscles we need to find our place in the community of people who care about the world, people who are willing to raise their voices to stand up for change.

creative facilitator's playbook

Say It with Art:
Visual Arts and Crafts

As the guests at the Hollyhock retreat center on Cortes Island, British Columbia, waited in the dinner line, they couldn't help but see the circular art piece, six feet in diameter, hanging on the dining room wall. The title: "The World We Want for our Great-Great-Grandchildren." Six individual pie-shaped wedges, fanning out from a center circle, featured snowcapped mountains, people of all races holding hands, windmills, solar panels, cities overflowing with greenery, babies, parents, animals of all kinds and more.

We had made the art piece a few nights earlier with the youth and adults at a Power of Hope camp taking place in one corner of the Hollyhock campus. Groups of eight youths and adults each decorated a wedge with their hopes and dreams for the future. We then taped the pieces of paper together to make one large mandala. The next morning we placed the communal art piece in the middle of our group space, where it served as the centerpiece for a session on Caring for Our World.

"Are you with those youth?" we were asked time and again by Hollyhock guests as we passed them on the wooded paths. "I never knew young people cared about these things," they'd marvel referring to the art piece hanging in the dining room. This single art activity fulfilled a multiple purpose, igniting conversation among the camp participants about their values and hopes as they envisioned a desired future, and at the same time introducing the adults at Hollyhock to the depth of passion young people hold for the future. The cost of the materials was negligible, the benefits incalculable.

Humans have been making their mark since the dawn of time, and yet many of us deprive ourselves of the joy of playing with color and image, scoffing it off as child's play or giving in to the inner voice that says, "You're no good at this, so why even try." When we invite adults, and even teens, to draw, they sometimes complain that they feel like they are back in kindergarten. But once they get into it, with the help of some gentle encouragement, they begin to surprise themselves and enjoy their creations.

Putting color to page offers a wide range of benefits, from deepening a group conversation to helping people explore their values and concerns and even healing mind and body. A growing body of research fostered by the art therapy movement points to the healing effects of creating visual art. Studies of adult women with heart disease, for example, show that drawing their illness helps them increase their understanding of their condition. This in turn supports the healing process. Women living with cancer receive benefits such as enhanced self-worth, an increased ability

A young boy at Ugandan camp for war-affected youth finds solace in drawing.

Credit: Cyrus Kwalya

to focus on the positive aspects of their lives, and the ability to hold an identity not defined by their disease. Study after study shows that making art decreases stress and anxiety.[20]

It turns out that crafts such as knitting reap similar benefits. Studies conducted by British physiotherapist Betsan Corkhill found that the rhythmic and repetitive aspect of knitting raises serotonin levels and provides a calming effect, a relief from distraction, akin to that of meditation. Knitters also benefit from the satisfaction and creative excitement of completing a creative project, and their right brains are stimulated by the colors and textures of the yarn. "I am convinced that knitting has somehow reset my brain," wrote one study participant. "The repetitive, meditative, and creative aspects are what has gently helped me back to a more fulfilling life." Said another, "The only time I could significantly reduce the pain was either when I took a large amount of pain killers or when I could concentrate on knitting. Knitting became my drug of choice."[21]

What the social scientists have discovered through research, we see in action as youth spend countless hours in our programs drawing, painting and working with crafts. "Through the visual arts you can express things symbolically that you can't put into words," said PYE arts facilitator Jackie Amatucci. "When people get engaged in an arts activity, there's a quiet— a deep silence that comes over the group. They are totally immersed in their creativity, and it becomes magical—it feels sacred." Once people cast aside their beliefs that they can't do art, they drop into a flow state. "The pride and the joy of creating something of personal meaning actually changes a person. I've seen it time and again with young people. They'll start by making a pair of earrings; then they make a necklace; then they are designing things for other people. They're unstoppable."

Jackie finds the same in retreats she leads for adults. "Once adults start making art, it is almost impossible to get them to move on to anything else. It's as if the adult self takes a backseat to the inquisitive, excited child that wants to explore and play and create. The tactile nature of making art brings people right in." One year we experimented with asking adults at the Hollyhock Summer Gathering to make I-AM posters to introduce themselves to the rest of the crowd. The art tent was abuzz with activity for days, and some of the posters were ingenious works of art.

When leading visual arts activities it's important to pay special attention to quelling the inner critic, because it seems to hold particularly strong sway in this realm. Here's an example of what we might say to introduce a drawing activity:

> We're going to be doing a visual arts activity—but it's important to remember that *this is not a test*. In fact it has nothing to do with being good or not. It's simply an opportunity to put color to paper and see what it reflects back at you.

If people have a hard time getting started, encourage them to simply choose a color, close their eyes, make a shape on the page and then let that shape guide their next move. Give participants the choice of using literal or abstract images—or a combination of the two. And yes, stick figures are beautiful too! We often invite people to include words with their images, but we always emphasize image. We are ever surprised by how readily people take to the visual arts once they realize that they don't have to be good.

You can use visual arts activities in youth programs, classrooms, conferences and business seminars to get big results at a very low cost. You just need paper and colored pencils, crayons or oil pastels (our favorite because of their brightness). Visual arts activities are useful to use as group process tools as well as for individual exploration and enjoyment.

Group Art Activities

Whole-group art activities are powerful tools for developing group cohesion and shared visions. And, lest you need a gentle reminder, you don't need any arts experience to lead them. Two of our favorites for getting your program off on a positive note are creative name tags and I-AM posters (see page 67). Following are some of our other favorites:

Group Mandala

Drawing a group mandala—a circular piece of art like the one mentioned in the opening of this chapter—is a good way to open a discussion on a theme and to express visions of a shared future. Youth workers in

Kampala, Uganda, drew a mandala to identify their gifts and strengths. Students at the Linnaea Farm School on Cortes Island in British Columbia drew one to depict the school culture they wanted to co-create. Over 100 people drew a mandala of their hoped-for visions for the 21st century at a turn-of-the-century New Year's Eve event we facilitated in our community.

Materials: large paper, crayons, oil pastels or markers, masking tape
- To prepare for the activity, tape together pieces of paper to make one very large sheet—say six feet square. Using a pencil and string, draw a large circle that goes as close as possible to the edge of the paper. This is your mandala. Then draw a smaller circle of about 18 inches in diameter in the center. This will be the centerpiece of your final

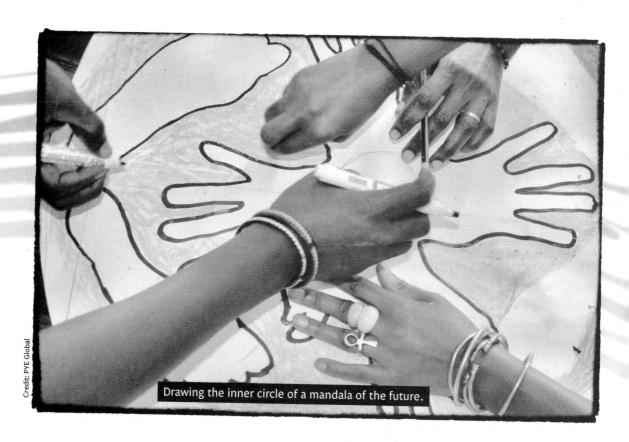

Credit: PYE Global

Drawing the inner circle of a mandala of the future.

mandala. Next draw the pieces of the pie from the inner circle to the outer circle. Do the best you can to make them even. Number the wedges on the back for easy assembly. Cut the pattern into pieces.

- Introduce whatever theme you choose to the whole group, and give a wedge to each small group. Give the centerpiece to the final group. A few examples of themes include "our ideal community," "the school culture we want" or "the future we desire."
- The group members then discuss the theme and come up with a way of illustrating their ideas. They can build their piece around a central image or not. Make sure they decorate the side of the paper that does not have the number written on it. Encourage everyone to use strong colors.
- Finally, assemble the piece and unveil it to the whole group. You can add some fanfare to the presentation by asking for a volunteer to share a poem or spoken word piece or by singing a group song.

Images of Our Collective Work

Collective art pieces bring people together around their shared work. An example is the activity Peggy led at the environmental conference we talked about on page 46. She hung a large hand-drawn map of the Columbia River watershed in the main conference room, and over the course of the weekend participants drew pictures of their individual projects along the shores. You can adapt this idea for any group that is working for a common purpose in a geographic area.

Paper Quilt

This is one of our favorite activities for building a group identity. It's quick and easy and costs very little. The end product is a paper quilt made up of 8½″ × 11″ art pieces on a theme, one made by each participant. You begin with a theme, such as "the gifts we bring to the community," "the gifts our organization brings to the world," "the gifts we bring to the students in our school" or "our strengths as leaders."

Materials: 8½″ × 11″ paper, crayons, oil pastels or markers, masking tape
- Without divulging the purpose of the activity, give each person a sheet

of 8½" × 11" paper. Ask participants to place their papers vertically in front of themselves. *Warning! It's important that the papers are all in the same direction or the quilt won't work out!*

- Introduce the theme, then ask each person to come up with a word and image to depict on their paper. If, for example, the theme is "the gifts we bring to our team," each person comes up with a quality (such as enthusiasm) or an action (such as listening) and makes a picture incorporating the word into the drawing. Each drawing then becomes a patch in the quilt.
- Count the number of participants and decide how many patches across and how many down you want for this quilt. For example, with 24 people you might want six pieces across and four down. In this case, once participants have finished their pictures, ask them to get into groups of six. They share their pictures with one another and then place them side by side to make a panel, taping them from behind. Make sure to tape the entire seam or the quilt will fall apart.
- Then tape all the panels together from the back. And voila—You have a paper quilt!

We've used the paper quilt with great success with groups as large as 125 in various settings with youth and/or adults. Once complete, you have an art piece that can be displayed in schools or organizational offices. We once concluded a workshop with the staff of an NGO in Kampala, Uganda, with this activity. The 35 team members were so delighted with their creation that they marched it down to the office of their executive director, who promptly told them she would use it as the cover of their organization's next annual report.

Group Picture on a Theme

Drawing a group picture on a theme is a good conversation starter for small groups of four to eight. Participants in a youth/adult dialogue drew images of their ideal community. Young women in a girls' empowerment weekend traced the outline of one girl's body and then filled it in with images representing the strengths of women. Participants in our facilitation trainings draw group pictures of the ideal facilitator. We then hang the images on the wall to form a gallery representing the variety of ideas in the group.

Materials: Large paper or rolls of paper, crayons, oil pastels or markers

Pass-around Drawing

This activity helps people find their flow with visual arts. We've used it with great effect with adults in Creative Facilitation programs. (Young people seem to find the activity less satisfying.)

Materials: 18" × 24" paper, crayons, oil pastels or markers

- Break into small groups of six or eight sitting around a table. Give each person a blank piece of paper, and place oil pastels, crayons or markers in the center of the table.
- Ask participants to close their eyes and imagine a time they felt happy

Pass-around drawing staves off the inner critic.

Credit: Peggy Taylor

and creative. Have them begin drawing an image that represents that feeling. Once the drawings have gotten started, ask everyone to pause.

- Preface the next instruction by saying "What I'm going to ask you to do next may make you feel uncomfortable, but please go along with it anyway." Then ask people to pass their picture to the person on their left. Now everyone gets to add images to the new picture just received. After a minute or two call out "Pass the picture to the left."
- Ask people to imagine they are giving the originator of each drawing a gift as they add new images to each picture. Invite them to use words as well as images, but with a focus on images.
- Once the pictures have gone all the way around the circle, each person adds some final touches, then looks at their picture as a whole and adds a short title.

This activity releases a lot of creative energy and generates a good deal of delight. The groups have fun talking about the process and comparing their pictures. Of course, the real learning here has to do with freeing the voice through visual arts.

Two Heart of Facilitation training graduates, Adam Rosendahl and Julien Thomas, have developed an entire community art happening called Late Nite Art, loosely based on this activity. In the San Francisco Bay area and in Vancouver, BC, they hold regular soirees in which participants move around the table, drawing a shared art piece while enjoying local food and wine and engaging in lively conversation. (For more information, visit www.facebook.com/lateniteart and www.facebook.com /pages/Late-Nite-Art/224871310903431.)

 Individual Art Projects

Working on individual art projects opens the door to our inner lives and gives expression to our deepest thoughts and concerns. We find that projects that connect beauty with meaning inevitably induce magic. We often start by asking participants to think of a word, a value or a personal quality to use as a focal point for an art piece. Here is a sampling of easy-to-lead individual activities:

Art with a values message is a winning combination.

Credit: PYE Global

Balloon Lanterns

These lanterns are quick and easy to make and give everyone the chance to focus on their own inner light.

Materials: Small balloons, colored tissue paper, glue, string or wire

- Blow up small balloons. Cover them with three or four layers of colored tissue paper dipped in glue (or Mod Podge), leaving enough space at the top to insert a light. Once they dry, pop the balloon. Punch holes in the sides of the lantern to attach string or wire.
- You can add messages to the lanterns using words or images. We often string the lanterns onto a cord and drape them along the side of our gathering space. You can use battery-operated tea lights to illuminate the lanterns. *Caution: Do not use flames of any kind! These lanterns are highly flammable.*

Prayer Flags/Blessing Flags

Creating small flags decorated with blessings provides a context for exploring our hopes, dreams and visions for the world and then sharing them with our community.

Materials: Cotton muslin, old sheets, or even heavy paper; acrylic paints and brushes, magic markers or oil pastels; string for hanging the flags; tape

- Cut the cloth into pieces about a foot square. Begin with a discussion about the act of blessing—what it is and how it focuses our intentions. A blessing often begins with the words "May you…" or "May we…" or "May the world…"
- Invite each person to decorate a flag with a blessing or a wish for the world. Once the flags are dry, you can tape or tie them to a long string and hang them in a common area.

Who I Am on the Inside/Who I Am on the Outside

Using shoe boxes or simple paper or cloth masks, participants get to reflect on the difference between what they show on the outside, and who they are on the inside.

Materials: Shoe boxes; light cardboard to make a box or cloth or paper to make into masks; supplies for decoration: magazines for collage, glue, markers, oil pastels, feathers, paint and anything else you might have on hand.

- Begin with a discussion about how we appear on the outside vs. who we are on the inside. What parts of our inner selves might we like to share more freely?
- Participants then decorate their boxes/masks: the images on the outside represent their outside selves; those on the inside represent their inside selves. Let participants know they won't be required to share the inside of their boxes/masks.
- In small groups that include at least one adult, give time for participants to share whatever they wish about their outer or inner selves.

Fashion Freestyle

We love to create arts events that bring together participants from diverse sectors of a community, feature a performance, raise money for a good cause and don't cost much to produce. Here is one such project we developed with artist and clothing designer Lynn Mizono. Several years ago Lynn attended a Power of Hope camp armed with sewing machines and mountains of fabric. The youth responded with zeal! Twenty-five of the 40 campers made clothing from scratch, and the camp's open mic featured a high-spirited fashion show. Spurred on by this enthusiasm, we worked with Lynn to design a weekend youth conference and community arts event called Fashion Freestyle. We ran our second Fashion Freestyle in our community on Whidbey Island, Washington, in 2008.

It was surprisingly easy to organize. We put the word out that we were looking for people with sewing machines and a bit of experience who would like to spend three days sewing with young people. We had our 30 volunteers within a few days—along with the 30 machines we needed to borrow. Lynn invited two young clothing designers to join her as design consultants, and a final volunteer offered to bring a big chest of supplies to make jewelry to match the outfits. We then signed up 30 young people: 15 from our island and 15 from inner-city Seattle. Island families hosted the Seattle youth.

We turned a wing of our local middle school into five sewing studios. Each one became a mini community of six participants and six volunteers. We opened the conference with our community-building process (Chapter 4), and Lynn offered some salient words of wisdom about the creative process. A favorite for us all was "Every mistake I make becomes my next best idea."

The following morning the youth and volunteers jumped into the mounds of fabric and worked all day, barely taking time for lunch. "I have never seen kids be so focused for so long," said a local teacher. In the evening everyone took a break to write poetry, and in a Sunday morning plenary we explored the social justice aspects of clothing by following the path of cotton from the fields to the sales table as a finished garment.

By mid-Sunday afternoon, the outfits were complete. A local theater director helped us integrate the poetry, some songs, a hip hop dance and the runway walk itself into a fashion show that we held in a local church hall. One hundred and fifty people crowded in, leaving barely enough room for the long runway. The show raised awareness about social justice issues related to clothing and brought in over $650 to provide food for homeless teens living in the woods on Whidbey Island.

The program provided a broad range of learning for both the mentors and the youth. "I had never even considered sewing without patterns before this weekend," said one mentor. "Now I design most of my own clothing. My creativity took a big jump." One young participant said, "It was like magic. Everyone was so supportive—all the youth and all the adults. I want all my friendships to be more like that."

The magic didn't end there—and this is what we love most about community arts happenings. Mary Fisher and Dorit Zingarelli, two of our sewing volunteers, were so shocked to hear about the number of teens living in the woods on our island that they decided to do something about it.

"We have to make sure they have enough food to eat," said Mary. She had wanted to start a small service project on the island, and decided this was it. So she and Dorit formed an all-volunteer organization called WIN (Whidbey Island Nourishes). Five years later, WIN is a thriving local organization that makes over 1,600 healthy meals a month with the help of over 100 volunteers. They work with schools and community organizations to make sure the children in our community are sufficiently nourished, and now they have started programs to educate young people about food and health. It's not exactly the "small service project" Mary was first envisioning! (For more information, visit whidbeyislandnourishes.org.)

Natural Baskets

Baskets hold; baskets carry; baskets have been around for thousands of years. The purpose of this activity is to connect with natural materials and create a usable art piece you couldn't have previously imagined.

Materials: grasses, small branches, twigs, rags, yarn, string, paint, feathers and other natural objects

- If you are near a wooded area, go out as a group and gather a variety of sticks of all shapes: bent, gnarled and straight. Place them in a big pile on the floor.
- Using cotton or hemp string, tie sticks together or weave them to make a basket of any size.
- Decorate with feathers, paint or natural objects such as moss or pinecones.

"This is one of the most powerful arts workshops I can ever remember leading," said Jackie Amatucci. "It required collaboration because one person had to hold the sticks while another person secured them in place. They had to create a bottom and sides so the basket could carry things. Other than that I gave them no instructions. The ten baskets were so individual and artful that we could hardly believe we had turned this pile of sticks into objects of such beauty."

Artist Trading Cards

This is a perennial favorite among youth and adults. Using magazine images and recycled playing cards or postcards, you design art pieces that represent your values, provide inspiration, make social commentary or generate laughter. You can collect these for yourself or give them as gifts.

Materials: recycled playing cards or postcards, magazines for collage, glue, pens

- Using a playing card or postcard as a base, participants design mini collages or art pieces that make personal or social statements about themselves and/or their concerns in the world. The trading cards can represent something the artist desires or disagrees with or a way the artist wants to be in the world. Words from magazines can be used to make a poem or a proclamation.

We've decorated a wall at camp with artist trading cards; we've shown them off in parades at open mics; and we've used them as a kind of guerilla art initiative, putting messages in places where people would least expect to find them. Artist trading cards have become so popular among artists that you can find hundreds of examples on the internet.

Making a statement with artist trading cards.

Credit: Jackie Amatucci

The Art Barn: Building the Heart of the Community

We set up an improvised community art studio, called an art barn, at each of our camps. Both youth and adults take their first creative risks in the art barn as they make name tags or draw personal posters. They return to the art barn for workshops and at free time when they want quiet and relaxation. For many, the relaxation and fulfillment they find here leads to a desire to develop more artistic skills. You can create a mini art barn or kiosk in a classroom or at a conference. You can also develop an art space in a public building or at a fair. Prepare to be surprised by its magnetic effect.

We call Jackie Amatucci the Queen of the Art Barn because she showed us how to transform the art space into the heart of the camp. With her varied skills as a teacher, artist, enthusiastic coach and ready listener, she creates an atmosphere within which everyone thrives. Here are some tips from Jackie on ways to create and facilitate a warm and healing space for visual arts and crafts.

Set up the art barn in a central place

It's more important to have your art space centrally located than to have it in a beautiful studio. This optimizes the chance that people will get drawn in during their free time. An art barn can be as simple as a few tables and chairs set out under a covering to protect participants from the rain or sun.

Create a welcoming, non-judgmental atmosphere

As the facilitator of the art barn, it's your job to radiate a feeling of welcome. No pressure to succeed—people are simply encouraged to jump in and have fun. Be aware of all the ways you can help participants move into exploration mode rather than judgment. Remember that the art barn is not a professional art studio. Rather, it is a place where people can express their values and concerns and put their voice into the world through visual arts and crafts.

Provide as wide array of supplies as possible

When I put out bowls of feathers, beads, buttons and scraps of material, along with magazines, paper, acrylic paint, beading string and glue, it's like a tactile invitation. The next thing I know self-directed fun takes over. Choose basic supplies, such as colored paper rather than commercial pre-printed stickers. It's the difference between having a coloring book with all of the images preset and having a blank piece of paper upon which your personal choices become an adventure in themselves.

Encourage imitation

Playing off someone else's idea helps the more reticent participants get started. I encourage everyone to be inspired by each other, and the next thing you know, they are launching themselves into their own ideas.

Look for leadership to emerge

When the art barn is open for free time, youth share their skills and ideas freely. This creates confidence, particularly for the shyer youth. At one camp, a young woman from a First Nations band shyly asked me if she could teach a session on beading. Several of us gathered. She handed out tiny beads and thread and went around to help each of us like a master teacher. Gifting us with her skill gave her pride. A significant part of the art barn experience for youth is that friendships are forged and a deep sense of belonging to the community emerges.

Follow your intuition

I'll never forget one weekend youth conference where several very young boys arrived to join my workshop. It was kind of like, Whoops, how did they get here? They were much younger than anyone else at the conference, and they didn't really know how to fit in. Looking at these youngsters, I came up with the idea of making "power sticks." I invited the boys to paint and decorate sticks to represent aspects of their personal power. When I saw them begin to have sword fights with their sticks I said, "You know, if these are your power sticks it's important to respect them and not let them be broken or handled by others without your permission." To my

Young people love to make jewelry.

Credit: Sara Dent

surprise, they picked up on that idea and began to hold their sticks with reverence. They put their hearts into decorating those sticks and the results were magnificent. Years later, I ran into one of the boys, and he said, "Jackie, I still have my power stick!"

 ## The Value of Art

Over and over again we hear things like, "I haven't made art in over twenty years, and this feels so good!" It is never too late to bring your artist self back into play. Get some oil pastels and start adding dashes of color to your journal or message pad. Take up knitting, crocheting, pottery or sculpture. You can make artist trading cards for friends and family or hang a big hand-painted flag in front of your home. You don't have to be good; you just have to do it! And just like with those young people in the wake of Hurricane Katrina, life itself might take on a brighter shade.

Stocking Your Art Barn

Here is a basic list of supplies suggested by Jackie. You can keep costs low by gleaning scraps from leather shops, frame shops and fabric stores and by shopping at garage sales and second-hand stores. "Don't be afraid to ask. People are usually eager to donate to youth art projects," said Jackie.

Paper goods

Mat board—recycled from
frame shops
Card stock of various sizes
Large sheets of paper
(18" × 24")
Rolls of paper 24" to 36" wide
Pads of decorative papers
Colored tissue paper
Coffee filters (restaurant size)
to decorate with food
coloring
Decorative wrapping paper
Magazines: particularly ones
with positive ideas and lots
of color
Playing cards for Artist Trading
Cards

Adhesives

Glue sticks
Paper glue or Mod Podge
Glitter glue
Gesso

Paints

Acrylic paints
Oil pastels (Portfolio series by
Crayola is best)
Colored pencils
Multi-colored Sharpies
Paint brushes of various sizes
Containers for water for clean-
ing brushes

**Jewelry and decorative art
supplies**

Colored wire or florist wire
Scraps of leather, cloth, lace
ribbons, buttons
Colored glass
Beach glass
Beads of all kinds
Wire for jewelry making
Jewelry supplies: stretchy
string, wire, jewelry find-
ings, hemp string

Mask-making supplies

Plaster of Paris gauze cloth
Balloons
Vaseline
Heavy muslin

Magic Markers
Feathers, beads, ribbon

Sewing supplies

Embroidery thread of all colors
Needles of various sizes
Knitting needles
Yarn
Lace and edgings

Tools

Dremel tool for drilling holes
Scissors
Hammers, screw drivers, pliers
Wire cutters
Glue guns
Paper cutter
Hole punches
Mat board cutter

Miscellaneous supplies

Blue masking tape
Cello tape
Christmas lights for decorative
use
Rubber stamps and pads
Small decorative mirrors
(4" × 4")

Paint with Words: Creative Writing and Poetry

Our students were set to perform at a school assembly and we were overcome with anxiety. The performance would be the culmination of a month-long writing and photography project on community and identity with 15 students at Anacostia High School in southeast Washington, DC. Knowing the cacophony of shouts and taunts that usually characterized this school's assemblies, we feared we were leading our students like lambs to the slaughter. The hallways at Anacostia High School were raucous, and the police ubiquitous. Several times we had had to stay sequestered in the classroom while they and their dogs conducted drug searches of the locker areas.

As our project progressed, our classroom became an island of calm. The students wrote countless metaphors about their lives and extended them into poems. They read for each other and listened with deep appreciation. Once they had crafted their final pieces, musicians joined the process and, taking direction from the students, they wrote and recorded musical backgrounds for the poetry. The format for the assembly was simple and unadorned. Each student would step to the microphone and deliver her offering, with the music recorded for each piece playing in the background.

Singer Thao Nguyen and facilitator Sara Kendall put music to words at Y-WE Girl's writing camp.

Credit: Deborah Koff-Chapin

The auditorium was packed with restless students waiting for the performance to begin. At first we had to work hard to quiet the audience, but a hush descended as soon as the first performer, a young man, stood in front of the mic and began to share his poem about the death of a close friend. The themes of the poems ranged from grief over the death of a parent to the hurt and misunderstanding based on differences in skin color, class or style of dress. Some poems were ironic, others funny, still others deeply moving. Regardless of the content, the honesty and lack of artifice was totally captivating. The students sat rapt as they heard their own life experiences reflected back to them. The reaction of the group taught us an indelible lesson about the depth young people are capable of achieving—both in their speaking and in their listening.

Creative writing is both a healing salve and a practical tool for personal and group development. According to the work of Dr. James Pennebaker, a social psychologist from the University of Texas, writing has health benefits both physical and emotional. Dr. Pennebaker's typical experiment involved people writing freely for 15 to 20 minutes each day for three days about their most traumatic experiences or about something for which they had strong emotions. The control subjects wrote for the same amount of time about trivial subjects. The participants who wrote about trauma or emotion showed a marked rise in their immune response, a decrease in doctor's visits over time and a significant increase in their sense of well-being. The control subjects, on the other hand, showed no change whatsoever.[22]

In another study Dr. Pennebaker showed that writing can also help people overcome life disruptions. This study included a large group of people from a high-tech firm who unexpectedly lost their jobs. The researchers asked one group to write for 30 minutes a day for five days about their experience of losing their jobs. A control group did no writing. The group of writers ended up finding new jobs significantly faster than those who didn't write.[23]

We have been happily surprised to see how readily young people take pen to paper once they realize that writing is a means for expressing their own thoughts and feelings. After just one creative writing workshop, a 15-year-old girl who had previously had an aversion to writing, became an avid author. She went on to start her own zine—a personal magazine that she published regularly throughout high school and sold in local stores. We've seen person after person take on the practice of writing after a single workshop.

Young women in a homeless shelter began writing with a passion after their journalism teacher learned how to free write in our Creative Facilitation training. "This is all great, but my girls will never be able to do it," she said, when she first learned the technique. A few months later she reported, "I couldn't have been more wrong. One week I was so busy I didn't have time to plan for my journalism class, so I thought I would just try free writing. We started with 30 seconds, and they loved it and wanted more. I built the time up in increments until they were writing for ten minutes without stopping. Now, that's all they want to do in journalism class!" She and the girls found another way to use free writing in the shelter. They placed a journal on a table in the living room and invited the youth to write about their experiences while living there, thus created an ongoing group journal. "Everyone loved it," she said. "I have to say, I am happily surprised."

Adults are equally surprised and delighted when they're introduced to activities that free their voice through writing and poetry. We've learned to leave plenty of time for reading aloud, because once people realize they *can* write, they want to be heard.

There are two power techniques that we rely on over and over again to liberate the writing voice: metaphor writing and free writing (also called stream-of-consciousness timed writing). You can use these two seemingly magical techniques separately or in combination to explore a variety of themes and achieve objectives as diverse as self-awareness, team building and healing—and they are effective across cultures and generations.

 ## Metaphor Writing

Several years ago Charlie led a creative writing program in a facility for teen women in Idaho. He passed out writing journals and asked each person to decorate her journal with an image that said something about her life. One young woman drew a feather peeking out of light, fluffy clouds. When asked what the image meant to her, she said, "I drew the feather because it represents my culture. I'm Native American. And the clouds? I was trying to draw a windstorm. I am a 'feather in a windstorm.'" As she uttered these words, a wave of resonance passed through the group.

Metaphor is a means of communication that connects head and heart. Think about how powerfully "I am a feather in a windstorm" describes that young woman's life compared to, "My life is out of control, and I don't know which way to go." No. She simply said, "I am a feather in a windstorm," and we can feel what she is describing.

Metaphor is foundational to the way we think and make sense of our lives. We speak in metaphor so naturally that it is often invisible to us. Metaphor functions as a bridge between rational logic and emotion, imagination and sensory experience. It bypasses the thinking mind and activates the right brain. When you work with metaphor, you connect people with a deeper part of themselves.

When we introduce the subject of metaphor to adults, they often look at us with eyes wide as if to say, "Oh no. You are *not* going to make us write a metaphor, are you?" In youth programs, the students start wrangling with each other about the difference between simile and metaphor. Unfortunately, this rich artistic tool is too often taught in a dull technical way that doesn't engage people, and it's rarely used as a means of exploring issues and plumbing one's depth.

We introduce metaphor through presenting ones that young people have come up with in other situations. This kick-starts the imagination, and before you know it, the images are flowing. Here are some examples from the Anacostia High School program. Not surprisingly, their images mirror their urban experience: "I am a car in fifth gear, with the parking brake on," said one young woman to describe herself. "I am a traffic

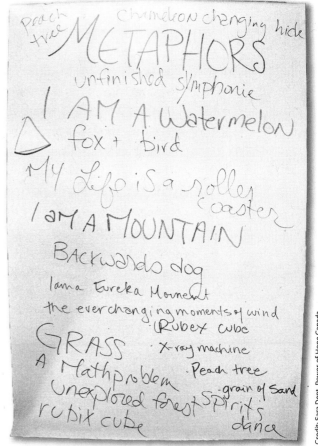

Metaphors waiting to inspire free writing.

light that never turns red," said another. A young man with a particularly sunny disposition—who would enter the classroom each time with a new dance move—described himself this way: "Inside me is a stadium full of thousands of people ready to stand and cheer!" Metaphors don't have to be fancy, and they don't have to express every last thing about you. They just have to ring true. In one workshop a young man who had difficulty connecting with his peers hung his head in defeat and said, "I can't come up with anything. I'm just a single leaf on a tree." And there it was—the perfect metaphor!

Here are some things to say when coaching people to come up with metaphors:

- Keep your metaphor to eight words or less.
- Look to the natural world for ideas.
- Close your eyes and see if an image presents itself.
- Remember, it doesn't have to be fancy; simple is good.
- It doesn't have to represent everything about you; it just has to be true.
- Think about the feeling you are trying to express, and then come up with an image that represents that feeling.

Though people are often stumped at first, they usually succeed in identifying a metaphor, and with that comes a sense of creative accomplishment. When they then share their metaphors with a group, they often do so with a mix of timidity and pride. It is important to recognize the feeling of vulnerability that often accompanies this creative challenge. It helps immensely to appreciate each metaphor by repeating it aloud with enthusiasm. Once participants have generated metaphors, there are many ways to work with them.

Group Dynamics

To get a quick picture of dynamics within a group, you can ask participants to come up with an image that represents their shared situation. For example, you can ask teachers to come up with metaphors that represent themselves as teachers. In an organization, the metaphor might be about each participant's experience as a member of the team. Once the metaphors are generated, write them on a flipchart and look for common themes. Charlie once asked an entire high school class to craft metaphors that represented their school culture. When the students compared the metaphors, they recognized that they all fell into two themes: boredom and the suppression of difference. This helped them understand how not showing their uniqueness or differences directly related to the boredom they experienced. What followed was a passionate conversation about the kind of unspoken community norms the students were buying into. It was a powerful first step in shifting to a more positive and lively school culture.

In a workshop with staff members at a youth drop-in center, the metaphors told a compelling story of how burnout was affecting many members of the team—an issue that had not been on the radar of management. Once it was out in the open, the team engaged in a constructive conversation on ways to address burnout. It is important to note that using creative techniques like metaphor can provoke a deep dive into what is going on beneath the surface, and you need to be prepared to deal with what arises. When a group establishes sufficient trust prior to doing the metaphor exercise, people can often make swift strides in addressing the emerging issues without being sidetracked by defensiveness and division.

Self-introductions

Metaphors can energize what might otherwise be long, drawn-out introductions at a conference. At an adult leadership gathering we facilitated, rather than having participants talk about their work, we asked them to simply share their name, where they came from, their field of work, and then a metaphor that represents him or herself as a leader. The addition of the metaphor kept everyone captivated through all 60 introductions. You may have to give some examples to get the flow going, but the results are guaranteed to energize your group. Here are some possible examples: I am a candle shining in the dark; a rudder on a sailing ship; a sheltering tree; or an ignition spark.

Metaphor Free-Flow

To get metaphors flowing, ask participants to stand in circles of six to eight people. One person in each group starts by saying "I am [a metaphor]." Go rapidly around the circle, with each person saying a new metaphor. Ask people to say whatever comes to mind, whether it makes sense or not. Continue around the circle for a second, third and even fourth round. As the process unfolds, the metaphors become increasingly potent. The speed of the activity and the need to listen to one another helps bypass the judging mind. Every once in a while a particularly juicy metaphor will come forth. You might ask someone to volunteer as a scribe and capture as many of the metaphors as possible for later use as starter phrases for free writes.

Short Group-Poetry Performance

Here's a way to use metaphors to structure a short group poem. People in groups of five or six each come up with a personal metaphor on a shared theme, such as:

- my life right now
- my relationship to my creativity
- my experience as a teacher, student, social entrepreneur, youth worker

They then stand in a line and each person states his metaphor prefaced by "I am."

Timed Free Writing

Free writing is our favorite technique for breaking through writer's block and helping people connect to their voice. It's equally effective for people of all writing abilities, from best-selling authors to those who are barely literate.

Advice from the Front Lines

Writer and facilitator Nadia Chaney leads lots of writing workshops with teens. Here is her advice on how to make writing accessible and exciting:

Writing often causes anxiety—perhaps because it is so associated with schooling. When giving writing workshops I try to be sensitive to things that may trigger this anxiety. For example, I avoid writing instructions on blackboards. I never correct spelling or grammar, and if someone asks, I just say "Do it your way." In the early stages of drafting a piece I suggest orienting the paper in

different ways, connecting writing with music and drama, and working in groups or with partners. More than anything, I encourage participants to follow their own impulses in writing. At the same time, I believe that there is a lot of self-confidence to be gained when a piece of writing "feels done." So I do encourage multiple drafts, lots of sharing and, as the drafting process continues, teaching genre-based tricks of the trade. That felt experience of loving writing can open up a lifetime of self-expression and powerful articulation.

Introducing Timed Free Writing

Many people are so stilted in writing that they freeze once the pen is in hand. When introducing free writing it's important to include a lot of encouragement and permission to make mistakes. To prepare for free writing you can ask participants to come up with a metaphor to use as their starter phrase, or you can provide a phrase of your own. Here are some examples:

- A time I knew I had a friend...
- In a heart-centered world...
- A challenge I have overcome...
- A time I felt powerful and creative...
- If you really knew me...
- What I love about my life right now...

Each person writes a starter phrase at the top of a blank sheet of paper. When we describe this practice we consciously work to get under the radar of the most defended writers:

> We are now going to introduce a technique that is used with great success by all kinds of people—from best-selling authors to people who can barely read. It's called timed free writing. It's called "free" because it's all about letting your thoughts freely move from your mind to the page without letting your inner critic get in the way. It's as if you turn the on spigot and let the thoughts flow from your mind to the page like a stream. It's called "timed" because you'll have a specific amount of time to write. We'll give you a starting time and tell you when to stop. Once I say "Go," you just turn on the faucet and let your thoughts flow. Spelling doesn't matter. Punctuation doesn't matter. Your entire piece might be one long sentence. Or you might have all kinds of short phrases. Whatever comes out is just right. There is no reading over what you've written and no erasing or crossing out. Just let the thoughts flow. If you get to a place where you don't know what to say, write whatever you are thinking at the moment. For example, "I don't know what to say now and it feels like..." By continuing to commit words to the page, new thoughts will emerge naturally. It's almost impossible to do

Hip Hop Hope: Turning a Cultural Phenomenon on Its Head

When young volunteers started leading free-styling workshops at our camps in the late '90s, it took many of us right up to the creative edge. Freestyle is a style of rap spoken over instrumental beats. The words that come tumbling out are completely improvised and often straight from the heart. Dan Edwards, a young African American staff member, had a passion for hip hop as a force for visionary social change. This visionary force in rap culture goes right back to its origins and has become a global cultural phenomenon, and we witness it in every country we visit. It is no surprise that the Arab Spring was fueled by the passion for change expressed by local hip hop poets whose songs became overnight anthems.

To play with this energy, we created a new program called Hip Hop Hope, based on many of the elements of hip hop culture. This program is an example of how adults can support youth empowerment through using the very forms that sweep through youth culture.

Hip Hop Hope is generally held as a residential camp over a long weekend during the school year. It is different from our other camps in that we embrace the specific outcome of producing a CD. While presenting the goal of recording a CD, we talk about the relationship between process and product. We emphasize how the success of the recording will be determined by how effective we are in building a supportive community where people feel free to be themselves, find their true voices and take creative risks.

For many of the young participants this is a first experience of being in a creative, supportive community. They are initially drawn to the program because of their passion for hip hop music, and suddenly they are challenged to step into a deeper level of self-awareness and personal growth. Alfonso is one example. He was sent to Hip Hop Hope by a Seattle community center youth program. When he arrived, he made it clear that the only reason he was there was to rap, and his image of a rapper was based on the mainstream rappers he idolized. Some of the staff gently but clearly challenged him to find his own personal form of expression, to confront the stereotypical ways women were portrayed and to move beyond a knee-jerk reliance on profanity for lyrics. At first it was hard going for Alfonso, but eventually he left behind the "bad boy" rapper identity and began to write about his experiences living as a young black man in a culture that projects stereotypes and fear on him. He received huge affirmation from the group for being real.

The people who volunteer for Hip Hop Hope love the art form, understand its history and see how it can be a force for positive change. They invent ways of shifting negative cultural forms into uplifting forms of expressions. Common in hip hop culture is a freestyle rap competition where rappers see who can improvise the most clever and harsh put-downs of one another. In an evening arts event at Hip Hop Hope, the staff transformed the battle to put the other down into a competition to see who could most cleverly and powerfully lift up the other person. Time and again, the youth were on their feet cheering as contestants demonstrated their prowess at praise and acknowledgment.

The impacts of the Hip Hop Hope experience are far reaching. Youth new to performance come away with a huge sense of pride and self-confidence. Many continue performing in their communities. As a result, thousands of adults get exposed to the visionary voice of young people through a form of expression they had previously discounted. And for so many youth, a popular expression of youth culture has become a doorway to self-worth and personal power. To hear Hip Hop Hope recordings go to www.powerof hope.org/media/music.

Credit: Maya Hasson

Heartbeat Jerusalem: Palestinian and Israeli youth communicate through hip hop.

this activity wrong. You'll know if you are doing it right, by looking down to see if your pen is moving. If it is, you're on track. It's important to know that you won't be reading your whole piece to anyone, so you can write anything you want.

As you are doing your free write, imagine your pen is a paintbrush that is painting the page with words. Be as descriptive as you can be. Take some risks with language, and try out new things. When I say "Go" read your starter phrase and then let your pen take off as you explore the meaning of the metaphor or starter phrase as if you are unpeeling an onion. Follow your thoughts wherever they go.

Time the writing and give participants a 30-second warning to finish their current thought. Once the free write is complete, ask participants to read their writing silently to themselves. Then invite people to read part or all of their pieces aloud.

Sharing with the Group

Once one person breaks the ice by reading his work, others are eager to jump in. To encourage the writing process, it's important to keep the sharing safe and fun. Here are two things to keep in mind:

Use a structured form for feedback: Reading a free write can be a raw, vulnerable experience. And, after all, these are completely unedited pieces. They are not perfect. Ideas on how to improve the writing are generally not helpful at this point. Rather, invite participants to feed back to the writer the words, phrases or ideas that really landed with them. Over and over again we see young people's faces light up as they receive this type of feedback from their peers and mentors. A timid smile, accompanied by a sigh of relief says, "Yes, I can do this."

Take advantage of caveats: Most people will preface their reading with caveats like, "I know this is no good" or "I wrote this very fast, so it's probably not good." We just let them state their caveats. When participants hear a convincing argument about how terrible the writing they are about to hear is going to be and then they are gifted with a moving eloquent piece, they gain perspective on the validity of their own judgmental voice.

 ## Easy-to-Lead Writing Activities

Here are several activities to use in all kinds of venues with youth and/or adults.

Writing Your Life Workshop

Metaphor combined with free writing followed by sharing makes for a powerful 75-minute workshop for young people or youth and adults together. (If you have adults in the group, be sure they are aware of the boundaries around what personal stories they can share with youth.) Begin by introducing metaphor. Then ask each person to come up with a metaphor to represent his life, write it at the top of a blank sheet of paper and then do a timed writing. We usually let the time go until everyone has one to two pages of writing. Encourage sharing with the group, but never coerce. After each reading we use the structured method of feedback mentioned above. This simple design more often than not opens the door for profound sharing. At one workshop, a young woman read a piece about the death of her beloved grandfather. We later learned that she had previously avoided mentioning her grandfather's death. Now she was talking freely about it, and her grieving process had begun.

Synchronicities often occur. In one workshop, for example, all of the participants wrote about substance abuse in their families. In another, everyone's piece was about the death of a loved one. As piece after piece was read, tears flowed. A quiet and comforting conversation followed as the youth and adults acknowledged the hurt and challenge these situations bring. Each Writing Your Life workshop is an adventure all its own.

Group Poetry

You can use this fun and flexible activity to explore a theme while developing creativity and teamwork. We use this in classrooms, workshops and even as an evening arts activity for a large group. Begin by asking each person to generate a metaphor on a theme identified by you or the group.

It could be a metaphor that represents one's life as a 15-year-old, life as a youth worker or teacher or social change agent, or one's relationship to one's own creativity. Choose whatever theme fits the group and the situation.

- Once everyone has come up with a metaphor, ask for volunteers to write them on chart paper as each person reads hers aloud. If some people don't have metaphors, you can catch them the second time around the circle.
- Next, break into groups of four to six people. Each small group then chooses one metaphor for everyone in their group to use as a starter phrase for free writing. Each person then writes that metaphor at the top of a blank piece of paper. Reassure participants that whatever metaphor they pick will work fine, so they don't have to get bogged down in the search for just the "right" one.
- Everyone does a free write for about five minutes, using the metaphor as a prompt. Describe the free writing as a process of peeling an onion, getting to deeper levels of meaning evoked by the metaphor.
- When the writing is complete, ask participants to read through their writing and underline two or three phrases of eight words or less that they like for some reason. It might be the sound of the words or the meaning or something else.
- Pass out strips of paper, and ask participants to write each underlined phrase on a separate strip.
- Then each group puts all their group's phrases together to form a poem. A little reassurance is often needed about now. "Don't worry, we've done this hundreds of times and it always works out," we often say.
- Once the poem is formed, let the small groups know that their final task is to come up with a way to perform their poem for the larger group. They are to use at least three art forms in their performance. This can include reading, improvisational dance or movement, percussion, vocal sound, visual arts and more. Colorful scarves and percussion instruments come in very handy for the performances.
- Set up a performance space and be prepared to be surprised and delighted!

Youth and adults love this activity. They are nearly always proud of the poems they come up with, and they have fun with the performance. To prepare people for performing, we remind them that this is a quick and dirty performance, no big deal. At the same time, we ask them to act as if they have been rehearsing for six months, and this is their big debut.

Pass-Around Poem

Here is another creative writing activity that liberates the poetic voice. Organize participants into circles of six or eight. People need pencils and paper and a firm surface, such as a book, to hold in their laps to write on.

- Ask each person to come up with a metaphor that represents her life and write it at the top of a blank sheet of paper. Alternatively, you can choose a theme for the metaphors based on the situation.
- These metaphors represent the first lines of poems. Then ask each participant to add a second line to her poem.
- Each person then passes her paper to the left and receives a paper from the right, reads the first two lines, adds a third line and then passes the paper to the left.
- The poems continue all the way around the circle, with a line added by each participant. Ask people to imagine that with each line they write, they are giving a gift to the person who began that particular poem— even though they don't know who the author is.
- Once the poems gets back to the original authors, they are to read the entire poem, add a final line and give the poem a title, which they write at the top of their page.
- Now take the time for everyone to read their poems aloud in the small groups.

People are inevitably enthusiastic about their collaborative creations. As with the group poem above, you can also perform these poems. Each small group chooses one poem to perform to the larger group.

Both the group-poetry process and the pass-around poems are great activities to use to honor someone at a birthday or some other significant event.

Word Collage and Found Stories

Here are two ways to get the story voice flowing through a solo activity.

Invite participants to choose a theme that is personally meaningful. Using words and phrases cut from old magazines and books, they form poems on the theme. They glue the words and phrases to paper and decorate with collaged pictures or colored pencils.

Another activity is to make copies of four pages or so of an old novel. Pass them out to everyone in the group. Each participant then circles words to sequentially form a whole new story, crossing out all the other words and decorating the pages if they choose. When participants read their stories to one another, you will all be surprised by the variety of stories that come from the same set of words.

 ## The Gift of Writing

Find creative ways to use metaphor and free writing throughout your program. Before starting in on a group conversation, for example, give everyone a few minutes to do some free writing on the theme. After a particularly powerful group experience, carve out some time for integration through free writing. One of the greatest gifts you can give to youth or adults is access to their writing voice.

12

Raise the Curtain: Theater Improvisation

During our first visit to Uganda, we led a short arts workshop for health care workers at Mulago Hospital's Pediatric Infectious Disease Clinic in Kampala. We met with our eight participants in a tiny office alcove off of a narrow hallway adjoining the clinic. No chairs, just room to stand in a circle. It was mid-afternoon and faces drooped with weariness.

We began with an imaginative name game, and before we'd even got once around the circle, eyes began to light up. The energy rose. We then played a series of theater games they could use with their HIV/AIDS teen group to encourage more active participation in their workshops. When we got to a game called Pass the Ball, things really took off. We began by passing an imaginary ball around the circle and then called out qualities to change the characteristics of the ball, making it bigger and bigger then light as a feather, heavy as a rock, sticky and smelly. As the ball continued to move around the group, the energy shifted from engaged to raucous. Finally the ball turned into an imaginary piece of fine chocolate and was relished by all with laughing and smacking lips. The racket attracted the attention of the young patients from the clinic, who climbed on the outside windowsills, attempting to get a clear view of the action. Clinic personnel came in at least three times to ask us to keep it down. As the hour drew to a close, the benefits were self-evident. "I came here so tired

I didn't think I could do another thing," said one nurse. "Now I feel like I've been on a vacation."

Viola Spolin, a key figure in the development of American theater, well knew the fun and regenerative value that comes from playing theater games. As a young social worker with a love of acting, she began working at Hull House in Chicago in the late 1920s. The settlement house provided housing, food and classes in life skills, culture and recreation for impoverished families and new immigrants. Spolin developed a series of theater-based games that fostered social skills and community connection and, above all, brought joy into the lives of these mothers and children living in bleak circumstances. Spolin is now considered the grandmother of the theater improvisation movement in North America. She later turned to using theater games in professional acting training, but her games and those developed by other improvisers remain powerful tools for non-professionals—people who want to become more conscious, confident actors in their own lives.

Theater improvisation is increasingly finding its way into leadership and team development. "Applied improvisation is being taught in blue-chip companies and in more than half of the top business schools around the world," says the website of the Applied Improvisation Network (AIN). AIN has over 2,400 members and is growing rapidly, with actors, business people and academics who use improvisation tools to improve relationships and increase creativity, innovation, authenticity and spontaneity.[24]

Theater for Everyone

The world of theater improvisation offers a treasure trove of games and activities you can use to increase the imagination, build confidence and self-esteem, develop presentation skills and increase comfort with public speaking. You can use them to build community and connection in groups, to show people how to bring play into their lives and work, and to teach people to think on their feet. Theater improvisation is also great for developing leadership and collaborative skills and for delving into personal story.

Even if you don't have any theater experience, you can learn to use improvisation games with groups of any age. To be quite honest, early on we let our lack of acting experience get in the way of leading theater activities. We now use them as a central part of our work. So we're here to tell you that you too can do this. As Viola Spolin said, "Everyone can act. Everyone can improvise. Anyone who wishes can learn to play in the theater."[25]

With that in mind, we have organized this chapter into two sections. First are games that ignite the imagination. These are good to use as a warm-up for any creative endeavor, including the second set of activities: games for storytelling and public speaking. In the next chapter you'll learn about methods for using theater to explore social issues, another application of theater games.

Tips for Leading Theater Games

Facilitating theater games is a lot of fun, and it does require some skill. Here are some things to keep in mind when you are leading any kind of theater activities.

Make it safe: Anyone can enjoy playing theater games as long as you raise the risk incrementally. Start with easy, low-risk games that engage the imagination. If your participants are resistant, you are probably raising the risk level too quickly.

Share agreements: Since playing theater games requires a good deal of risk-taking, begin by asking for some special agreements such as "Let your inner critic out to play for the next hour" and "Be willing to try something new." Remind participants that you are not asking them to do anything well; you are just asking them to jump in and participate.

Engage the body: Non-verbal activities that engage the body provide an easy entry point for theater games. As people move, they relax and their mental blocks fall away. A good way to do this is by using games in which one person leads for a moment and everyone copies. This gives the leader the satisfaction of being followed and gives the group a way to participate without having to think too much.

Share your own delight: Theater games are a lot of fun, and they can become riotously funny. Show your own enthusiasm for the quirky ideas that come out. It's easy to do, because a lot of quirky ideas actually *do* come out. By honestly appreciating imperfect offerings you demonstrate that you are not looking for perfection.

Give clear instructions and demonstrate: Keep your instructions clear, crisp and short. Assume that your group will understand. (They will let you know if they don't!) Whenever possible, model the activity with a fellow facilitator or a participant.

Look for the multiple benefits of activities: Even the simplest game reinforces multiple skills and capacities. For example, let's look at a name game in which each participant says his name, takes a shape and has it repeated by the group. Yes, people learn each other's names, but they also gain so much more. They get to take a creative risk, put their voice into the room and expand their repertoire of movement and sound through mimicking others. They also sharpen their listening and empathic skills. As you become aware of the multiple purposes of each activity, you will be able to choose the right one to use in any given moment. The larger your repertoire of games, the more options you'll have.

Prepare a sequence of activities ahead of time: Before leading a theater-based session, make a clear plan that achieves your goals. Make sure your activities move slowly from low to higher risk. Build in time to reflect on what participants are learning about their own creativity and ability to be spontaneous. Think ahead about ways you might simplify your plan if you run up against time constraints.

The Magic of Improvisation

Don't be surprised if some of your participants cringe when you tell them you are about to play theater games. Lots of people are afraid of them, and it's no wonder since many of us have been introduced to improvisation through watching professional actors. You can ease people's fear by providing some background about improvisation and assuring them you won't be forcing them to do things that are too scary.

Begin by letting people know that improvisation is simply the act of making things up. It's what young children do naturally when they play, and with a bit of coaching we can all do it. There are also some rules and structures to help you along the way. As with any art form, getting into it requires taking baby steps—one little creative risk at a time.

The term "improvisation rules" may sound like an oxymoron. Doesn't improvisation mean freeform? Actually it doesn't, and as with any other art form, structure helps make things happen. Here are three basic rules that make the games work better. As you read them, you might notice that they are also useful maxims for living.

Rule #1: Say Yes

This quite possibly is the most important rule of improvisation. It means that when another player makes an imaginary offering to you, you always say yes and then add to your partner's idea. So, for example, a player comes up to you holding something in his hands and says, "Hi, Mom, look at the beautiful kitten I brought home for you." It is your job to accept the offering without question. You have to act as if you are your partner's mom and that he has indeed given you a kitten. "Oh, Billy, thank you so much. You know I've wanted a kitten for so long. Can I hold it?" You accept the imaginary kitten and the scene continues. Now let's imagine you say no to your partner. Here's the scenario:

A: Hi, Mom, look at the beautiful kitten I brought home for you.
B: What kitten? What are you talking about? There's nothing in your hands. You're crazy.

Effectively, the scene stops right here. This is called *blocking*. The game is over. Or you might say no to your partner disguised as a yes: "Oh, thank you, Billy. But that's not actually a cat; it's a piece of chocolate." This is still a faux pas because even if your partner can find a way to continue the scene, his idea has been rejected and the energy is broken. So getting back to improvisation, here is how it flows:

- Partner A makes as rich an offer as possible to partner B, and through his actions and words implies how old she is, or what her relationship is to him, along with some story to play with.
- B fully accepts the offer, adds some new information and passes it back to A.
- They go back and forth, playing in the field of imagination.

It's fun and it's that simple. No one has to *try* to be funny. People are just naturally funny when they make things up on the spot.

Rule #2: First Idea, Best Idea

Our inner critics move so fast that they quash great ideas before we have time to consider them. While doing improvisation, the real genius emerges when you act first and think later. This is a way of outwitting the critic and discovering how brilliant you actually are. The problem here is that you might say something embarrassing. When adults do improvisation together, that's okay. In fact, the goal of improvisation is to get "beyond the mind" to that place of flow by quieting the critic as much as possible. In cross-generational settings, however, you need to keep a little piece of your critic in place to set some boundaries around appropriateness.

When we're working with youth, we often just say, "Okay, let's have an agreement of keeping it clean." They immediately know what that means. We might also say, "We are so surrounded by sex and violence in our media, that we often fall into those realms when we do theater games. Let's really challenge ourselves to think out of the box and not make such easy choices." Youth like this challenge. Depending on your group, you may have to restate this challenge now and again.

Rule #3: Make Your Partners Look Good.

Some people may think that theater improvisation is a competition, with the goal to be the funniest or most clever. You can argue that this attitude is a form of "blocking." The game actually works best—and is lot more fun—when the players try to set each other up for success. The best way to do this is to make offers that encourage action. Let's demonstrate this with our earlier example:

> A: Hi, Mom, look at the beautiful kitten I brought home for you.
> B: Oh, Billy, thank you so much. You know I've wanted a kitten for so long. Can I hold it?
> A: Sure Mom, but be careful. This kitten is slippery.
> B: [*Mom takes the kitten and immediately struggles to keep it from slipping out of her clutches.*] Oh, you're right, it's like trying to pet Jell-o. Here, you take it. [*She tosses the kitten to A.*]
> A: [*Physically struggling with the kitten.*] Quick, get a towel! We'll try wiping it off.
> B: [*Offers a towel.*] Be careful, that towel has magical powers.
> A: Thanks. [*He wipes the kitten and it suddenly becomes gigantic.*] Um, Mom—we're going to need a bigger litter box.

You can see how one action builds on another, and the two players are each affirming the other's choice, creating an imaginative and active scene that is highly engaging to watch.

While this is a great rule for adults to remember, it's crucial for teens, who too often fall into put-down mode.

Games That Ignite the Imagination

These activities ignite the imagination, induce relaxation, get people laughing and provide chances to take creative risks. You can use them individually or in a sequence. Just as athletes warm up before playing a sport, these games will warm up your creativity before starting a challenging project or sitting down for an important meeting.

This Is Not A...

This starter game is low risk and lots of fun.

Materials: A variety of simple objects, one for each group. For example, stick, water bottle, magic marker.

THIS IS NOT A...

IMAGINATION | RELAXATION
LAUGHTER & PLAY | CREATIVE RISK

5 MINUTES FOR GROUPS OF ABOUT 10 PEOPLE.

MATERIALS : AN EVERYDAY OBJECT FOR EACH GROUP SUCH AS A STICK, A WATER BOTTLE, OR A MAGIC MARKER

ASK PARTICIPANTS TO FORM CIRCLES OF 8-12 WITH ONE LEADER IN EACH GROUP.

THE LEADER HOLDS THE STICK & SAYS:

THIS IS NOT A STICK, IT IS A COMB*.

BUT IT IS A STICK...

? WHAT THE...

*IT DOESN'T HAVE TO BE A COMB; COULD BE ANYTHING!

THEN HE DEMONSTRATES USING THE STICK AS A COMB, MAKING APPROPRIATE MOTIONS & SOUND EFFECTS.

SCRUNCH.. SCRATCH.. SCRUTCH..

THE LEADER THEN PASSES THE STICK TO THE PERSON ON HIS LEFT.

PERSON #2 REPEATS THE LEADER'S DEMONSTRATION OF THE COMB, COPYING HIS MOVEMENT & SOUND AS ACCURATELY AS POSSIBLE. WHILE SAYING:

THIS IS NOT A COMB...

SHE THEN GIVES THE STICK ANOTHER IDENTITY, SAYING:

THIS IS A PAIR OF SCISSORS.

snip snip!

SHE DEMONSTRATES THE PAIR OF SCISSORS WITH MOVEMENT & SOUND AND THEN PASSES THE STICK TO THE LEFT.

PERSON #3 REPEATS #2's DEMONSTRATION OF THE PAIR OF SCISSORS, COPYING THE SOUNDS & MOVEMENT AS ACCURATELY AS POSSIBLE WHILE SAYING:

THIS IS NOT A PAIR OF SCISSORS.

HE THEN GIVES THE STICK A NEW IDENTITY & DEMONSTRATES THE NEW OBJECT IN MOVEMENT & SOUND.

AND SO IT GOES, AROUND THE CIRCLE.

Credit: Sam Bartlett

- Ask participants to form circles of eight to twelve, with one leader in each group. This is a go-around game, so each person will have a chance to play in sequence.
- The leader (A) holds the stick (or other object) and says, "This is not a stick, it is a [fill in the blank with another made-up object—a microphone, for example]. He then demonstrates using the stick as a microphone, making appropriate motions and sound effects.
- The leader then passes the stick to the person on his left (B).
- B repeats the leader's demonstration of the microphone, copying his movement and sound as accurately as possible while saying, "This is *not* a microphone." She then gives the stick yet another identity, saying "This is a [fill in the blank—say, a pair of scissors]. She demonstrates the pair of scissors with movement and sound and then passes the stick on to the person on her left. ·
- And you continue around the circle.

Tips: Encourage players to use exaggerated movements and sounds to demonstrate their objects. Getting the body and voice into the action helps people let go of self-consciousness. Ask participants to copy the person before them as accurately as possible. If a participant tells you all their ideas have been taken, remind them that the stick can be anything and does not have to be limited by its actual size and shape. There is only one criteria: You can't repeat anything that has already been done.

What Are You Doing?

This second low-risk game ignites the imagination, generates laughter and has the side benefit of helping people learn names.

Ask participants to form circles of eight to twelve and choose a leader in each group. Everyone needs to know the name of the person to the right.

- The leader (A) mimes an obvious movement, such as sweeping the floor.
- The person to her left (B) asks, "[A's name], what are you doing?" A answers in a way that is at odds with her movement. For instance, if she is miming sweeping the floor, she might say, "I'm washing the dishes."

- B then begins to mime washing the dishes and the person next to him (C) asks, "[B's name], what are you doing?" Even though he is miming washing the dishes B now says he is doing something completely different such as, "I am flying a kite."
- C then mimes flying a kite, and so on around the circle.

Tips: Remind players to use people's names when playing this game. Challenge them to use imagination to suggest all sorts of actions, such as sailing a ship, climbing a tree or even flying a spaceship. The more imaginative you can get, the more fun you'll have. And once again, keep the rule that you can't repeat anything that has already been done.

Pass the Ball

Here's another low-risk game. Along with activating the imagination, this game demonstrates the mind-body connection by showing how our thoughts affect our physical experience. Ask participants to stand in a circle. You can play this in circles of eight to ten or larger.

- The leader stands outside the circles and calls out the directions.
- The leader hands an imaginary ball to one person in each circle and says, "Please pass this imaginary ball around the circle. It's about the size of a tennis ball. Really see its size and shape as you pass it around."
- After the ball has gone around the circle once, the leader calls out changes in the quality of the ball by saying, "The ball is slowly getting lighter. Now it's getting lighter and bigger. Now it's very large and light like beach ball. Keep passing it around."
- The leader continues to change the quality of the ball: "Now it's slowly getting heavier…and heavier…and heavier. It's very heavy. Help each other pass this rock-heavy ball."
- "And now it's the size of a soccer ball. Keep passing it around. It's getting sticky. It's very sticky—and it *stinks*! Keep passing it. Now it is very hot. Now it is a precious tiny thing."
- After calling out several changes, give the groups the power to transform the ball themselves. Anyone in the group can now call out a new quality when the ball comes to her. Remind them to let the ball go

around for a bit with its new quality before someone transforms it yet into another thing.

- The leader eventually brings the game to a close.

Tips: This activity can lead into a discussion of how our imaginations affect our bodies. Encourage participants through side coaching to really see the ball as it comes to them. Receiving the ball as the giver sees it builds an early experience of "saying yes" as we described earlier in this chapter.

Magic Clay

Now we're beginning to raise the risk. It's good to do at least one warm-up before playing this game. Magic clay is a miming game that increases spatial awareness, imagination, attention and focus. Be sure to demonstrate this activity by making a fairly simple object. Encourage people to take their time with this activity.

Ask participants to form circles of four to six people.

- The leader begins by giving a piece of imaginary clay to one person (A) in each circle.
- Using mime, A slowly molds the clay into a usable object, let's say a hat. She then demonstrates using the hat by putting it on her head and showing it off.
- She then passes the imaginary hat to person B standing next to her. He first plays with the imaginary hat, and then compresses the "clay" into a ball and makes a new object. He demonstrates the new object and passes it to C, and the players continue around the circle.

Tips: Remind people to *go slowly*, and ask them to refrain from guessing what the object is until the sculptor has demonstrated using it. You might challenge the group to do this exercise in total silence, using their powers of observation.

Non-Verbal Freeze Tag

This game enhances the imagination while demonstrating the power of non-verbal communication. It also serves as a warm-up for doing

MAGIC CLAY

 SPATIAL AWARENESS · ATTENTION · IMAGINATION · FOCUS

 TAKES TEN MINUTES

FORM CIRCLES OF 4-6 PEOPLE

THE LEADER BEGINS BY GIVING A PIECE OF IMAGINARY CLAY TO ONE PERSON IN EACH CIRCLE.

PERSON #1 USES MIME TO SLOWLY MOLD THE CLAY INTO A USABLE OBJECT SUCH AS A HAT.

SHE THEN DEMONSTRATES USING THE OBJECT. IF IT'S A HAT, SHE PUTS IT ON HER HEAD & SHOWS IT OFF.

THEN: SHE PASSES THE IMAGINARY OBJECT TO A PERSON NEXT TO HER & HE BEGINS TO PLAY WITH IT.

AFTER HE HAS DEMONSTRATED USING THE OBJECT THAT WAS PASSED TO HIM, HE COMPRESSES THE IMAGINARY CLAY INTO A BALL & MIMES MAKING A NEW OBJECT.

HE THEN DEMONSTRATES THE NEW OBJECT BEFORE HANDING IT OFF TO THE NEXT PERSON IN THE CIRCLE.

THIS PERSON TAKES THE OBJECT, DEMONSTRATES USING IT, AND THEN TURNS THE CLAY INTO YET ANOTHER OBJECT. CONTINUE AROUND THE CIRCLE.

TIPS: DEMONSTRATE MAKING A FAIRLY SIMPLE OBJECT. ENCOURAGE PEOPLE TO GO SLOWLY WHEN THEY ARE FORMING THEIR OBJECT.

ASK PARTICIPANTS TO REFRAIN FROM GUESSING WHAT THE OBJECT IS UNTIL THE PERSON HAS DEMONSTRATED USING IT.

Credit: Sam Bartlett

improvisation scenes with dialogue. A theater artist once led this activity for 125 youth within the first hour of an environmental conference we facilitated, and the youth were riveted. Ask your group to form a circle or sit in an audience facing a playing area.

- Participant A steps into the playing area and strikes a pose with her body and freezes.
- Participant B steps into the playing area and takes a pose in relationship to A to imply a story.
- Participant C comes in and taps either A or B, who leaves the playing area. The untapped person remains frozen in his shape. C then strikes a new pose in relationship to that person to imply a completely new story.
- Participants continue to come into the playing area, tap out one player, and take a shape in relationship to the remaining player to imply a new story.

Tips: Encourage participants to hold their shapes with an unmovable freeze. Ask participants to take the time to fully appreciate each new shape before jumping in and tapping someone out.

Improvisation Carousel

This activity gets even the shyest participants into playing improvisation scenes, because everyone plays in pairs, with no one else watching. This sometimes breaks the ice so successfully that shy actors are able to play scenes in front of an audience in the next game, Verbal Freeze Tag. After playing this game in a workshop, one participant tearfully reported, "I've sat on the sidelines for years watching people play improv and never dared to participate. Now I know what I've missed." We've played this game with as many as 90 people in a large room.

Begin by arranging your group in two circles facing one another so that the inside circle faces out and the outside circle faces in. Each person needs a partner.

- Tell the outside circle (B) that they will be the first ones to initiate scenes. When you say "Go" everyone in the A circle faces a partner and strikes a frozen pose. Each partner in the outside circle (B) then moves in and begins a two-way scene that includes dialogue and movement. B gives A some material to work with by letting her know things like who she is, how old she is and what she's doing. B might say, for example, "Mom, I'm sorry I stayed out so late without telling you." Or "Hey, Alisha, you want to jump rope with me?" A responds by joining in the scene with dialogue and movement, and they play the scene until you yell "Freeze."

- Everyone freezes in place. You then say, "Inside circle remain in your frozen position. Outside circle move one person to the right and begin a scene with your new partner."
- Do three or four scenes this way and then switch to give the A circle a chance to initiate the scenes. This time the people in the outside circle will hold their frozen postures and people on the inside circle move one person to the right and begin a fresh scene. Continue moving the inside circle one person to the right for three or four scenes, then bring the game to a close.

Finding an Improvisation Class

Want to increase your skills as a facilitator or trainer, or just bring more fun and flow into your life? Take a theater improvisation class. You can find them at local theater schools, community schools and colleges. A good teacher can help you become more comfortable in front of groups and able to think on your feet.

But choose your class carefully. Look for an introductory class that focuses on self-development and leadership rather than on learning the craft of improvisation. People don't often advertise improvisation classes in this way, so look for words like "introductory," "low-risk," "fun" or "educational." Improvisation classes that are designed for actors will likely be too technical, and the risk level may be so high that it shuts down your creative flow.

Your theater improvisation class should begin with a well-facilitated warm-up that helps you shed your self-consciousness. It's the job of the teacher to provide this kind of facilitation and to know how to help you quiet your critical mind. Not that you shouldn't sometimes feel nervous in an improvisation class, but overall it should be a positive, nurturing experience. If you find yourself feeling put down or shut down, look for another class. Trust your instincts on this.

Tips: This game gets very loud, so it helps to have a noisemaker, such as a percussion instrument, to signal the freezes. If it gets too raucous, ask players to speak in a stage whisper. Even though the scenes start with one partner in a frozen pose, make sure players know that they are engaging in active scenes that include movement and dialogue on the part of both partners. Also encourage the players to vary their scenes to include a range of emotions.

Verbal Freeze Tag

A combination of the two previous activities, this game is fairly high risk but lots of fun. Once participants let go of judgment, they get right into it. Ask your group to form an audience with a designated playing area.

- Participant A steps into the playing area, strikes a pose and freezes.
- Participant B steps onto the playing area, strikes a pose in relationship to A, and then launches into an interactive scene that includes movement and dialogue. Once again, B needs to give A some information about who she is, how old she is and what they are doing.
- A responds to the scene using both dialogue and movement. The pair continues the scene until an audience member (C) yells, "Freeze." The players then freeze and wait for C to come in and tap one of them out.
- C takes the exact pose of the player he has tapped out and goes on to start a completely new scene with the remaining player. His partner responds and they improvise a scene together until another audience member yells, "Freeze." And on it goes.

Tips: Ask participants to let the scenes go on long enough to gain some momentum. Remind players to take the exact pose of the person they tap out. Encourage them to enter the scene even if they don't have an idea of what they want to do. They can simply get into the position of the person they tap out and see what comes to mind. The think-on-your-feet nature of this game makes it pretty common for participants to "block" one another. Be sure to remind players from the sidelines to say yes to the suggestions being offered.

Make an Object

Here is a great game for building teamwork. Participants work together in small groups to come up with a way to demonstrate a common object. They then "perform" their object for the rest of the group by using their bodies and voices to become the object.

Ask participants to form groups of five to seven.

- Give each group the name of a common object such as fruit smoothie maker, elevator, helicopter, grand piano, roller coaster, refrigerator or television.
- Each group has ten minutes to come up with a skit that demonstrates the object. They are allowed to make sound effects, but they can't use words. Some of the group can be the object while others use it. Everyone in the small group has to take part in the skit.
- The groups then perform their skits one at a time. After a group has completely finished a skit, the audience guesses the object.

Tips: Encourage participants to use sound effects. Remind the audience to refrain from guessing until the group on stage has finished the skit. Once the performances have begun, encourage players to add improvisation to their skits.

 ## Games for Storytelling and Public Speaking

Public speaking is said to be the number one fear among North Americans. What a sad state of affairs, given that we live in participatory democracies. Young people often step out of their shells quite naturally through playing theater games. The following games help people of all ages gain comfort in telling stories and in speaking out in front of a group of any size.

Yes, and...

This easy-to-play storytelling game ignites the imagination and demonstrates the first rule of improvisation: say yes. Playing this game early in a program, meeting or conference raises the creativity quotient by setting up a "Yes, and..." culture in the group. Ask participants to form circles of three or four people and decide who will go first (A).

Credit: Sam Bartlett

- A begins by making up a story. It can be any story, past, present or future. After setting the stage through three or four sentences, A stops at the end of a sentence.
- B picks up the story with the words "Yes, and…." B then continues to tell the story in the same voice as A. This means, if the story was started in the first person, the story continues in first person. B adds three or four sentences and stops at the end of a sentence.
- C then picks up the story with, "Yes, and…," adds to the story and stops at the end of a sentence. The story continues around and around the circle with each person picking up with the words, "Yes, and…."
- Let the storytelling go for seven to ten minutes and then call "Stop."

Tips: Make sure participants know they are to come to the end of a sentence before passing it to the next person. Encourage participants to stand while playing this game, because people tend to add more gestures and energy to their stories while standing.

Conducted Story

This activity makes speaking in front of a group quite easy. Begin with five or six people standing in a line facing the audience. These are the storytellers. A "conductor" sits on the floor facing the line of storytellers.

- To start the game, the conductor points to one of the players (A). A begins telling a story, any story.
- When the conductor points to a new player (B), A falls silent and B picks up the story mid-sentence, even mid-word.
- The conductor continues to move the story from one teller to another by pointing.
- The conductor gradually picks up the pace of moving from one teller to another looking for interesting places to make the shift.

Tips: Clarify that each new storyteller has to pick up the story exactly where the other teller left off without using words like, "As I was saying." The idea is to be of one voice, transitioning as fluidly as possible from one person to the next.

Sensitivity Line

These next two games provide a fail-safe way to get even the shyest participants to speak in front of a group. The first game is done in silence and is a warm-up for the second. Begin by asking the group to form an audience.

- Invite five or six volunteers to stand in a line facing away from the audience. They should be standing close to each other but not touching.
- When the facilitator says "Go," one person in the line (A), in silence, turns to face the audience.
- A must remain facing the audience until another person (B) randomly turns to face the audience. A then must turn back so that *only one person is facing the audience at any time*. B cannot turn back until another player turns to face the audience to take his place.
- The players continue to randomly turn to face the audience, signaling for the person facing the audience to turn back. When the participants get into a flow, they look like a set of revolving doors.

Tips: To get volunteers, we usually tell them that this game is the easiest part of an upcoming sequence. Ask the players to try to sense when another person has turned rather than crane their necks to look. As they get going, encourage them to pick up the pace of turning. You might be surprised by how funny this gets.

Sensitivity Line with Stories

This is where the fun really comes in. Begin with a line of five players standing side by side and facing away from the audience, as in the previous game. In this activity, rather than standing in silence, each player tells a story whenever she is facing the audience.

- When the first person (A) faces the audience, she starts telling a story. It can be a true story from her life, a fantasy or a folk tale. It can be funny, sad or outrageous. The theme is up to her.
- When the second person (B) turns to face the audience, he interrupts A as if she is not even talking and launches into his own story.
- A immediately stops her story mid-sentence—even mid-word—and turns her back to the audience.

SENSITIVITY LINE

PERSONAL PRESENCE | FOCUS | 10 MINUTES | FAIL-SAFE WAY TO GET EVEN THE SHYEST PARTICIPANTS TO SPEAK IN FRONT OF A GROUP. ULP...

BEGIN BY ASKING THE GROUP TO FORM AN AUDIENCE.

THEN: INVITE 5-6 VOLUNTEERS TO STAND IN A LINE WITH THEIR BACKS TO THE AUDIENCE. THEY SHOULD BE STANDING ABOUT 8 INCHES APART — CLOSE BUT NOT TOUCHING.

WHEN THE FACILITATOR SAYS, "GO," ONE PERSON IN THE LINE (A), IN SILENCE, IS TO TURN TO FACE THE AUDIENCE.

(A) MUST REMAIN FACING THE AUDIENCE UNTIL ANOTHER PERSON IN THE LINE RANDOMLY TURNS TO FACE THE AUDIENCE.

(A) THEN MUST TURN BACK SO THAT THERE IS ONLY ONE PERSON FACING THE AUDIENCE.

THE PLAYERS IN THE LINE CONTINUE TO RANDOMLY TURN TO FACE THE AUDIENCE.

ULP...

THE RULE IS: ONLY ONE PERSON CAN BE FACING THE AUDIENCE AT ANY ONE TIME, AND EXCEPT AT THE VERY BEGINNING, THERE MUST ALWAYS BE ONE PERSON FACING THE AUDIENCE.

WHEN THE GROUP GETS INTO A FLOW, IT LOOKS LIKE DOORS REVOLVING SEAMLESSLY TOWARD & AWAY FROM THE AUDIENCE.

TIPS: ASK THE PLAYERS TO TRY TO SENSE WHEN ANOTHER PERSON HAS TURNED RATHER THAN CRANE THEIR NECKS TO LOOK.

AS THEY GET GOING ENCOURAGE THEM TO PICK UP THE SPEED OF TURNING.

TO GET YOUR FIRST VOLUNTEERS, YOU CAN TELL THEM: THIS IS THE EASIEST PART OF THE ACTIVITY!

ONCE ONE OR TWO GROUPS OF VOLUNTEERS HAVE GOTTEN INTO A FLOW WITH THE SENSITIVITY LINE, IT WILL BE TIME TO MOVE ONTO THE SENSITIVITY LINE WITH STORIES.

SENSITIVITY LINE WITH STORIES

| STORYTELLING | PERSONAL PRESENCE | 15 MINUTES OR MORE DEPENDING ON THE SIZE OF THE GROUP | THIS IS WHERE THE FUN REALLY BEGINS. IN THIS PART OF THE ACTIVITY, EACH PERSON IN THE LINE TELLS A STORY WHILE FACING THE AUDIENCE |
| LISTENING | FOCUS | | |

WHEN THE FIRST PERSON (A) FACES THE AUDIENCE, SHE IS TO START TELLING A STORY. IT CAN BE A TRUE STORY FROM HER LIFE, A FANTASY, A FOLK TALE. IT CAN BE FUNNY, SAD, OR OUTRAGEOUS. WHATEVER SHE WANTS.

I WAS HANGING BY MY FINGERNAILS TO THE TOP OF...

WHEN THE SECOND PERSON (B) TURNS TO FACE THE AUDIENCE, HE INTERRUPTS (A) AS IF SHE'S NOT EVEN TALKING AND LAUNCHES INTO HIS OWN STORY. *AND I HAD ALWAYS HAD 17 THUMBS ON EACH FOOT...*

PERSON (A) IMMEDIATELY STOPS HER STORY MID-SENTENCE AND TURNS BACK FROM THE AUDIENCE.

EACH THUMB WAS A DIFFERENT COLOR AND AS I SOON FOUND OUT A DIFFERENT FLAV...

WHEN PERSON (A) TURNS TO FACE THE AUDIENCE AGAIN, SHE PICKS UP HER OWN STORY MID-SENTENCE AND CONTINUES ON UNTIL ANOTHER PLAYER TURNS & INTERRUPTS HER. WHAT YOU END UP WITH IS 5 OR 6 PARALLEL STORIES INTERRUPTING EACH OTHER.

...THE ICY DRAIN PIPE, 14 STORIES ABOVE THE CITY STREET. I SPOTTED A CLOTHESLINE...

FACILITATION TIPS:

INSTRUCT THE PLAYERS TO LET THE STORIES GO A LITTLE LONGER AT THE BEGINNING SO THE AUDIENCE CAN GET THE GIST OF EACH STORY.

AS THE GAME GOES ON, THE PLAYERS ARE TO INTERRUPT EACH OTHER MORE & MORE FREQUENTLY. THEY CAN ALSO LOOK FOR GOOD MOMENTS TO INTERRUPT.

BLAH BLAH BLAH BLAH HBL AH BLAH BLAH BLAH... BLAH BLAH BLAH BL

THIS GAME IS SOMETIMES UPROARIOUSLY FUNNY. IF YOU HAVE A VERY ADVENTUROUS GROUP, AND WANT TO TAKE THIS GAME TO THE NEXT LEVEL, YOU CAN INVITE FOUR PARTICIPANTS TO JOIN THE STAGE WITH TWO STANDING NEAR EACH END OF THE LINE. THEIR JOB IS TO ACT OUT THE STORIES AS THEY ARE TOLD.

I DID NOT REALIZE I WOULD STILL HAVE SENSATION IN MY...

SNORT SNORT

- When A chooses to face the audience again, she picks up *her own story* where she left off mid-sentence and continues until another player turns and interrupts her. You end up with five parallel, unrelated stories told in an interrupted fashion. The effect is a bit like channel surfing on a TV.

Tips: Instruct the players to let the stories go a little longer at the beginning so the audience can get the gist of each story. As the game goes on, the players are to interrupt each other more and more frequently. They can also look for good moments to interrupt. This game is sometimes uproariously funny. After a time, the leader can choose to end the game by asking all the players in the line to face the audience and continue their stories together. The cacophony of noise crescendos until the leader claps her hands to bring the tellers to silence.

Sensitivity Line on a Theme

In this version, each player speaks on the same theme, based on a starter phrase such as "If I really knew I was creative, I would…" or "My ideal community would be…" or "A time I took a risk was…." This offers an opportunity to speak to the audience from the heart. We provide the starter phrase before asking for volunteers so they can choose whether to participate. In this version players speak only once, and they don't interrupt one another.

Ask for five or six volunteers to stand in a line with their backs to the audience.

- When you say "Go," the first person (A) turns to face the audience, starts with the starting phrase and speaks for 30 seconds or so.
- When he is done, he turns back. Person (B) then turns to face the audience, starts with the same starting phrase and speaks for about 30 seconds. She then turns back.
- One by one, the players turn to face the audience, speak to the theme and then turn back.
- When the last person is done, the players all turn and face the audience and take a bow.

Tip: This is a powerful format for a short public performance on a theme.

 ## Scary but Worth It

We know from our own experience how scary it can be to lead theater improvisation games for the first time. You might want to try out some games with a group of friends to get the feel for them. But do give it a whirl. It will open up a whole new dimension to your facilitation, and your participants will thank you. And the games don't stop with the ones described in this chapter. You can find hundreds of theater games on the internet.

13

Imagine Change: Issues-Oriented Theater

It was 1998 and a gender dynamic at the first camp of the season was making us very nervous. A group of sophisticated inner-city boys were not buying into the community agreements that precluded coupling, and they seemed to have their eyes on several 14-year-old girls from a rural community. After repeatedly having side conversations with the youths about this, we decided to address the situation with the entire community, using interactive theater. Theater artist John Scott began by offering several scenarios relating to personal relationships and boundaries.

Finally he set up a scene in which a girl was being bothered by the advances of an older boy. As a young girl stumbled through the scene trying to figure out a way to fend off a boy's advances, an 18-year-old girl (from the same community as the older boys who were worrying us) jumped up and said, "I'll show you how to do it." She took the young woman's arm, marched right up to the guy, looked him in the eye and said, "I'm NOT interested!" She then made an abrupt 180-degree turn and walked away, the younger teen in tow. The group broke into laughter and a lesson was learned.

The scenario led into an open discussion in which the girls let the boys know why it is important to them to have a place where they can be themselves without being approached sexually. This session marked a definite shift in the group energy around this issue. We were able to relax, knowing that the young women had gained their own strategies and power in the situation, and they had successfully communicated their needs for safety and respect.

The group session was a based on a body of work developed by Brazilian theater director Augusto Boal. Called Theater of the Oppressed (TO) or Theater of Liberation, Boal's work is useful for exploring issues, liberating the imagination and motivating change. Boal's innovation was to break down the barrier between actors and the audience by inviting audience members to become "spectactors," a combination of spectator and actor. The spectactors could volunteer to come on stage to influence the outcome of scenes devised by the actors.

In his popular "forum theater," the players present a five- to ten-minute scene in which there is an oppressor and one or more oppressed characters. They play through the scene once and then begin a replay. This time audience members—the spectactors—call out "Freeze" when they have an idea for a better strategy the oppressed person could have taken to gain power in the situation. They take the place of that actor, rewind the scene and act out the new idea. The facilitator—called the Joker—looks for the good in the idea, points it out and then starts the scene again, giving more and more people a chance to step in to offer new ideas. When someone's idea is successful, everyone can feel it.

Boal, who grew up under an oppressive regime in Brazil, asserted that if you want to oppress people, you begin by taking away their imaginations. Forum theater counteracts oppression by reinvigorating the imagination so that people can discover alternative ways of being, thinking and solving problems.

Boal's work has made its way all over the world, with practitioners using it to empower people to solve issues in their communities. PATH, a large public-health NGO, ran a program in Kenya called IMPACT using Magnet Theater, a version of Theater of the Oppressed, to prevent HIV infection among out-of-school youth. Their success demonstrates how arts-based methods can have a huge impact and spread quickly. According to their reports, "PATH supported 3,408 performances that reached

649,947 youth in the Coast, Rift Valley, and western provinces and trained 430 theater troupe members in HIV and AIDS content and the Magnet Theater process."[26]

Theater of the Oppressed has grown to include a large body of work. Our purpose here is to introduce you to the method and give you a few easy-to-lead practices to get you started. You can use the following activities in a variety of settings.

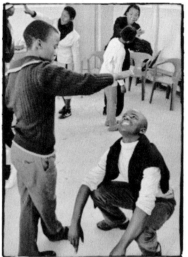
Credit: PYE Global

Playing Columbia Hypnosis activity in South Africa's Eastern Cape.

 ## Columbia Hypnosis

This game, designed by Augusto Boal, gives participants the opportunity to explore the dynamics of leading and following. Ask people to form pairs and decide who will be A and who will be B.

- Tell A players they will be the leaders first. Each will hold up one hand, palm open about six inches in front of partner B's face.
- When you say "Go," A begins to slowly move around the room. B is to follow the hand as if A is a hypnotist. A can walk around the room, move up and down, side to side, crawl on the floor, whatever occurs to him. B needs to keep her face six inches from A's open palm at all times. Tell A that it's his job to give B an interesting and enjoyable experience.
- After a few minutes ask everyone to freeze, and then switch so that B leads A.

Tips: With younger participants it's important to stress that the leader's job is to give the partner an interesting and enjoyable experience. Invite people to vary the speed of their leading. Be sure to encourage people to take care of themselves physically and to watch for nearby players, to prevent accidents. Possible debrief points include the following: Who preferred leading and why? Who preferred following and why? What made this activity safe for people? What does this activity teach us about leadership?

Playing family portrait: the enthusiastic family!

Credit: Jesse Sternburg

Family Photos

This is not an activity from Theater of the Oppressed, but we find it useful as a warm-up for building statues on a theme. (See "Sculpting Emotions.") Ask participants to break into groups of five or six. Each group will be a "family." In this activity you will be taking imaginary photos of each family.

- Give each group two chairs to serve as the frame of their family photos.
- Begin by asking participants what makes a good photo: facial expression, positioning of the people, etc. Then ask each group to imagine

Frozen statue: this is what "wonder" looks like.

Credit: Jesse Sternburg

they are posing for a family photo. Once they are in place, within the frame of the two chairs, ask them to hold perfectly still. Go around and take an imaginary picture of each family.

- As you go around the circle of groups for the second time, ask each group to depict a specific kind of family—the happy-go-lucky family, the spiritual family, the shopping mall/consumer family, the supportive family, the furious family, the independent family, the co-dependent family, the snobby family. It's a good idea to keep this lighthearted. You can touch on more serious themes, but from a lighthearted perspective.
- To leave people in a good frame of mind, be sure the last pose for each group is a positive one.

🖐 Sculpting Emotions

This activity teaches emotional intelligence in an embodied way by having people demonstrate, observe and experience specific emotions. It is done in pairs, with one person being the sculptor and the other being imaginary clay. The sculptor forms the clay into a statue to depict a particular emotion. Begin by demonstrating three methods the sculptor (A) can use to manipulate her clay (B).

1. A asks permission to touch B and then gently moves B into position.
2. A asks B to mimic A's shape and facial expression, avoiding physical touch.
3. A moves B's body by pulling an imaginary string that is attached to B's hands, elbows, feet, etc. Again this provides a way to move a person's body into position without touching.

Once you have demonstrated the sculpting process, ask partners to choose to be A or B. Begin with A sculpting B to represent one particular emotion. Some possibilities include surprise, sadness, compassion, fear, fury or love. Once the sculpture is complete, B partners stand totally frozen. A partners then walk around the room as if strolling through a sculpture garden. Ask what they notice about the statues. Are there similarities? Differences? How do they feel as they look at these sculptures? Ask the clay to drop their poses and shake their bodies to release the emotion.

Then switch to having the B partners sculpt the A partners to represent a new emotion that you assign. This time B partners walk around to view the results. Continue the process of debriefing. What do people notice? What are they learning from being the clay? From being the sculptors? From being the observers? You can include any emotions. Be sure to end with a positive emotion for each group. Ask the clay to shake their bodies as they come out of each pose to discharge the emotion they have been representing.

Group Sculptures

This exercise provides a means for a group of any size to explore issues. Ask participants to come up with a situation, theme or issue. Possible themes include pollution, the typical high school classroom, peer pressure or violence.

Organize participants into groups of six or eight. Ask half of the groups to silently move into sculptures that illustrate the theme. The other groups then walk around and observe the sculptures and reflect on what they see and feel. Have players shake out their bodies after holding their poses.

The Next Step

To learn more about Theater of the Oppressed, and related approaches to using theater for social change, look for classes (held in most major cities) or conferences run by the Theatre of the Oppressed organization (www.theatreoftheoppressed.org). We also recommend Augusto Boal's book *Games for Actors and Non-Actors*.

Share Our Stories: Storytelling and Witnessing

Some years before Jason arrived at Power of Hope camp, his dad had left the family. In a Painting with Words workshop Jason took a risk and wrote a poem for the first time. The poem was addressed to his father, and it gave voice to feelings that he had kept hidden for a very long time. The workshop participants loved Jason's poem and encouraged him to develop it into a performance piece for the open mic three days later. Backed up by guitar and hand-held percussion, Jason delivered his piece to a group of 75 supportive people. When he finished, he was enveloped by a wave of applause and shouts of "Go, Jason!" and "We love you, Jason." This proved to be a momentous breakthrough for Jason, both in terms of building his self-confidence and in helping to heal the wound left by his father's rejection. Gaining the ability to put a story that has meaning and depth into a form that can be shared and witnessed is life changing. Jason left camp with a lighter heart and a newfound sense of self-worth.

Anthropologists trace storytelling back at least 27,000 years, to the early cave dwellers. "[It] is one of the few human traits that are truly universal across culture and through all of known history," writes science journalist Jeremy Hsu in *Scientific American Mind*.[27] Stories pass information through history, teach us how to live in communities and build empathy in our social interactions. Neuroscientists tell us that we

yes!

Credit: Sara Dent, Power of Hope Canada

A young woman joyfully shares her story.

are far more likely to remember information if we are introduced to it through story rather than bullet-point data. While data stimulates just a small part of the brain that processes language, story activates widespread areas. If the story contains references to our senses—as in "the silky water" or "his gravelly voice"—it arouses the sensory cortex; "the sugary orange" excites the olfactory region of the brain; "slogging through the mud" turns on our motor cortex. Even more interesting is the emotional resonance set into motion by story. When we tell a story, our listeners actually "feel" the experience. The emotion of the teller ignites corresponding areas in the listener's brain to simulate the experience as real. In this way, sharing our stories is a potent empathy builder.[28]

Over the years personal storytelling has taken its place in the center of our work because of its beneficial effects. Whether you have lived through unimaginable horror or walked an easier path, every life is a tale filled with love and joy, rejection, loss, heartbreak and upheaval. When we tell our stories and are simply witnessed without judgment or advice we are embraced in a cloak of healing. There is nothing like hearing one's peers and elders say, "I hear you, and I'm sorry you've had to bear this." This basic human act of witnessing reaps benefits across generations and cultures, bringing us relief, insight and comfort. As poet Maya Angelou has said, "There is *no agony like* bearing an untold story inside of you."

PYE facilitator Hanif Fazal founded Step Up, an award-winning empowerment program for youth in Portland, Oregon. Step Up participants are students who have been identified as the most likely to fail and drop out of school. Starting in eighth grade (12 or 13 years old), they attend a

five-day residential empowerment camp, go to tutoring/mentoring sessions after school and meet for regular retreats that build on the themes
offered at the camp.

"Personal storytelling is perhaps the most essential element in the
program," said Hanif. "Most of these students have lived difficult lives. I
believe that in every challenging situation there is a gift, so we help young
people reframe their stories by looking at their lives in different ways."
When Hanif introduces the importance of storytelling to his young
participants, he places a cup on the table in front of him and holds up a
big pitcher of water. As he tells a version of the following, he slowly pours
water into the cup until it overflows.

We're each going to tell our story at this camp. And the question
is, Why share? What's in it for me? When you were little and Mom
said, "You need to share with your sister," you said "No, no, no."
Sharing was all about giving something up. You lose something—
it's a resource that's getting depleted. The nice thing about sharing
your story is that there is an endless source to draw on.

I'm going to share a metaphor with you to help make sense of
this. Someone once told me that the only time you see the world
clearly is when you're born. It's as if you are an empty cup. But then
life starts happening. When you're four, say, Dad and Mom start
fighting all the time. Your cup starts getting filled up with some fear
and pain and helplessness. Then at six, Dad leaves home. Your cup
fills with sadness and worry and a lot of anger. Each time you're hit
with something hard, that cup fills some more until finally your
cup is full—filled to the brim. The next time something happens
there is no more room in the cup, so it overflows into your life.
You might get high or drunk or start a fight. You just can't take it
any more.

Our job as human beings is to empty the cup. How do we do
that? If we yell and scream—yes, the cup gets emptier but it fills
right up with shame and remorse. Eventually you get to the place
where you just don't care anymore. How can we empty the cup in
ways that don't fill it back up with things we don't want? This is
where sharing comes in.

Every time you talk about what's going on, your cup empties a little bit. The more you're able to empty your cup, the more room there is for other things that maybe you haven't experienced in a long time. Like happiness, joy and peace. Or how about love and nurturance? Our job is to continue to empty that cup every time life hits us, so that there is room within us to feel what we want to feel and to do what we want to do. Every time you share, you feel that empty space. You just let go of a ton of shame and sadness, and now you have room to breathe. When I look back on my own life, I can see that things really began to change when I was able to empty the cup.

 ## Using Visual Art to Enhance Storytelling

A few years ago we began working in the East Cape of South Africa through an organization called African Solutions to African Problems (ASAP). This is a region that has been hard hit by the AIDS crises and has a high percentage of child-headed households. In a workshop of youth workers and health care workers, we introduced a storytelling activity called My Life As a Stream in which people draw a picture of their lives using the metaphor of a stream. In doing this activity, the adults discovered the potency of their own life stories and the personal impact of sharing their stories with empathetic listeners. In a subsequent youth camp, the facilitators decided to lead My Life As a Stream with the young people. After returning home, we learned that several of the youth workers had started monthly groups where upwards of 400 teens were coming together to continue the arts-empowerment work they had begun at their camp. Their favorite activity? My Life As a Stream. The youth would share their life stories with one other and weep as the group listened in silent support, allowing them to express the sorrow and loss they had held so silently.

When you work with young people in an arts-rich environment, their stories begin to spill out. You become privy to their world—and for many, it's a world with altogether too much violence, neglect and abuse. As you

Credit: Autumn Preble

Telling our stories builds empathy.

hear young people's stories, it's natural to want to give them advice and show them how to work things out. But when it comes down to it, we've come to the conclusion that the altogether best we can offer is a sincere listening ear. It's a surprise to hear a young person say, "I feel so much better now," when you haven't offered them a bit of advice or attempted to solve their problems. (This, of course, this does not deny the importance of actively working to improve the conditions of young people. And it's not to say that we shouldn't provide help if a child shares a story of current abuse. In North America caregivers, including mentors and volunteers, are legally required to report circumstances in which a young person is in danger of personal harm or of harming others.)

✋ Becoming a Story Listener

We consider the practice of storytelling and listening a sacred act that puts us in touch with the gift that is each individual's life. As we tell our stories we weave our experiences together into a rich tapestry. It takes some personal training to be able to evoke the healing power of story, and it all starts with listening. How do we become a deep and effective story *listener?* In our Heart of Facilitation sessions we give each participant the opportunity to tell his own life story to a small group for 30 to 45 minutes. This is of great benefit for the tellers. For many people in their 20s, 30s, 40s or even 50s this is the first time they have ever told their life stories to a receptive audience.

Our small-group storytelling is hugely important for the listeners as well as the tellers. Sometimes it's hard for the listeners to realize that their role is to simply listen, to stay open and empathetic and to refrain from offering advice or trying to fix another person's life. Only with practice do the listeners come to realize what an active role that really is. As we learn to bear witness in this way, we build the emotional capacity to listen fully and hold another's story without judgment. We encourage people to listen from their highest selves. Not from sympathy, in which you feel sorry for the person, but from empathy, holding the person in high regard, capable of living the story of her life.

When we tell our stories, not only do we feel comforted by the attention we receive, in the act of telling we gain new insight into our lives. Here is what Sam Keen and Anne Valley-Fox have to say about the benefits of storytelling in their book *Your Mythic Journey*:

> When we tell our stories to one another, we at one and the same time find the meaning of our lives and are healed from our isolation and loneliness. Strange as it may seem, self-knowledge begins with self-revelation. We don't know who we are until we hear ourselves speaking the drama of our lives to someone we trust to listen with an open mind and heart.[29]

When we learn to listen empathically to one another, we gain perspective on our own lives, and our loneliness is alleviated. At camp we often hear young people say, "Before this camp, I thought I had the worst life in the world. Now I know it's not so bad. I no longer feel so alone." Or "I've really come to appreciate my life."

The Value of Each Life

When you invite people to tell their life stories, it's important to emphasize that each person's life is sacred and valuable, and each person's story adds to the richness of the community. If one person has had a more tragic life than another, this doesn't make her life story more valuable. The gift of story comes when people speak authentically from their hearts regardless of the intensity of their experience. One time, for example, a young woman told the story of losing of her cat. She was an only child, and this cat had been like a sibling to her while she grew up. When the cat died, it was as if she had lost her best friend and sister. Her sense of loss was so raw that it struck a chord deep within all of us.

Heart Circles

We learned about the value of sharing life stories in a structured way when Fran Peavey, an activist who had worked to stop French nuclear testing in the South Pacific, volunteered at camp. Prior to her visit, there always seemed to be an unexpected emotional outburst sometime during camp. It was as if emotions were getting stirred up through the camp experience but had no place to go. Fran brought us a ceremony called the Heart Circle, designed by several Maori grandmothers in New Zealand with instructions to take it to North America. "Your people need this," they told her. Essentially, the community creates a ritual listening circle and people are invited to step into the center to speak to the question, What do I need to do to step into more power in my life? We've found that when young people stand in a witnessing circle to respond to this question, what they need to do is to tell their life stories and be heard.

We won't give you specific instructions on how to hold a Heart Circle, because we were asked to pass it on only in person, but suffice it to say that holding some kind of safe space for life storytelling can add a healing element to your work with youth. Once we institutionalized the Heart Circle, it became a safe channel for stories to emerge, and the unexpected emotional outbursts disappeared from our camps. Though it's not always easy for adults to listen for hours to life stories, young people clamor for it.

A Cautionary Note

Please keep in mind while reading this chapter that getting people to share too much or to share prematurely is not helpful, and can even be harmful. We believe it is never appropriate to coerce people into telling their stories. Everyone's story is his own. Whenever entering into story-telling activities, we remind people that they are the gatekeeper of their stories. There is no merit to "telling all." Similarly check your own enthu-siasm for drama that might cause you to be overly curious and to probe for details. The purpose of personal storytelling is to provide an outlet for personal sharing in whatever form and to whatever extent a person wishes.

 ## Activating Our Own Stories

Telling stories is as natural as sharing the experiences of the day with your family or gossiping on the phone with a friend. But ask people if they can tell stories and many will say no. So the place to begin is with some activities that surprise people into discovering their ability to tell stories. For a set of activities that activate the storytelling voice see pages 216–222.

Following are some additional easy-to-lead storytelling activities that you can use with groups of youth and or adults.

Talking Circles

A good way to acclimate people to listening and speaking from the heart is to use a simple circle process in which one person speaks while every-one else listens. You can use a talking object, such as a stone, which the speaker holds while talking. Only the person holding the stone speaks. The circle process comes in handy for debriefing activities or exploring themes in small groups.

The Three-Minute Story

What story could you tell about yourself in three minutes that would sig-nificantly shift people's view of you? When we pose this question, people often think that three minutes is not long enough, but when they try it, they find out differently. This is a great activity to do in groups of four to eight people to help them practice telling stories and to increase intimacy.

One person in each small group volunteers to go first. He launches into a true story about his life. The leader calls time after three minutes and then gives three minutes for the listeners to appreciate the storyteller. Ask the listeners, "What strengths, gifts and values did you learn about this person through listening to the story?" After three minutes of appreciation, you move on to the next person in each circle and so on. If you are short on time, you can skip the appreciations or keep them to a minute; however, they are often the richest part of the experience. When you introduce this exercise, let people know that for some of them three minutes will breeze by, while for others it will seem an eternity. Make sure the group gives the full three minutes to each person.

My Life As a Stream

This is our all-time favorite storytelling activity. Ask participants to imagine that their life is a stream that began at their birth and has flowed to the present time. Using 18″ × 24″ drawing paper and oil pastels or crayons, they are to draw their personal streams with twists and turns to represent the people and experiences that have formed them (see picture below).

A Human EYES student tells the story of her grandmother's life.

Draw your stream to represent the major events and influences, both positive and negative, that have made you into the person you are today. The twists and turns represent major turning points. Your stream might become large and deep, or it might get small and shallow. There may be rocks or waterfalls. You can use both images and words to represent people and experiences. When you get to the present, illustrate or write a few of your hopes and dreams for the future in the stream going forward.

Be sure to remind people that this is not a visual arts test. Their picture does not have to be a beautiful art piece.

Changing the World One Person's Story at a Time

Here is a storytelling project that Meghan Chaffin and Jessica Armstrong, two young volunteers, initiated at The Power of Hope program in Bellingham, Washington. Their plan was elegant, inexpensive and easily replicable. The project brought together middle school students with college acting students in a creative collaboration that provided members of the wider community a window into the inner lives of the adolescents living among them. They called it the Monologue Project, and it worked like this.

The Power of Hope team began by facilitating workshops for middle school students on community building, self-reflection and creative writing. Each young person wrote at least one life story in the form of a 150- to 350-word monologue that was then delivered to acting students at a local university.

The actors chose pieces to perform and then created a show for the younger students. The show held some unexpected benefits. "For many of the youth this was their first experience on a college campus," said Jessica. "And they got really inspired by meeting the actors. It gave them a peek into what it might be like to go to college."

The performance was powerful. "It was very moving—much more than I thought it was going to be," said middle school teacher Joel Gillman in a local paper. "One parent said it was one of the most moving experiences of his life."[30] As a result, the acting students decided to do a public performance with some of the sixth graders performing right along with them. They ran several performance workshops for the young writers, and in the end, 15 college actors and 7 middle school students performed at a cozy theater in an old firehouse.

One by one the actors stepped from the

This is simply an opportunity to visualize your life as a whole as it has flowed from birth to the present and on into an imagined future.

Once the pictures are complete, ask people to look at their images and add a title. People then share their pictures in groups of four to six. Choose a time frame for sharing, depending on your group. Young people may be comfortable talking for only five to seven minutes; adults may go for 10 to 15. Time the group as they go through the process.

If possible, end each storytelling with a few minutes of appreciation for the teller. We have used this activity with great success in youth

back of a bare, dark stage into a spotlight and launched into a monologue. "How can you tell if someone is honest about his passion?" pondered one actor. "I know a lot of people talk crap, but there are others out there who really mean what they say when they say they have a passion for something. I can feel it." Another spoke through the voice of an adult berating her for eating too much: "Can't you mooch off someone else?" she asked. Still another confessed to a friend that she had stolen her jacket. "I'm sorry. I really am. It's just that, well, you seem to have everything.... It was just jealousy I guess. I wanted something cool. Something to make people see beyond the boring person I seem to be." The mood ranged from funny (a boy falls off his bike and lands in a big pile of dog poop) to sorrowful (a girl not having the courage to talk to a friend who has been lost to drugs) to courageous (a young man sharing what it's like living every day with cancer).

The two shows sold out and even generated enough to cover some of the expenses of the project. "I thought it was a great experience," one student said. "It was really touching. I'm just a middle school student, and seeing my words spoken through good acting was thrilling. When I first wrote it, I thought it only applied to me. [Now I realize] that everyone has a broader sense of themselves. You're not just narrowed down to a category."

Power of Hope volunteers then took the Monologue Project to communities in other parts of Washington State, demonstrating how you can bring the stories of youth to a community while at the same time instigating a broad array of cross-generational and cross-cultural connection. And all on a shoestring budget.

programs, college classrooms, adult conferences and business team-building workshops. When working with youth, be sure there is an adult in each group.

Timeline with Free Writing

Another way to prepare people for personal storytelling is to ask them to list five positive and five challenging events that have shaped them. They place these events along a timeline and choose two or three events as the basis for free writing. This process both elicits emotion and heightens memory, preparing them to tell their life stories in groups.

Write Your Life Workshop

See page 191 for instructions on how to use metaphor and free writing as the basis of a life-story workshop.

Telling Stories All Day, Every Day

On the second day of a Creative Facilitation training we led in Santa Fe, New Mexico, an educator and grandmother from a local Pueblo told us, "I learned something special last night. Instead of telling my six-year-old granddaughter a story, like I usually do, we played the Yes, and… game [in which people take turns telling a story]. And I discovered that she is a storyteller, too!" We can tell and listen to stories anytime and anywhere. We hope through playing with the storytelling activities in this book you will discover that within every person—including you—there is a whole world of stories waiting to be shared.

Join the Chorus: Music, Rhythm and Dance

The 40 educators gathered in the outdoor pavilion represented several countries from the Middle East. The participants came from communities on opposite sides of the deep conflicts that have long plagued the region, and the undercurrent of conflict was palpable. The group had already been together for a week when Charlie and PYE facilitator Nadia Chaney came in to deliver a Creative Facilitation workshop. A lot of tension had surfaced, and it was still simmering. They thought it would be helpful to get the group singing together, so early in the workshop Charlie introduced a three-part song from Ghana, West Africa. The group learned the song quickly and surprised themselves with the gorgeous sound they produced together. When he brought the song to a close, the group fell into silence and then broke out in wild cheers. People looked at each other in awe. During the next break, several participants came up to him, amazed by what had just happened. "I never sing in groups like this. I do not know how you got us to do that. It was absolute magic!" said a young Palestinian. Singing together is magic for sure, but it is a magic that any one of us can learn to conjure.

An increasing body of research from around the world supports what many singers know from their own experience: singing is extremely good for us on many levels. The act of singing together releases endorphins, the feel-good chemicals in our brains. Singing for an audience builds self-confidence and has broad, long-lasting effects on general well-being. Of all the kinds of singing, group singing has the most positive and dramatic effect on people's lives. A 2008 Australian study revealed that choral singers rated their life satisfaction higher than the general public even when they faced significant problems and challenges. According to a 1998 study, after participating in a singing program for just a month, nursing-home residents showed significant relief from anxiety and depression.[31]

Like exercise, singing is an aerobic activity that increases circulation by getting more oxygen into the blood, affecting our mood for the better. Singing requires deep breathing, and that in turn reduces anxiety. In a 2000 study by University of California researcher Robert Beck, choral singing was shown to increase immunoglobulin A and cortisol (which boosts immune response and reduces stress) by 150 percent in rehearsals and 237 percent during performances.[32]

No doubt some of the positive benefits of singing come from rhythm. Our bodies are based on rhythm—the beat of our hearts, women's monthly cycles, the cycles of life and death. Mickey Hart, musicologist and longtime drummer for the Grateful Dead, tells the story of how he first recognized the deep power of rhythm to heal when he was taking care of his grandmother, who had fallen into dementia. One day he sat down in front of her and began to beat a soft and steady drumbeat. She had not spoken a word in over a year. She opened her eyes, shed a tear and then began to repeat his name, "Mickey, Mickey, Mickey." "That was one of the key experiences in my life, which showed me what the power of rhythm can do," said Mickey. "Rhythm was reconnecting her to the world that was fading away."[33]

The late social work educator and scholar Henry W. Maier spoke to the role rhythm plays in fostering group cohesion. "Have you noticed that when people jog, dance or throw a Frisbee in rhythm with each other, they seem to experience momentary bonding and a sense of unity? At these and other moments of joint rhythmic engagement, they discover an attraction for each other regardless whether there has been a previous sense of caring. In fact it is almost impossible to dislike a person while being rhythmically in 'sync.' Rhythmic interactions forge people together. Rhythmicity provides a 'glue' for establishing human connections."[34]

Singing in the woods, supported by beat boxers.

Our experience with young people impresses this on us over and over. Once they get over their initial resistance, they fall into singing, drumming and dancing with wild abandon. Adults—other than having stronger initial resistance—are no different. We thrive in the rhythm of connection.

Since rhythm, song and dance don't lend themselves to written descriptions, and rather require learning through active participation, we have put all three together in this one chapter with resources for further exploration. From our own experience, supported by scientific evidence, we enthusiastically assert that song, dance and rhythm belong where people gather. They cause happiness—body and soul!

 ## Join the Chorus

Our friend Shivon Robinsong, founder and codirector of Victoria, British Columbia's 300-member Gettin' Higher Choir, is one of the most effective and joyful champions of the power of song in community. This non-audition choir, filled with many people who had never previously sung, is an institution in Victoria. Shivon has a passion for taking singing into unlikely places; whether in non-profit board rooms or organizational trainings and retreats, she finds that, with the right approach, people everywhere love connecting through song. "I find that people are longing to sing together," said Shivon. "They thrive on what I call vitamin H (for harmony), and the more I see how it benefits people's lives, the more I understand it to be an essential nutrient for body/mind/spirit." Shivon asserts that "everyone needs to sing. It's a matter of life and breath!"

Shivon's success is only one indication of the growing popularity of community choirs. The natural voice movement in England has a network of 320 song practitioners, who lead choirs and workshops to restore singing as a natural human activity. "Singing together is simply the best, most powerful way to make friends and build lasting communities," they assert on their website.[35] Research on choral singing has proven that the

Shivon Robinsong and her 300-voice Gettin' Higher Choir.

Credit: Sara Dent

practice increases community involvement. Studies in Italy even show that towns with lots of choirs have higher levels of voter participation.[36]

As musicians ourselves, we were eager to incorporate singing into our work with youth, and indeed singing quickly became a much-loved activity. We find that young people, like all people, love singing. Shivon said, "Singing is about listening, making friends with the sound of your own unique voice, and finding your place in a vocal community." When a previously shy young person makes friends with the sound of his own voice for the first time, the impact is enormous and long lasting. Singing is a pillar of our work with groups because listening to one another, raising self-awareness and self-acceptance and experiencing a sense of belonging is central to awakening our potential—that is exactly what happens when we sing.

We weave song into daily life at our camps, starting on the first night. We sing first thing in the morning when we gather for a community meeting, and we close each evening activity with a calming song to end the day on a unified, soothing tone. We sing during plenaries, in workshops and at the open mic. After camp has ended, the singing vibe continues; we've heard countless reports of youth singing their way home on ferryboats and buses.

At a camp in Brazil, one staff member in particular, Augusto, discovered his passion for singing and leading groups in song. A few weeks after camp he formed a youth choir with many of the campers and their friends. They called their group Voices that Cure, and began singing in nursing homes, prisons and community events.

All it takes is one person who is charged up about singing for the healing and connective power of singing to start making waves. We'll offer some suggestions here on ways to get even the most reluctant singers to bring out their vocal power.

The Vocal Boot Camp Warm-Up

When you first tell a group you are going to lead them in singing, don't be surprised if you hear a few groans and observe some people squirm and try to hide. Too many of us have been told somewhere along the line that we don't have a good voice. And then we never sing in public again. You, as the song leader, play an important role in empowering people to begin to sing again. Start by demystifying the whole process. We tell people,

> We can all sing. In fact, every one of you has a beautiful voice whether you know it or not. And the singing we're going to do now is not supposed to be good. We're just going to sing. So even if somewhere along the line you were told to "please mouth the words," now is the time to sing out.

We begin song sessions by inviting participants to stand in a big circle. We then ask people to indicate their comfort level with singing with groups. "On a scale of one to five raise the number of fingers to show how comfortable you are: One means, I am not comfortable at all and five means I love it." This is an important first step because it gives those people who are feeling uncomfortable a chance to make it known to the group and hopefully let go of their inhibitions just a bit. It also gives the song leader the chance to acknowledge and welcome the different levels of experience and comfort that are in the room and to make that okay. We usually add something like "I am so happy to see some zeros, ones and twos because you get the chance to really surprise yourself!"

We then state "There are two basic rules for singing. The first is: you *must* open your mouth." People usually chuckle at this understatement, and we explain that often, out of shyness, people try to sing through a very small opening.

> So our first job is to open our mouths wide. Let's take a deep breath. On exhale let's see how wide you can open your mouth and say the syllable "ahh." Great! Let's do that again!

Notice how we find ways to affirm the group early on; building the group's confidence in singing starts with the first sounds they make. We go on to explain that singing gives our whole bodies a buzz and we can feel that when we let go of the tension we normally, unconsciously carry around.

Relax the jaw: We call the group's awareness to the tension we all carry in our jaws, and ask them to take a moment to massage the hinges of their jaws. We then teach a sure-fire theater warm-up that allows us to relax our faces and jaws more so that the sounds we make can start to vibrate our bodies, beginning with our faces. We instruct people to clasp their hands together and hold them in front of their faces, take a deep breath and make a sound on the exhale while shaking their hands back and forth. It is amazing what happens; jaws go slack and people make the weirdest sound. This activity usually ends in a lot of laughter.

Engage the breath: We then focus on the second rule of singing: You *must* breathe—and breathe fully—in order to sing. We use the following activity to engage the diaphragm. "Please repeat the following phrases: *hing ya! hing yee! hing yay!*" The group repeats these phrases loudly in unison several times. Point out that we can feel our diaphragms contract each time we say *hing*.

Make a sound: Now it's time to make a tone. We use the syllable "ya" to stretch out the upper and lower ends of our vocal ranges. While making the sound we follow an arc with our hands as we see how high we can go, and then swoop down with our hands to see how low we can go. We finish the vocal boot camp by making a tone together. We ask the group to either match the note, sing a higher note, or a lower note and see what happens.

This whole process takes about ten minutes, and it is important on several levels. It gets people more in touch with their bodies and their breathing, which makes them more likely to embrace singing un-self-consciously. It also gets people breathing in unison and making sounds together. It's a very short step from here to actually singing. Finally, the activities themselves actually work in helping groups produce sound confidently so that when you actually get to singing a song, people step into it fully. It speeds up the pleasurable payoff that comes with singing.

Making the Magic Happen

What follows are some tips for leading groups in singing.

Check your attitude: Engaging a group of people who are new to singing can be challenging. It is up to the song leader to fill the enthusiasm gap that is often present when you begin. Cultivate a willingness to step into the gap, and trust that you can take the group with you. They will love it! Enthusiasm for something you love to do is infectious and hard to resist. Let your enthusiasm flow!

Warm up your group: Preparing to sing makes all the difference. You can use the vocal warm-up sequence described above or a condensed version if you are short on time. At least have the group shake their bodies to relax, massage their jaws for a moment, and make a tone together before you launch into a song.

Keep it simple: We advocate teaching songs that people can learn by ear, without using song sheets. Looking at a book or piece of paper separates you from your group and therefore breaks the energy and sense of connection. Similarly reading the words separates participants from each other and the music. We prefer short three- or four-part songs that can be learned quickly and sung over and over again. Once people get the hang of the song they can sink into it and really enjoy the vibration of the harmony and the connection to their fellow singers.

Identify the origins of songs: Whenever possible, identify where the song has came from. What is the cultural and historical context? Refrain from teaching songs that are part of sacred ceremonies in cultures other than your own.

Affirm your group: Just as with any sort of arts activity, people participate more fully when the leader affirms how well they are doing. Phrases like "You sound great!" are a big help. If the group is struggling, you might say "You almost have it. This is beautiful."

Challenge your group: Challenging the group goes hand in hand with affirming it. If a song is challenging, let the group know: "This is challenging, and I know we can get this. Are you up for it?" If your group is singing quietly you might say: "On a scale of one to ten of vocal power, I'd say we are at about a seven. Let's see if we can bump this up to a ten!" or "I know there is more power in this room. Let's hear it!" We often call the group's attention to the essence of what we are doing by asking "Are you ready to create some beauty here today?" Who can say no?

Take command: Sometimes the group gets excited and people start side talking. This can be frustrating for the rest of the group and definitely gets in the way of learning the song. You can gently but firmly call the group back to focus by saying something like "I want everyone to take a deep breath together right now and just listen."

Use your hands: It helps the visual learners in the group to see your hand following the notes in the song as they rise and fall. To do this hold your hand horizontal to the floor about mid-body in front of you and then follow the notes in the song. This may be difficult to do at first, but practice with an easy song and you'll get the hang of it.

Add one part at a time: Once you have taught the parts separately, you are ready to put all the parts together. Begin by having the group with the melody line sing through the song; then add one harmony at a time. This way, you can get each group firmly established in their part. Once the song is in full swing, have some fun with it. Raise your arms to indicate singing more loudly and lower them for singing quietly; invite some parts to sing more loudly than others, etc.

Move your body: People respond to body movement. Freeing yourself to move naturally with the rhythm of the music really helps people get "in the groove" with the song.

Know your songs well: You get so much more mileage out of knowing a few songs very well than from having a huge repertoire. If there are tricky parts to the timing of a song, make sure you have mastered the challenge yourself before you engage the group.

The World Unity Chant

This is an all-time favorite part song that combines five religions into one song that has become a favorite at our Hip Hop Hope programs and camps. As the whole group sings the chant, various youths jump into the circle and rap free style about their hopes and dreams of the future. You can sing this song with youth or adult groups ranging in size from 15 to 250. Begin by letting people know you will be singing a song from five religious traditions. Explain the meaning of each line as you teach it. The song was composed by Sophia, a singer in Southern California with a line added by Nancy Watters. You can find the words and music at www.pye global.org/world-chant/.

 ## Reclaim Your Voice

PYE facilitator Rebekka Goldsmith is a professional singer and improvisational artist who uses her theater and music skills to facilitate vocal empowerment workshops for youth and adults. She specializes in helping people reclaim their voices through a combination of theater games, rhythm and vocal improvisation. Rebekka leads workshops and retreats for people from 12 years old to the mid-90s, and she trains teachers and music educators in ways to bring more creative exploration into their mainstream music teaching. "Keep your expectations realistic when working with a group around sound and rhythm," she advises. "You want to have fun without judgment. This helps people get over the fear of doing it wrong and helps them reclaim their voice and their inherent rhythmic capacity."

Rebekka offers the following beginning sequence of activities to build people's trust in their voice and vocal power. Many of these activities are also helpful in preparing people for public speaking. After all, it's all about trusting your voice.

Sound and Movement

This game involves the whole group and gets people accustomed to expressing sounds while heightening focus and listening. It also gets everyone laughing, which helps relax and connect the group. Everyone stands in a circle.

- The leader (A) begins by looking to the person on her right (B). A then makes a distinct sound accompanied by a movement. An example would be, swinging her right hand in front of her while issuing a loud WHOOOSHHHHHHH.

Credit: PYE Global

Dance breaks out at the Dream a Dream program in Bangalore, India.

- Person B then turns to the person on his right (C), copies the movement and WHOOOSHHHHHHH sound as accurately as he can.
- C then passes it on, and the sound and movement continue around the circle. Once it goes all the way around the circle, A passes that same sound to B one more time so that the sound and movement are begun and ended by person A.
- Then it is B's turn to come up with a completely new sound and movement and pass that around the circle. Then it's C's turn to come up with a new sound and movement, etc.

If you have a group of ten people or fewer, you can continue the game until everyone has had a turn to come up with a sound and movement. As the coach, encourage people to build the intensity by sending the sound faster and faster around the circle without dropping the volume. Urge them to be spontaneous when it is their turn to make up a sound and movement.

Sound Ball

This activity builds vocal power by having participants spontaneously come up with new sounds and pass them across the circle. It's a great teaching tool for public speaking because it involves giving and receiving energy. Participants stand in a circle.

- The leader (A) begins by making a sound and sending it to a person across the circle (B), using a hand gesture as if it's a ball.
- As B "catches" it she repeats the sound with the same intensity and velocity with which it was sent. B now comes up with a completely new sound and sends that to another person in the circle (C).
- C catches the sound and then sends a new one to yet another person, etc. The group continues to catch and send sounds across the circle.

In the heat of the game, people often forget to catch the sound before sending a new one. Remind people when they forget. As the game gets going, urge people to go faster and faster. If you have a large group, you can break up into pairs. Have the partners stand about ten feet apart and play sound ball as twosomes.

Call-and-Response with Sounds

Rebekka starts call-and-response games by pointing out that it is a centuries-old practice used in African culture, various religious communities and in some forms of music to engage the entire community. Begin by having everyone stand in a circle. Make a variety of sounds, one at a time, and ask the group to mimic you. Sounds can include short melodic passages, percussive sounds, animal sounds, whispers and shrieks. "Play with the whole range of ways you can make sounds," she says. "This will stretch the vocal range of your participants. The sounds will likely bring up some laughter. Usually people are able to recreate the sounds I make."

Point out how good participants are at parroting your sounds and how well they are listening. "This goes a long way in calming some people's fears of being tone deaf. Very few people are in fact tone deaf. Most of it has to do with strengthening our ears and getting out of our way so that our bodies can do what they naturally do."

Call-and-Response Rhythm

You can also do call-and-response with a clapping rhythm. Clap four bars of four beats each, and have the group clap back the same rhythm. Vary the clapping and challenge the group to continue echoing the sound. You may be amazed by how well people will do. Most of us have far more innate musicality than we realize. You can then move to singing a series of four-bar riffs, with the group copying each one. And then to singing two bars of music followed by two bars of silence. "People know instinctively when to come in," Rebekka says. "I'll ask, 'How did you know where to come in?' and they'll say, 'I just felt it.' and I'll say, 'That's your innate musical instinct.'"

Call-and-Response Go Around

Once your group is comfortable with you leading the call-and-response, you can go around the circle, with each person leading four call-and-response rhythms in a sequence. Rebekka recommends doing four because it gives people time to get into it. "Even if they fumble at first, by the third and fourth time they usually get the idea."

After doing this exercise, take some time to check in with the group about how they are experiencing their own and each other's voices. You can also ask questions about their creative intuition. You might ask, "Who came up with something that surprised you? Who did something you thought about before?" This can flow into a conversation about creative exploration.

Rebekka doesn't make any judgment about the way people made their sounds or the sounds they make. "I say, 'We used our voices, and listened to each other. What did you notice about that?' Responses from the group might be something like, 'I never would have made that sound that I just copied.' To that I would respond, 'So you now get to add that to your repertoire of sound 'cause you've made it and you can do it again.'"

Toning

This exercise is based on Rebekka's work with master improviser and teacher Rhiannon. Toning connects people with themselves and the group as a whole. To prepare your group for this activity of making extended sounds together, introduce the idea that silence and sound are complementary and that often we can most easily tune into sound if we have our eyes closed. If we close our eyes, our ears can hear more. (Give the option of looking down rather than closing eyes.) Here are Rebekka's instructions for leading toning:

> We'll start in silence. At some point, I'll count to three and we'll all take a big breath together, and we'll make a long sound. It might sound messy because we will be singing different notes or pitches all together. If you have ever heard an orchestra warm up, you might remember that they all warm up at the same time, not listening to each other. It's a jumble of sound. This exercise is not about creating a beautiful piece of music, it's about creating our own sound within a group. Now let's all begin.

After toning a few times as a group, you can say,

> This time as we go forward, keep holding long tones, one per breath at your own pace. Let the tone you make come from your intuition. Try not to think of what tone you should make but what tone wants to come out. At some point you may want to start exploring a variety of tones or sounds on each breath. If that happens let yourself explore and let it keep going.

The group may stop on its own after a short while. If they continue, they will often move into a deeper sound exploration, with a whole variety of sound occurring simultaneously. Let this go on for a while. Sometimes the group will naturally come to a close and sometimes you might need to give an instruction to the group to find a way to bring it to a close. Rebekka usually says something like, "Keep listening and let's find an ending as a group."

When the sound stops say, "Stay in silence with your eyes closed and notice how your body is feeling." Rebekka often follows the toning with a one-word check-in. Reponses are usually words like *open, warm, vibrating, connected, awake, alive, refreshed, relaxed.* "I use that opportunity to talk about how everything is made up of vibration so we can really shift things in ourselves by creating sound, and how these shifts can be magnified by making sound together."

Rhythm Jam

You can do this activity with voice or small percussion instruments. The game increases rhythmic awareness while heightening group awareness. The leader begins by making a repetitive, rhythmic sound. Go around the circle, with each person adding his own rhythm to build a tapestry of sound. Once everyone is in the game, begin to deconstruct the jam, with the leader first going silent. Continue around the circle, with one person after another withdrawing her sound. End in silence. Rebekka suggests doing this with a group of five to ten. If you have a larger group, half of the group can simply listen and then take a turn as a new ensemble.

Note: It may be helpful for you as a leader to start the rhythm with a steady beat—like a steady, moderately slow clap. This will help anchor all of the rhythms to follow.

Get Your Move On

One of the best ways to embody learning experiences is by bringing movement into your program through stretches, movement games, freeform dancing or official dance steps. Nothing wakes up a group faster than movement.

Gentle Stretches

Every group usually has someone who will volunteer to lead a few minutes of stretching or easy yoga moves. We recommend veering away from challenging and complicated yoga poses and staying with slow easy stretches that everyone in your group can get into regardless of age or agility. Adding image to stretch increases the fun and effectiveness. For example, say, "Slowly reach up one arm after the other as if you are plucking apples from a tree."

Yes, Let's…

This fun and energetic movement game gets everyone into their imaginations and their bodies while at the same time building an attitude of "yes" in the group. Move chairs to the edge of the room and delineate a play area. The leader comes up with an action for the entire group to do such as flying around the room like airplanes. She proclaims loudly, "Hey, everybody, let's all fly around the room like airplanes." The group loudly responds in unison, "Yes, let's!" Then everyone runs around the room pretending to be airplanes.

Anyone in the group can add a new directive at any time. "Hey, everybody, let's hop like bunnies." "Yes, let's." And everyone hops until a new directive is called out.

To end the game, a facilitator can call out, "Hey, everybody. Let's all sit back down in our seats." During the game you may have to remind people to give some time for each action before jumping in with a new one.

Go, Stop, Fall

This whole-group movement game, taught to us by dance artist Christian Swenson, is energetic and fun and teaches a lesson in non-verbal communication. Begin by explaining that the game has three commands. "Go," "Stop" and "Fall." Model each of these. "Go" means walking around the room. "Stop" means freezing in place. "Fall" means gently dropping to the floor and slowly rolling around.

Stage 1: The leader begins by calling out "Go." He then plays with the three commands, attempting to give the group a pleasurable experience. The leader can then invite a volunteer to be the caller. This can be exhilarating. One young person proclaimed as he watched the group respond to his instructions, "Nobody has ever done what I asked before!"

Stage 2: Once the group has got the hang of following commands, say that now anyone in the group can call out a command at any time. Start in silence and wait for someone to begin. When young people play this game, you predictably get into a mess as people start calling commands one on top of the other. This provides a teachable moment about how we share space and leadership as a group. If the participants get in a muddle, stop them and ask what they might do to make the game work better, and then begin again.

Stage 3: Here's where the game gets very rich. Ask the group to find ways to issue directives non-verbally in total silence, simply through action. Anyone in the group can change the action at any time. Typically the group will go into a silent flow with one another.

Debrief: This activity has good possibilities for discussion. What was it like for the folks who led in stage 1? How did stages 2 and 3 differ? Who preferred the verbal commands? Who preferred the non-verbal? What did we learn about working together as a group?

Dance Circle

This all-time favorite movement activity works with groups ranging from 10 to 125 participants. The structure of this activity beautifully demonstrates how facilitators can set up the group so that everyone gets to lead for a moment.

Begin in one large circle. Tell participants you are going to turn on some danceable music, and then ask for a volunteer to be the first leader. The volunteer will begin by doing an easy-to-follow repetitive dance move from her vantage point as part of the circle. Everyone in the group will join in and follow her move for ten seconds or so. She then passes the leadership to the left, and that person will start a new move, with everyone joining in. The leadership moves all the way around the circle, with each person coming up with his own movement to lead.

There will undoubtedly be some people who are uncomfortable dancing, never mind leading dance. To calm the fears, model one or two very simple moves, explaining,

> Your move can be as simple as waving your left hand up and down. The key is to do it in rhythm and do it like you mean it. As if you believe that this is the best dance move in the world. And then everyone will enjoy it.

You can vary the music to fit a desired mood. For example, use upbeat music when you want to raise the energy in the group, or gentle watery music when you want to quiet things down at the end of an evening program.

Young Women Empowered mentors jump into a dance circle.

Credit: Young Women Empowered

 ## Dare to Take a Risk

Remember that you can lead song and movement even if you think of yourself as tone deaf with two left feet. This is a chance to take yourself out on a limb and model risk-taking. If you make a mistake, just say, "Whoa, that didn't work!" Often people will laugh, and then you try again. You can even ask the group what didn't work. If you believe that everyone in the group is learning and working together, you get support from your group. In this way you all have more fun, and you teach people not to be afraid to take a risk.

Resources for Songs and Rhythms

Here are some places to find easy-to-sing, short songs and rhythms for group singing.

- *Unicorn Natural Voice Camp Songbooks*: Volumes 1–4. Short, easy-to-lead repeatable songs: nickomoandrasullah.com.
- *Victoria Sings Short Stuff*. A songbook of short songs for community singing: soundthinkingaustralia.com.
- *Sounds for the Great Turning*. Short songs written by several song leaders, broken down into parts for easy learning: songsforthegreatturning.net.
- *Singing in the African American Tradition*, Volumes 1 and 2, taught by Ysaye Barnwell with George Brandon. These sets of choral and congregational songs will really get you in the groove: ymbarnwell.com.
- *Slap Happy: How to Play World-Beat Rhythms With Just Your Body and a Buddy*, by Alan Dworkin and Betsy Sansby. This is a great introduction to body percussion. We also recommend Betsy's teaching CDs for community choirs: dancinghands.com.

Other Resources

- Rebekka Goldsmith's work: www.rebekkagoldsmith.com.
- Community Choir Leadership Training: Shivon Robinsong and Denis Donnelly lead an excellent training for community choir leaders once a year in Victoria, British Columbia: communitychoirleadership.com.

part 4

facilitation tools

Building
on Strengths

Some years ago psychologist Martin Seligman got fed up with psychology's focus on what's wrong with people and became curious about what is right. If the purpose of psychology is to make us happier, he wondered, why weren't psychologists asking the question, What makes people happy?

Seligman himself asked the question, and his research turned up some interesting answers. First of all, some people are just born happy. You probably know at least a few people like this. They have a sunny disposition, and it takes a lot to throw them into a funk. Fortunately Seligman discovered three simple things everyone else can do to increase happiness:

- Discover what you are good at.
- Identify what you love to do.
- Do more and more of these things every day.

While it may sound simple, this philosophy actually flies in the face of cultural norms across the world. Acknowledging our strengths is too often seen as boasting. Too much praise is believed to spoil children and inflate egos.

Guerilla art at the Culture Jam Camp.

Credit: Culture Jam

The tide is shifting on this, however. In recent years the field of youth development has been moving away from a problem-based to a strength-based focus. Strength-based facilitation is founded on the idea that people thrive when their talents and gifts are acknowledged. Since most of us have not been brought up in this milieu, leading with a strength-based approach requires changing some deeply ingrained habits both in how we treat ourselves and in how we lead groups.

When leading from strengths, the goal is to enable the group and individuals to recognize their specific strengths so they can put them to use to achieve their goals. Think for a moment about how you praise people you are working with. Typically you might say, "Good job," "Great," "Fabulous work." These are all generic praises that don't feed the core of a person. Okay, the person did a good job, but what does that say about him? To identify strengths, we need a robust vocabulary to draw on. So rather than "Good job," you might say, "I really liked the way you used your *creativity* to solve that problem." Now the participant knows that you see him as creative. Maybe no one has ever told him this before. See the sidebar "The Vocabulary of Praise" for a list compiled by people in our trainings.

 ## Strength-Based Activities

Since most of us weren't brought up in a strength-based milieu, practicing strength-based facilitation begins with practicing on ourselves. Draw up a list of your own gifts and strengths, and share it with a colleague. Be honest and unashamed in your assessment. Begin to notice these gifts and acknowledge yourself for them as they show up in your work and life. To further enhance your self-awareness you might make an art piece that displays these gifts.

Something I Like About Myself

Another way to strengthen your self-assessment is to do the following partner exercise suggested by life coaching trainer, Dave Ellis. Stand and face your partner. For three minutes complete the following sentence: "Something I appreciate (or like) about myself is…" Don't over think it, and to keep the flow going feel free to mention big things like "how loyal I am to my friends" or "the way I commit myself to a project and then stay with it," and seemingly insignificant things like, "my choice of shoes." Every four or five times say, "Something I like about myself is *everything!*" Approach this activity like a spoken version of free writing. At the end of three minutes switch and listen as your partner does the same.

Stating your gifts and strengths gets easier with practice. Doing the activity helps shed the cultural proscriptions against positive self-assessment. And remember, you are not doing this to flaunt your ego; you are doing this to be of more use to the world and the people you work with.

The Vocabulary of Praise

Able	Candid	Discerning	Genuine	Motivated	Secure
Accepting	Capable	Dogged	Good listener	Musical	Sensible
Adaptable	Carefree	Dramatic	Graceful	Natural	Serene
Adept	Caring	Dreamy	Gracious	Observant	Skillful
Adorable	Catalytic	Dynamic	Grounded	Open-minded	Smart
Affable	Centered	Eager	Gutsy	Organized	Solid
Affirming	Charismatic	Earthy	Happy	Original	Spirited
Agile	Cheerful	Easygoing	Healthy	Outgoing	Spiritual
Aglow	Clear	Edgy	Helpful	Passionate	Strong
Agreeable	Collaborative	Effective	Honest	Patient	Sweet
Alert	Comforting	Elegant	Humble	Perceptive	Tactical
Altruistic	Composed	Emotive	Imaginative	Persistent	Tenacious
Amazing	Concise	Empathic	Impassioned	Playful	Tender
Amiable	Confident	Empowering	Independent	Poetic	Thoughtful
Amusing	Cosmic	Encouraging	Intelligent	Positive	Tolerant
Angelic	Courageous	Energetic	Inventive	Powerful	Tough
Artistic	Creative	Engaging	Intuitive	Principled	Trustworthy
Artsy	Cuddly	Enthusiastic	Joyful	Prescient	Unique
Assertive	Curious	Exciting	Just	Proactive	Unstoppable
Athletic	Daring	Fair	Kind	Proud	Vibrant
Audacious	Dazzling	Fascinating	Kinesthetic	Radiant	Vivacious
Authentic	Decisive	Feisty	Laid-back	Receptive	Warm
Available	Dedicated	Flexible	Literary	Reflective	Wise
Awake	Deep	Focused	Lively	Reliable	Witty
Balanced	Delicate	Forthright	Logical	Resilient	Zealous
Beautiful	Determined	Frank	Lovable	Resolute	Zesty
Bold	Devout	Friendly	Loyal	Resourceful	
Brave	Dignified	Fun	Luminous	Respectful	
Bright	Diligent	Funny	Magical	Reverent	
Broad-minded	Diplomatic	Generous	Magnetic	Sassy	
Calm	Direct	Gentle	Mindful	Savvy	

Appreciation Circles

We are constantly impressed by the high standards held by the people we work with in our programs—ourselves included. These standards can backfire, though, in the form of self criticism. To counter this, several years ago, we began leading appreciation circles in the final staff meeting at camps. What a difference this made for us all! We had all bent over backward to do our best for the week. We had taken risks, tried new things and, of course, made mistakes along the way. It is easy to focus on those mistakes, hold them close and never really look at the positive. Taking the time to appreciate what we'd done *right* was priceless.

An appreciation circle takes just one to two minutes per person but works like a charm. Everyone takes a turn standing or sitting in the center of the circle and receiving praise in the form of single words, phrases or a few sentences. To make sure the praise lands, ask someone to write down what is said, and hand the positive feedback to each person afterward.

Naming Strengths

Once you've begun to identify your own strengths, you can begin to spot them in your friends, family, colleagues and the youth you work with. If you must, you can do this silently at first. Just notice the behavior and identify the strength behind it. While this might come easily with behavior that pleases you, it's more of a challenge when the behavior upsets you or gets in your way. Yet we would venture to say that hidden behind every behavior, good or bad, is a strength or multiple strengths. The strengths just might not be appearing in a way that pleases you. For example, a young person who is loudly vying for attention might be demonstrating the strength of persistence in asking to have her needs met.

 ## An Essentially Spiritual Practice

Consistently seeing the strengths in others requires rising above the emotional fray and taking a larger view. Taking the step of naming the strength may require some humility on your part, but it's well worth the try. Moving from complaint to appreciation opens up a whole new adventure in all our relationships.

Working with
Diverse Groups

When we started our first Creative Community camps in 1996, one impulse was to prepare teens to live in our increasingly multicultural world. As our planet gets "smaller" it becomes more and more important that we learn to connect with people from backgrounds very different from our own. "We need to prepare young people for the intercultural world they're going to be walking in the rest of their lives, because if they can't do that, they are going to be lost," said Hanif Fazal, PYE facilitator and founder of Step Up.

"People often think that difference disconnects us, but actually it's the judgments we make based on differences that create the great disconnect," said Hanif, reflecting on his years of working with youth from diverse backgrounds and leading equity trainings for educators and youth workers. "The willingness to have an open mind and engage with difference can really connect us. You gain empathy and compassion for other people's experience, and their willingness to reciprocate deepens."

Working with groups from diverse backgrounds is a true learning journey: fascinating, humbling—and sometimes harrowing. The territory of cross-cultural learning is fraught with strong opinions, deep feelings and misunderstanding. Using the arts can help us create a safe space for diverse groups to build the qualities of courage, empathy, forgiveness and connection that the journey toward understanding requires.

Credit: LIFEbeat

A family group at the LIFEbeat camp provides the opportunity for cross-cultural learning.

In this chapter we are not going to even pretend to take on all the issues related to working with diverse groups. What we will do is point to ways to educate yourself, and share a few practices we use in facilitating groups. We'll start with self-education. Cultural competency requires learning in two related areas: cross-cultural communication and equity work.

 ## Cross-Cultural Communication

For over 60 years, social scientists have been establishing the field of "cross-cultural communication" in which they study the behavior or norms of cultures throughout the world. According to Milton Bennett, noted cross-cultural theorist and trainer, cultures "can include any long term groupings…as long as the groups maintain the clear patterns of behavior and thinking of an 'identity group.'"[37] Thus many different—and some invisible—groups likely show up in your programs, including some based on race, ethnicity, gender identity, physical limitations, religion and age.

It's important to understand that there are two aspects to culture: Capital "C" Culture represents the visible dimensions of a group's identity, such as food, music, traditions and dress. The less visible aspect of culture, or small "c," is what academics call subjective culture. This represents all the subconscious ways the members of any cultural group interact with one another to communicate shared meaning. Anthropologist Edward T. Hall said, "Culture hides more than it reveals, and it does so most effectively from its own participants."[38] Understanding *your own* cultural and hidden assumptions when it comes to *communication styles*, *personal space* and *time*, to mention a few, is the first step toward understanding others. This is what ultimately will help you work more effectively with diverse groups.

Dr. Bennett offered this example. Say you are a North American leading a training program in South Africa, and no matter how hard you try, you can't get a good flow of questions going. You might assume that your participants are shy, or that they're not very interested in learning. In fact, it's more likely you are running up against a commonly understood difference in cultural communication. "North Americans generally feel it's the responsibility of the speaker to be clear, and that it's not the responsibility of the listener to try to figure out what he or she is saying," says Bennett. "As a result a North American group leader expects that if people don't understand, they will ask questions. In large swathes of the rest of the world, however, it's not considered the responsibility of the speaker to be clear. It's the listeners' responsibility to make sense out of what the speaker is saying. Therefore group members in South Africa are more likely to be contemplative, to go off and talk to others about what the speaker might have meant, to exchange stories, or to do something that doesn't involve asking a question of the speaker to generate more explicit understanding."

Dutch social psychologist Geert Hofstede's research of cultural behavior demonstrated clear values differences among cultural groups within organizations. He created a well-known framework that allows us to compare and contrast cultures along continuums or cultural dimensions.

The four best known dimensions are high versus low power distance, individualism versus collectivism, masculinity versus femininity, and uncertainty avoidance.

Cross-cultural trainer, Cecilia Utne gave Peggy this example of how differences in the category of "uncertainty avoidance" might play out in a cross-cultural collaboration:

> Say you are a facilitator from Bangalore, India and you are collaborating with Brazilian youth workers to adapt a program from your country for teens in the favelas of Sao Paulo. While you may have similar philosophies and goals for the work, when it comes to implementation, you may run into some cultural roadblocks. Brazilians as a whole score far higher on the scale of uncertainty avoidance (70 out 100) compared to Indians with a score of 40. This means that when it comes to program planning your Brazilian colleagues are more likely to insist on having everything written on paper and planned out exactly while you might find that unnecessary and burdensome to the process. Knowing the cultural differences around uncertainty avoidance could bypass misunderstandings and ease the process.

Cross-cultural misunderstanding between youth workers or educators and their students can have particularly deleterious effects. Take the case so common in the US, where you have predominately white teachers working with students of color. Studies show that African Americans generally have a more direct, emotional communication style than white Americans. Without understanding communication styles, a white teacher is likely to misinterpret the behavior of a more direct African American student as disrespectful and disruptive.

Learning from Difference

In the following example, Hanif shows how the diverse learning and communication styles that show up in a classroom offer a rich opportunity for students to learn about intercultural communication as well as what is required to live in a diverse world.

In a classroom of students from diverse backgrounds, you'll likely find all kinds of different communication styles: Some like to be loud, blurting out their thoughts without taking turns to speak. Others want everyone to speak in an orderly way. Some need the classroom to be quiet and focused. Others need it to be fun. How do you make a more inclusive classroom when you have five students who need it loud, five who need quiet, five need hands raised to speak, others don't. One idea is to ask the students to talk with each other about what they each need in order to be a really good learner. Help them become aware of their own cultural frameworks and how that affects their needs as learners. By asking them to reflect and see how their needs intersect with others, you raise their intercultural awareness in three ways:

First, they are learning that the way they see the world isn't necessarily the same way others perceive the world. And second, they become aware of what they need, and learn how to ask for it. Finally, they learn that intercultural engagement requires compromise: "I won't get everything I need but there will be space for some of it. And I can get comfortable operating in different cultural frameworks. Just because I like it quiet doesn't mean that's the only way I can learn. I also have to be able to get comfortable learning in loud environments." This creates a learning space for everyone, exposes students to multiple perspectives, models what healthy functional intercultural communication can look like and begins to break down the fear of difference.

Resources

The following are two resources that will help you increase your own understanding:

- *Basic Concepts of Intercultural Communication: Selected Readings*, by Milton J. Bennett.
- Geert Hofstede's website, where you can find comparisons of a series of culturally programmed attitudes across nations: http://geert -hofstede.com/national-culture.html.

Equity Work

Equity work is related to increasing social justice in our world through exploring issues having to do with power and privilege. Without understanding in this area, you can inadvertently cause harm and increase inequity. A lot of the current equity work in North America comes out of the US Civil Rights movement and subsequent social justice movements.

Acknowledging Privilege

When you are part of a dominant culture—whether it be white, male, heterosexual, or able-bodied, to name a few—you walk through a world that

Challenging Conversations: Avoiding the Pitfalls   *by Hanif Fazal*

Hanif Fazal has worked with diverse groups of youth and adults for many years, and is leading an equity initiative in the Open Meadow Schools in Portland, Oregon, using the Courageous Conversations approach. (To hear Portland teachers talking about their experience with Courageous Conversations visit pps.k12.or.us/equity-initiative/index.htm.) Here are his thoughts on avoiding the common pitfalls of conversations about equity.

Avoid shaming: The moment you shame yourself or the people in your group, or the moment you feel guilty, you weaken your ability to break out of an oppressive system. There is nothing wrong with feeling bad about the experience of others who don't have access to your privilege—but shame is debilitating. In my experience, people of color don't say to white people, "I want you to feel guilty." They would rather you own up to your privilege and do something about it. Time wasted on shame or guilt is time that is better spent in making change. We need all the creative energy we can muster. Passion, will and commitment should be your drivers.

Step away from judging: Judgment doesn't lead to change. Be really conscious of the judgment that comes up for you when people interact, engage or see things differently from you. How quickly can you notice the judgment, let it go and see the value that the person brings to the group?

When it comes to working with kids, it is easy to fall into judgment. The moment you hear yourself saying "This kid doesn't care; this mom doesn't care; this kid is disrespectful," you have to stop and switch the station on your mental radio. Ask yourself, What else could it be? What aspect of my cultural framework is ready-made for that part of you. You are represented in the power elite and in the mainstream media. Medical research is focused on your needs. Movies and media address your interests. You can buy bandages that blend with the color of your skin. The list goes on and on. Because the world is made for you, you likely don't notice the biases inherent in it. But when you are not part of the dominant culture, you are faced with adapting to the differences every day. Teenagers with brown or black skin in the US, for example, are far more likely to be treated with suspicion when entering a store than are white teens. Or a female politician with a strong, vocal leadership style might be referred to as "bitchy" while a man with a similar style might be viewed as assertive or strong. Similar difficulties arise for others in minority culture positions.

might be provoking the response? Kids have issues, and you need to be able to bring those issues to their attention without judgment.

Avoid disengaging: When leading Courageous Conversations, one key agreement we ask everyone to make is to stay engaged. When you do disengage, ask why. What aspect of my privilege allows me to disengage? What is the cost of disengaging for myself and for my community? Listen for the excuses that come up, such as "I'm not racist. I'm not sexist. This isn't for me. I already know this. These people just don't.... If the facilitators only...." Don't externalize the reason for disengaging. Notice it, and find out what you need to do to re-engage.

Notice breaks in your listening: When you verbally or mentally find yourself invalidating the experience of another or questioning the truthfulness of that person's perspective, you have a break in listening. It's a sign that you have moved back into being self-centered rather than other-centered. The minute you get self-centered, you have moved out of an intercultural dialogue. You have to constantly want to understand the perspective of the other.

Avoid the "I'm not" perspective: The moment you start saying "I'm not racist. I'm not sexist. I wasn't there 100 years ago when slavery happened. I wasn't there when women couldn't vote. That's not me," is the moment to catch yourself and ask, Where *do* I fit into this picture? Am I willing to have a healthy responsible conversation with myself about where I benefit and participate in the benefits of the dominant culture? Where I am contributing to the marginalization of other folks?

When we are unaware of our areas of privilege, we don't notice the more difficult experiences of others. So, for example, a male heterosexual facilitator will likely have less perspective on gender issues than a woman or a person who is gay, lesbian or transsexual. Someone born into wealth will likely not fully understand the challenges faced by those living in poverty. Who we are and the circumstances we were born into are not as central an issue as our lack of awareness. This is what works against change. Waking up to our own areas of privilege is an essential step in working with diverse groups. A good place for white people to start is with an article titled "White Privilege: Unpacking the Invisible Knapsack," by Peggy McIntosh, easily found on the internet. A lot of focus is put on white privilege, and rightly so, given the privilege that is inherent in being white. However, it's incumbent upon facilitators to explore their own areas of privilege to uncover the blind spots that result.

Learning About Equity

You need look no further than statistics of prison inmates in the US or comparative pay based on gender globally to get a picture of injustice. African Americans are incarcerated at a rate of over two and half times that of Latinos and over six times that of whites. Men still make, on average, 17.6 percent more salary for the same full-time work as women in the industrial nations.[39] In other nations the percentage is even more stark. The story goes on, with inequity based on race, gender, sexual orientation and age, among other factors.

If you are working with diverse groups—or are simply a caring human being—learning about equity is a required course. You can raise your awareness through courses that fall under the rubric of "undoing racism" or "diversity training."

Resources

- *Courageous Conversations About Race: A Field Guide for Achieving Equity in Schools*, by Glenn E. Singleton and Curtis W. Linton, is a great guide for educators and youthworkers.
- *Intercultural Communication: Globalization and Social Justice*, by Kathryn

Sorells, offers a step-by-step framework for how to use intercultural communication skills while tending to issues of equity and power.

 ## Practices for Facilitating Diverse Groups

Here are some guidelines we use in our programs. We provide these with the caveat that we are not experts in this arena—rather we are companions on the path with others who are working for a more just world.

Establish "learning from difference" as a shared goal: We find that young people readily respond to the challenge of learning from people different from themselves. We talk about the many benefits of being in a program with youth from diverse backgrounds, such as having an opportunity to learn, opening the door to more friendships and helping solve some real-world problems, the kinds of conflicts that come from misunderstanding. We acknowledge that it takes courage to cross cultural boundaries, but it's worth it. We gently encourage young people to get to know new people, but we let the process happen without forcing it. Here's where being in an arts-rich environment works its magic. When people from different backgrounds make art together, bonds of trust begin to form organically.

Create a space for multiple perspectives: Be as inclusive as possible in your approach by incorporating various communication styles, values systems and orientation to time, space and learning style. "In order to do this you need to be conscious of your own cultural conditioning as well as of others'," said Hanif. "What do the variety of people in your group need in order to feel engaged? What do they need in order to feel that their value systems are being recognized? Are the learning environments coming from your perspective, or do they encompass a variety so people can find themselves in any group you facilitate?"

Work with a co-facilitator from another culture or gender: This broadens the lens through which the facilitation team views the participants and increases the chances that the group members in turn will iden-tify with the facilitators. It also serves as a model of cross-cultural collaboration.

Include leaders who represent the cultures of the participants: Young people need leaders they can identify with culturally. At Creative Com-munity camps, in addition to having a diverse lead facilitation team, we make sure that adult volunteers who lead activities come from a variety of backgrounds. This includes all the kinds of cultures, including gender, sexual orientation, and age as well as race and ethnicity.

Make room for quieter voices: Members in a diverse group will repre-sent a range of learning and communication styles. Some will take longer to speak in front of the whole group—and some may never do so. Use ac-tivities in pairs and small groups as well as in the large group to find ways for each person to feel comfortable with speaking. We also use the arts to provide diverse ways for participants to express themselves.

Bring awareness around cultural communication and equity into your program: Many activities are available for exploring equity and cultural communication. A good resource is 52 *Activities for Improving Cross-Cultural Communication*, by Donna M. Stringer and Patricia A. Cassiday. Remember to meet the youth on their own ground. Rather than further-ing your own agenda, find out what issues are most important to them and work with those.

Establish an atmosphere of honesty: Encourage everyone to talk openly about cultural disconnects and to do so with the assumption that faux pas are not intended to be hurtful. Establishing trust sets the stage for learning.

Facilitating Across Generations

When Rick first moved from a city to a small town, he volunteered at the local youth center. He is an accomplished musician and a multi-media expert, and has an easy approachable manner. But after several sessions of volunteering, he quit in frustration. "I felt like I was doing little more than glorified babysitting," he said. Unfortunately this is too common a problem. Youth programs rely on volunteers, but often don't know how to engage the adults in ways that draw upon their talents and passions and foster meaningful connections with the youth.

Our solution is to treat all of our youth programs as intergenerational learning events in which youth and adults alike get to be on their creative edge. Volunteers and staff don't sit on the sidelines watching the young people do their thing. Rather, they participate in all aspects of the program right along with them.

The adults learn through participating in workshops and whole-group sessions, through leading activities themselves and through engaging in the high-quality interactions with youth that result from learning side by side. We encourage even our most experienced teaching artists to take creative risks too by moving beyond their tried-and-true workshops to experiment with new ideas. The resulting vibrant atmosphere keeps volunteers involved and sometimes even leads to long waiting lists.

Staff and volunteers at the Agrifirma, Brazil Camp in Bahia.

Credit: PYE Global

When you include volunteers fully, you need to educate them as to their responsibilities as adults doing youth work. They need to understand the nuances of being present and yet giving primary attention to the youth and maintaining necessary boundaries, both physical and emotional. Here are some ways we've learned to help volunteers have a smooth ride:

Make sure volunteers understand their role: The role of the adults is to participate fully while still being 100 percent responsible for the well-being of the youth. The beauty of the Creative Community camps is the balance of freedom within boundaries. The kind of freedom the youth feel is possible only if the adults are really paying attention to what's going on with the youth. This is a delicate, nuanced role that volunteers are usually able to negotiate quite gracefully, but *it is important to provide all adults with training and clear materials about risk management.*

Provide guidance on what to say and what not to say: While the youth have a lot of freedom to talk or write about anything they wish, adults have to pay special attention to boundaries. Our rule of thumb is to stay away from talking about personal sexual experiences or drug and alcohol use. Sometimes surprises come up. We once had a parent get very upset because a volunteer said she had dropped out of high school and was glad she had. The mom felt this gave her daughter permission to drop out of school too. Youth want to know the adults as people, but quite frankly, a little bit of self-disclosure goes a long way.

Remind adults to leave space for the youth to speak: It's often easier for adults to speak up in a group than for youth. We encourage the adults to refrain from monopolizing the conversation, even when they think they have the most amazingly insightful thing to say. Similarly, when a small group is facing a collaborative creative challenge, we encourage adults to wait for the leadership to emerge from the youth.

Be as clear as possible about expectations: We encourage first-time volunteers to simply participate and enjoy the program. They don't need to lead workshops to justify their presence. In fact, the primary role of every volunteer is to be present for the youth and to help with the overall flow of the camp. We urge people to be as open as possible and to practice flexibility. Our volunteers can be very hard on themselves, and it can take some coaching to help them settle in.

Expect new volunteers to have challenges: A Creative Community program can be challenging for adults new to the process. For some adults, a first intergenerational experience will trigger memories of their own teenage years. During the program itself they need to deal personally (or with the help of a friend) with the feelings of inadequacy, uncertainty and even trauma that may come up. We sometimes have to remind volunteers that the primary focus needs to remain on the youth.

For others, just finding their place in the mix can be hard. Volunteers' expectations about what they want to contribute are sometimes dashed when their ideas don't immediately fit into the program or when they compare themselves to the other staff and volunteers. We encourage new volunteers to be easy on themselves, go with the program and place their focus on the youth.

Hold a daily staff/volunteer meeting: We hold a staff meeting over lunch each day. The meeting starts with a quick go-around in which people share a high point and a low point of the day. We have time for discussions and questions, and then we prepare everyone for what is coming next in the schedule. It's important to strike a balance between hearing staff challenges and concerns, and keeping the focus on the youth and the camp.

Clearly articulate roles: We recommend that one person be in charge of logistics. This person can organize the staff around shared duties such as leading groups in washing dishes, doing morning wake-up calls, etc. We make colorful charts and issue reminders at the daily staff meeting.

Keep current with your communication: If you have an issue with a staff member or volunteer, talk about it as soon as possible. Things move so fast at youth programs that if you don't address issues as they come up, they can begin to fester. You might then find yourself avoiding the person to avert conflict.

It's equally important to give feedback with great sensitivity: Be careful not to shame or embarrass staff, volunteers or youth in front of their peers. Conversations on the side, using your best communication skills, can make a huge difference in the smooth workings of a program.

Acknowledge elders: Many of our camps have volunteers ranging from age 19 to the mid-70s. The youth are generally very open to the elders, but the elders sometimes feel insecure because of their age. Younger volunteers may feel uncomfortable communicating with elders when conflicts arise. It helps to have at least one older person on the logistics or facilitation team and to remember that this is an intergenerational community and that it's a priority to learn from all generations.

Practice lavish appreciation: Most volunteers expect a lot of themselves, and just about everyone has moments of insecurity at programs. Establishing a culture of praise helps keep everyone feeling positive and energized. Praise can happen person to person or as part of a group process. Check out the appreciation circle described on page 271. It's important to incorporate a praise circle into your final staff meeting so everyone leaves on a positive note.

Creative Facilitation Checklist

Facilitating arts activities is a lot of fun, but doing it well requires practice. The more you use the activities in the book, the more skilled you'll become. Here is a cheat sheet of things to keep in mind as you enter the fray.

- **Develop a Culture of Yes:** *Yes* is a powerful word that generates a number of benefits for the life of the group and each participant. Use activities such as the Yes, and… game (page 216) and Yes, Let's (page 259) to catalyze a positive group culture.
- **Share ways for the group to become quiet:** To cut down on chaos and avoid yelling, take time early in your event to share some methods (see page 81).
- **Start with the blank page:** When leading an activity such as My Life As a Stream, have people start with the blank page. Yes, it can be intimidating, but creativity blossoms as soon as participants engage with it.
- **Warm up the group slowly:** Start with easy creative activities and gradually increase the level of risk. If your group goes flat, you've likely asked too much of them too soon.
- **Structure activities so that everyone gets to lead:** In leading, participants get to take creative risks and receive acknowledgment from the group for their good ideas. With an activity like the dance circle,

for example, rather than ask the experienced dancers to show off their moves, set it up so that every person gets to lead for ten seconds.

- **Keep your intention in mind:** Be clear about your intention when you choose activities. If you want the group to learn names, for example, use games that use a lot of repetition, rhythm and associative thinking.
- **Use the arts to create beauty together:** Beauty touches our souls. Collaborative arts-based activities bring us together and inspire awe in life and each other.
- **Engage the body:** Get those bodies moving at least every 20 minutes. Body movement is both refreshing and relaxing, and it gives us access to our emotions.
- **Incorporate mirroring:** Structured activities in which one person comes up with an action and then everyone copies give people a chance to be seen and appreciated, and they get the rest of the group moving in new ways.
- **Give instructions quickly and clearly:** Keep them simple, and model the activity whenever possible. If participants don't understand, they'll tell you.
- **Tip your hat to resistance:** Don't assume everyone is going to be enthusiastic about every activity. If you're introducing something that might seem embarrassing, say something like, "I'll admit this will sound really corny, but I'm going to ask you to go along with it and try it out."
- **Avoid popcorn style:** When doing activities in a circle you'll save time and reduce anxiety by going consecutively around the circle. Letting people choose when they want to go takes more time and leaves the shyest people for last.
- **Vary the size of groupings:** Change up the energy and give people lots of chance to participate by switching between the whole group, circles of eight to ten, groups of three or four, and pairs.
- **Provide opportunities to perform:** When people have the chance to share their creativity in small or large ways, they receive a big dose of positive energy from the group.

Afterword

As we bring the writing of *Catch the Fire* to a close, we are busily preparing for our first international gathering of social artists meeting on Whidbey Island, near Seattle. Artists, educators, facilitators and community leaders are making their way from far-flung points on the planet to learn from one another and to celebrate their shared passion for serving young people and communities through creativity-based work.

The dedication of this diverse group, combined with the connections we make daily with people around the world who want to bring more soul and creativity into their work, is but the tip of the iceberg of a movement toward innovation and creativity that we believe is rapidly growing. Our world is calling for each of us to step into our most creative selves—and to help young people to do the same.

We hope that *Catch the Fire* has provided the inspiration and practical tools for you to step on your own path as a social artist, whatever form it may take. We invite you to connect with our growing community of collaborators by contacting us through our website at www.pyeglobal.org.

Notes

1. Ron Allen. "After Katrina, Finding Hope in Crayons." NBC News, April 10, 2006, nbcnews.com/id/12256191/3677250 (accessed May, 2013).
2. "High School Drop Out Statistics." Statistic Brain, statisticbrain.com/high-school -dropout-statistics/ (accessed May 2013).
3. "High Drop Out Rates/Low Graduation Rates." Education Evolving, education evolving.org/studentvoices/clearinghouse/high-drop-out-rateslow-graduation -rates (accessed May 2013).
4. Daniel H. Pink. *A Whole New Mind: Why Right Brainers will Rule the Future.* River-head Books, 2006.
5. Peter L. Benson. *Sparks: How Parents Can Help Ignite the Hidden Strengths of Teen-agers.* Jossey-Bass, 2008.
6. Peter Benson. "Sparks, How Youth Thrive." TED Talks, April 22, 2011, tedxtalks .ted.com/video/TEDxTC-Peter-Benson-Sparks-How (accessed May 2013).
7. Angeles Arrien. *The Four-Fold Way: Walking the Paths of the Warrior, Teacher, Healer and Visionary.* Harper San Francisco, 1993.
8. James S. Catterall. "Involvement in the Arts and Success in Secondary School." *Americans for the Arts Monographs*, Vol. 1 Number 9, 2012.
9. Edward B. Fiske. *Champions of Change: The Impact of the Arts on Learning.* President's Committee on the Arts and the Humanities, Washington, DC, 1999.
10. Karl Paulnak. Welcome Address at the Boston Conservatory of Music, 2009. bostonconservatory.edu/music/karl-paulnack-welcome-address (accessed May 2013).
11. Iain McGilchrist. *The Master and His Emissary: The Divided Brain and the Making of the Western World.* Yale University Press, 2009.
12. James W. Pennebaker. *Writing to Heal: A Guided Journal for Recovering from Trauma and Emotional Upheaval.* New Harbinger Publications, 2004.
13. "Creative Works." Human EYES Project, accesstomedia.org/humaneyes/hastings -community-school, (accessed May 2013).
14. Daniel Goleman, Richard E. Boyatzis and Annie McKee. *Primal Leadership: Realiz-ing the Power of Emotional Intelligence.* Harvard Business School Press, 2002.
15. Dave Ellis. *Falling Awake: Creating the Life of Your Dreams.* www.fallingawake.com.
16. Jon Young, Evan McGown and Ellen Haas. *Coyote's Guide to Connecting with Na-ture.* Owlink Media, 2010.

17. Ingrid Wickelgren. "The Education of Character." *Scientific American Mind*, September/October 2012.

18. Margaret Wheatley. "It's An Interconnected World." *Shambhala Sun*, April 2002, margaretwheatley.com/articles/interconnected.html (accessed May 2013).

19. http://www.pyeglobal.org/2012/12/04/charlie-murphy-building-a-group -rhythm/.

20. Heather L. Stuckey and Jeremy Nobel. "The Connection Between Art, Healing, and Public Health: A Review of Current Literature." *American Journal of Public Health*, February 2010, ncbi.nlm.nih.gov/pmc/articles/PMC2804629/.

21. Betsan Corkhill and Carol Davidson. "Exploring the Effects of Knitting on the Experience of Chronic Pain—a Qualitative Study." Stitchlinks.com, 2009, stitchlinks.com/pdfsNewSite/research/Poster%20Britsh%20Pain%20Society %20March%202009%20copy.pdf (accessed May 2013).

22. James W. Pennebaker. *Writing to Heal: A Guided Journal for Recovering from Trauma and Emotional Upheaval.* New Harbinger Publications, 2004.

23. Stephanie Spera, Drake Beam Morin, Eric Buhrfeind and James Pennebaker. "Expressive Writing and Coping with Job Loss." *Academy of Management Journal*, 37, 1994, homepage.psy.utexas.edu/HomePage/Faculty/Pennebaker/Reprints/Spera .pdf (accessed May 2013).

24. appliedimprov.ning.com.

25. Viola Spolin. The Spolin Players, spolinplayers.com/viola-spolin.html.

26. PATH. "Magnet Theatre: Involving audiences and encouraging change." PATH: A Catalyst for Global Heath, path.org/publications/files/CP_kenya_magnet_fs.pdf.

27. Jeremy Hsu. "The Secrets of Storytelling." *Scientific American Mind*, August/September, 2008.

28. Annie Murphy Paul. "Your Brain on Fiction." *The New York Times*, March 17, 2012.

29. Sam Keen and Anne Valley-Fox. *Your Mythic Journey: Finding Meaning in Your Life Through Writing and Storytelling.* Jeremy P. Tarcher/Putnam, 1989.

30. Amy Kepferle. "The Monologue Project: Students Have Their Say." *Cascadia Weekly*, April 25, 2007, cascadiaweekly.com/pdfs/issues/200717.pdf (accessed May 2013).

31. "Social Capital Benefits of Choral Singing." Social Capital Blog, July 1, 2010, socialcapital.wordpress.com/2010/07/01/social-capital-benefits-of-choral -singing/ (accessed May 2013).

32. Julia Layton. "Does Singing Make You Happy?" Howstuffworks.com, science .howstuffworks.com/life/singing-happy1.htm (accessed May 2013).

33. "Mickey Hart and the Healing Power of Rhythm." Hey Man, The Freewheeler, December 27, 2012, thefreewheeler.proboards.com/index.cgi?board=music2 &action=display&thread=7569 (accessed May 2013).

34. Henry W. Maier. "Rhythmicity: A Powerful Force for Experiencing Unity and

Personal Connections." *Journal of Child and Youth Care Work*, Issue 66, July 2004, cyc-net.org/cyc-online/cycol-0704-rhythmicity.html (accessed May 2013).

35. Natural Voice Practitioners' Network, naturalvoice.net (accessed May 2013).

36. Robert D. Putnam. *Bowling Alone: The Collapse and Revival of American Community*. Simon and Shuster, 2001.

37. Milton J. Bennett. *Basic Concepts of Intercultural Communication: Selected Readings*. Nicholas Brealy Publishing, 1998.

38. Edward T. Hall. *The Silent Language*. Anchor, 1973.

39. Catherine Rampell. "The Gender Wage Gap Around the World." *New York Times*, March 9, 2010, economix.blogs.nytimes.com/2010/03/09/the-gender-wage-gap-around-the-world/ (accessed May, 2013).

Index

About PYE

Partners for Youth Empowerment

PYE—Partners for Youth Empowerment is an international non-profit organization that partners with communities and schools around the world to activate the creative potential of young people. Our work is guided by a vision of a world in which all young people have transformative experiences that connect them with who they are, what they are capable of and how to take action on things that they care about. PYE delivers training to youth work practitioners in facilitating deep level youth engagement using the Creative Community Model. Our social network represents a growing hub of people dedicated to infusing education, youth work, and group work with creativity, depth, and passion. To find more resources and to connect with this international network please visit pyeglobal.org.

About the Authors

Peggy Taylor is a social entrepreneur, facilitator, creativity specialist, and a leader in developing creative approaches to youth development. She is an award-winning magazine editor and co-author of *Chop Wood, Carry Water: A Guide to Finding Spiritual Fulfillment in Everyday Life* (J.P. Tarcher/Putnam, 1984), which sold over 250,000 copies worldwide. Peggy's artistry includes writing, playing the folk harp and directing a 50-member singing group in her community north of Seattle, Washington.

Charlie Murphy is renowned for his group facilitation and program design work integrating the arts into youth development. He is an award-winning singer/songwriter with over 30 years experience in the field of experiential learning. In the '90s Charlie served as national director of training for the YMCA Earth Service Corps, a youth environmental organization. In 2005 he received an Ashoka Fellowship in recognition of his life-long achievements as a social entrepreneur and for his work with the Power of Hope program.

Peggy and Charlie are captivating facilitators and public speakers and have trained thousands of people worldwide in ways to bring meaning, depth, and joy to their work with groups of young people and adults. They are co-founders of PYE Global and the Power of Hope and work in venues ranging from schools and youth organizations to graduate programs, businesses, and leadership institutes.

If you have enjoyed *Catch the Fire*, you might also enjoy other

BOOKS TO BUILD A NEW SOCIETY

Our books provide positive solutions for people who
want to make a difference. We specialize in:

Sustainable Living ◆ Green Building ◆ Peak Oil
Renewable Energy ◆ Environment & Economy
Natural Building & Appropriate Technology
Progressive Leadership ◆ Resistance and Community
Educational & Parenting Resources

New Society Publishers
ENVIRONMENTAL BENEFITS STATEMENT

New Society Publishers has chosen to produce this book on recycled paper made
with 100% post consumer waste, processed chlorine free, and old growth free.

For every 5,000 books printed, New Society saves the following resources:[1]

41	Trees
3,728	Pounds of Solid Waste
4,102	Gallons of Water
5,350	Kilowatt Hours of Electricity
6,777	Pounds of Greenhouse Gases
29	Pounds of HAPs, VOCs, and AOX Combined
10	Cubic Yards of Landfill Space

[1]Environmental benefits are calculated based on research done by the Environmental Defense Fund and
other members of the Paper Task Force who study the environmental impacts of the paper industry.

For a full list of NSP's titles, please call 1-800-567-6772 or check out our web site at:

www.newsociety.com